THANK YOU,

PRESIDENT BUSH

THANK YOU, PRESIDENT BUSH

Introduction by GOV. JEB BUSH

Essays by GEORGE SHULTZ, ED MEESE, JAMES DOBSON, PHYLLIS SCHLAFLY, and Many Others

Edited by AMAN VERJEE and ROD D. MARTIN

World Ahead Publishing, Inc.

Published by World Ahead Publishing, Inc., Los Angeles, CA

World Ahead Publishing's books are available at special discounts for bulk purchases. World Ahead Publishing also publishes books in electronic formats. For more information, visit www.worldaheadpublishing.com.

First Edition

ISBN 0-9746701-1-1
LCCN 2004107069

Printed in the United States of America

10 9 8 7 6 5 4 3 2 1

Dedicated to the memory of Ronald Wilson Reagan, a defender of freedom and emancipator of millions. Thank you, President Reagan, for reminding all of us that the United States of America truly is a shining city on a hill.

CONTENTS

Editors' Note   i

Preface – AMAN VERJEE   iii

Introduction – GOV. JEB BUSH   vii

SECTION ONE: PRESIDENTIAL CHARACTER

Thank You, President Bush – DON HODEL   3

The Character of the President – GOV. MIKE HUCKABEE   9

The Rise of Opportunity Conservatism – TED CRUZ   19

SECTION TWO: FOREIGN POLICY

The Bush Doctrine: The War on Terrorism and America's
Choice – VICE PRESIDENT RICHARD CHENEY   39

A Changed World – GEORGE SHULTZ   51

Standing Up for American Sovereignty – PHYLLIS SCHLAFLY   69

President Bush, Terrorism, and Justice – ABRAHAM SOFAER   83

Aeschylus and America – JACK WHEELER   95

The Kyoto Protocol: One of the World's Great Religions
– ALEC RAWLS   109

SECTION THREE: ECONOMIC POLICY

The Bush Tax Cuts Have Paid Dividends – STEPHEN MOORE 127

A Supply-Side Perspective on the Bush Tax Cuts – ARTHUR
LAFFER   135

Of Debt, Deficits, and Economic Growth – AMAN VERJEE   167

The Second Term Diet – GROVER NORQUIST   189

Welfare Reform, Part II – STAR PARKER   197

Expanding Opportunity through Free Trade – HEIDI CRUZ 207

SECTION FOUR: SOCIAL POLICY

Compassionate Conservatism: The State of the Faith-Based Initiative – MARVIN OLASKY   227

Muted but Monumental: Achievements of Bush's Faith-Based
Initiative – DON WILLETT & SUSANNA DOKUPIL   235

The Feminism of George W. Bush – CANDICE JACKSON   261

Education and Health Care Policy – MICHAEL NEW   273

Defending America's Families – JAMES DOBSON   285

SECTION FIVE: THE ROLE OF THE LAW

A Legacy on the Courts – TARA ROSS   293

The USA Patriot Act – ATTORNEY GENERAL JOHN ASHCROFT 311

Protecting Civil Liberties and the Patriot Act – BILL BENNETT 321

The SAFE Act Will Not Make Us Safer – EDWIN MEESE III &
PAUL ROSENZWEIG   327

Conclusion – ROD MARTIN   349

Publisher's Note – ERIC JACKSON   365

*A*nthologies, like Presidential Administrations, face the choice of tailoring their focus in a manner that appeals to many or to a narrow few. It's fitting then that this book, like its subject, has chosen to reach out to as many people as possible. The works included in it range from popular to scholarly and from conservative to libertarian; not all readers will gravitate toward every chapter, but on the whole they will each find much to embrace.

The authors themselves are also a varied and amazingly accomplished group: the Vice President and Attorney General, former Bush Administration staffers, two sitting Governors (one of them the President's brother), former cabinet members, academics, commentators, and citizens of every stripe. In short, they reflect the diverse group of 50 million Americans who voted for George W. Bush in 2000 — their backgrounds and opinions vary, but they are united in their desire for an America that is rich in liberty, safe from threats, vibrant with commerce, and congenial toward religion.

Editors of a book such as this must not only choose their target audience but also their style. Again, we have aimed to be broad and inclusive. We've generally relied upon the popular and readable Chicago Style, although we've chosen to deviate from it when it strengthened the text (e.g. "the President," not "the president"). Yet we've used our red pens sparingly so as not to detract from the fine works of our contributors, who each in their own way articulate the case for a second George W. Bush Administration. Both individually and collectively, their case is most convincing.

The Editors

PREFACE

AMAN VERJEE

When former President Ronald Reagan passed away, he did so with his usual sense of timing. For just as the sad news reached the airwaves, the leaders of the free world were gathering on the shores of Normandy to commemorate the 60th anniversary of D-Day. Almost as if on cue, the most visible orators of this decade were available to eulogize Reagan as a defender of free markets and individual liberty. *Exit stage right, Mr. President.*

Coincidentally, his passing also occurred just as we were wrapping up the editing of *Thank You, President Bush.* The weeklong tribute paid to Reagan by the mainstream media put a general notion that had been kicking around my head into specific relief: the idea that there are two kinds of politicians — those who view politics as a tactical game, and those who view it as a moral pursuit. The former are invariably more popular in real life than they are in posterity, while the latter are often controversial during their tenures but well-remembered if their visions ultimately prevail.

Few remember this now, but millions of Americans cringed at Reagan's anti-Soviet "evil empire" posturing in the early 1980s, fearing that his simplistic rhetoric would provoke World War III. Many in Europe felt the same way—I remember listening to a June 1982 speech, which Reagan delivered to the British House of Commons, spiced with skeptical British commentary suggesting that Reagan was a cowboy President who knew nothing about the complexities of European communism.

Yet here we are, 20 years later, and we're all Reaganauts. No one campaigns to raise tax rates to pre-Reagan levels; the American mainstream firmly supports his foreign policy stance of projecting U.S. power; and few believe that communism—which enslaved over 2 billion people when Reagan took office—would have fallen so quickly without him.

Success, I suppose, ends controversy. Now that we know the outcome of the 1980s and 1990s—the Soviet Empire collapsing, Old Europe and Japan mired in recession after recession, and the American people prospering like never before—it's easy for the commentariat (both liberal and conservative) to forget the skepticism of the 1980s, and to celebrate President Reagan as a visionary. It's also easy to forget Teddy Kennedy calling Ronald Reagan a warmonger in 1984, thus feeding useful quotes to KGB propagandists. Or Senator John Kerry criticizing President Reagan's resistance to Soviet and Cuban land grab efforts in Central America, calling fears of a Sandinista invasion of Honduras "ridiculous."

Today, President Bush finds himself in almost exactly the same position as Reagan in 1984. He has pushed through large tax cuts in the middle of a recession, and the economy is at the beginning of a significant expansion. He has led a coalition of democracies to fight foreign despots who aim to take the freedoms of America and her allies, and he has done so without the help of the United Nations. Ted Kennedy and John Kerry have called him an irresponsible warmonger.

I believe that citizens of democracies have a responsibility to evaluate their leaders on more than just short-term political issues. We must judge them as history will no doubt judge them: on the strength of their vision.

Thank You, President Bush is therefore an important project because it describes and defines the values of a visionary leader. This is a collection of essays written by some of the nation's foremost conservative and libertarian thinkers, each contributing a chapter on a particular dimension of the most important presidential term of office in a generation. Collectively, this rich tapestry of policy issues evokes the values and ideals that this President will further and pursue.

It is easy to judge President Bush on short-term political questions—the integrity of the specific CIA intelligence used to determine the existence of WMD; an economic report showing unemployment rising or falling in a particular quarter; the President's speaking style on the stump; a farm bill here, a compromise with Congressional appropriators there—but history will forget these narrow questions. The electorate that focuses on these issues does itself a disservice.

Personally, I believe that the world in 2024 will be substantially as President Bush envisions it today. Democracy will have taken root and flourished in the Middle East; democratic nations will form alliances to serve their populaces, not unelected dictator-coddling elites; Social Security will be on sound financial footing; parents will have much greater choice in their children's education; and a global economic expansion, born of free trade and low taxes, will bring prosperity and opportunity to billions of people.

These are bold ideals that distinguish President Bush from Senator John Kerry, and they entail decisions that are politically difficult to make in the short term. For his willingness to make those decisions, President Bush has earned my gratitude.

Numerous others—both through their support and through their talent for arguing with me—have earned my gratitude as well. I would especially like to thank: Adam Ross, a good friend and colleague, a generous soul whose intellect and support were instrumental in delivering this book to you; Todd Gaziano of the Heritage Foundation, for his good wishes and for being a fellow traveler; and to each of the authors, who lent their talents and time to this important and historically significant project.

Finally, the editors would like to dedicate this book to former President Reagan. He was one of ours—the first, but not the last, President drawn from the conservative movement.

INTRODUCTION

GOV. JEB BUSH

It is an honor and a privilege to write the introduction to *Thank You, President Bush.*

For the past four years, our President has guided our country with steady leadership during times of historic change. In doing so, he has brought a renewed sense of honor, courage, dignity and strength not only to the Oval Office but to the nation.

President George W. Bush is the right man to lead this nation. He is a man for whom I have a great deal of respect, admiration and love. My brother is a man of character, faith, principles, honor and commitment. He is a man of his word; people respect that regardless of their politics.

The President's leadership has helped to create a strong America, economically, diplomatically, and militarily. This is because President Bush understands that the greatest strength of our nation lies in the character of our citizens.

Consequently, Americans are proud of their President

again, because he stands for the values that make us a good and decent country. In turn, that pride strengthens and galvanizes every American.

Come November, voters are going to have a very clear choice. It is a choice between keeping the tax relief that has created historic growth in our economy, and putting the burden of higher taxes back on the American people.

It is a choice between an America that leads the world with strength and confidence, and an America that is uncertain in the face of danger.

It is a choice between two visions of government: a government that encourages ownership, opportunity and responsibility, and a government that takes your money and makes your choices.

My brother's Administration has a record of sustained, superior achievement and a positive vision for the years ahead. We are fighting the war on terror, extending peace and freedom throughout the world, and creating jobs and opportunity here at home.

In the next four years, President Bush will build on the current economic growth and strengthen our recovery by making sure tax relief is permanent. In the next four years, President George W. Bush will continue to make America proud. I, for one, am looking forward to it.

The Hon. Jeb Bush,
Governor of Florida

PRESIDENTIAL

CHARACTER

CHAPTER ONE

THANK YOU, PRESIDENT BUSH

DON HODEL

Don Hodel is a former president of the Christian Coalition, and served as Secretary of Energy and Secretary of the Interior under President Ronald Reagan.

I am thankful that George W. Bush was elected President.

If the "mainstream" media is to be believed, we live in a time when most of the civilized world is wailing and gnashing its teeth at the rampant onslaught of American imperialism. Certain vociferous tirades from the Left in our country have made it clear that they don't think America can be trusted to self-govern, that we should relinquish control to a wiser, more global organization like, say, the United Nations.

Some on the Left in our country are apparently incapable of viewing the obliteration of the World Trade Center as an act of war. If we liken foreign policy to a boxing match, the liberal "blame America first" crowd would have us always on the ropes, with our gloves up, ever wondering where the next punch is going to land. Few of the talking heads realize what a blessing it is to have a President who is willing to stand strong for our national defense and the devastation that could result should he fail in that resolve.

When I served in the Reagan cabinet, I came to appreciate how the partisan leanings of the national media created a pernicious filter through which we had to make every effort to communicate to the American people. The conservative talk shows were in their infancy. There was no "fair and balanced" news channel, even on cable. The fact that a majority of the American people shared the views of President Reagan and those who stood patriotically for America did nothing to alter the incessant drumbeat of agitation against so many of the substantive proposals we sought to present, proposals that were consistent with the basic beliefs and opinions of most Americans. If anything, this has gotten worse during the intervening years as the manipulators in the media have become more proficient at misleading the American public.

It is amazing to me that President Bush has stepped boldly into this atmosphere, asserting his personal religious faith (which seems especially to antagonize his critics), his patriotism (which generates the same kind of animosity as that directed toward President Reagan's patriotism), and his determination to uphold the best interests of the United States against all nations and international organizations. He was no novice in politics and knew what he would garner in the way of opposition and criticism, but his stalwart integrity and intractable willingness to do what is right for the United States of America continue to drive him.

No one is surprised that his critics have relentlessly assaulted him for these stands. They have made their positions clear: only a weakened America will satisfy them; only an America that bows

THANK YOU, PRESIDENT BUSH

its knee to the whims of a foreign power or United Nations committees can be trusted; and the American people, as always, are too stupid to govern themselves. Sometimes openly opposing, sometimes subtly demeaning him, these closet socialists of the Liberal elite and their mouthpieces in the media seek to undermine public confidence in the American President at a time of international danger, while turning a blind eye to the threat of terrorism. Plainly from the daily violence of their rhetoric, the Left in this country seems not to care that more buildings may go down in flames as long as they can put their own man (or woman) in the White House. Apparently, they think they will deal with that problem when it arises. It is sad that those who seem to think that "patriotism" is a dirty word have so much impact on how our country is perceived in the world.

So, as we continue to take the war on terror to our enemies, as our President continues steadfastly to support our troops while his opponents pay lip service and systematically undermine our men and women in uniform, as our President continues to uphold his sacred duty to defend the Constitution from all assaults—both from within and without—in keeping with the theme of this book, let me tell you some of the things I am thankful for concerning President Bush.

I am thankful that we have a leader who listens to his advisors and makes the best decision he can based on what he thinks is right, rather than walking around with his nose stuck in a sheaf of poll results. It is true that power corrupts. The atmosphere in our nation's capital is particularly corrosive to honesty and decency. The political landscape in Washington, D.C., is littered with the detritus of personal ambition. "Potomac fever" has been an epidemic inside the Beltway for as long as there have been men and women answering the call to serve in the halls of power. Without values to govern ambition, ambition is blind and integrity is inevitably sacrificed on the altar of political advancement. President Bush has been a refreshing exception to that rule, determined to pursue the course to which he feels called regardless of the political fallout. This willingness to press on despite the slings and arrows of outrageous commentary shows a courage and character that have already done much to restore the office of the presidency to its former greatness.

I am thankful that our President speaks and acts with conviction toward creating a "culture of life," declaring a Sanctity of Human Life Day each year, re-instituting Ronald Reagan's Mexico City Policy, cutting funding for international abortion providers by $425 million, signing the Born Alive Infants Protection Act, eliminating funding for federal abortion counseling, and opposing the destruction of human embryos for stem-cell research. I am thankful that our President has signed the partial-birth abortion ban; has promised to sign a ban on cloning; has promoted adoption, abstinence education, crisis pregnancy programs encouraging life, and parental notification laws; and has supported extending state health care coverage to "unborn children."

I am thankful that since George W. Bush was elected President, not once has his character truly come into question; no women have come out of the woodwork with lurid tales of tawdry, adulterous affairs; no one associated with or formerly associated with the President has died under mysterious circumstances; no military secrets have been turned over to our enemies; and the word *impeachment* has never been seriously on any responsible person's lips. If our sports heroes are role models, how much more so is the President?

For eight years during the prior Administration, truth was treated as a tool to be twisted and manipulated by the spin doctors at the White House in numerous attempts to cover up a multitude of sins. Tragically, the mainstream media would dutifully report the latest scandal and then spend its time speculating on what stratagem would be used by the White House to deflect the demands for accountability, but there were precious few among the "watch dogs" in the media who expressed outrage over events or demanded any such accountability. Is it any wonder we are reaping in business today a harvest of broken promises and ethical crises? It is apparent that President Bush understands that not only does the President represent us to the world but that the presidency is the centerpiece of our national self-image and the exemplar of our character. His behavior and character is absolutely our business, and he has evidenced by his behavior and demeanor that he believes the office of the presidency is a sacred trust conferred by the people of this great country and not his by right to do with as he pleases.

I am thankful that our President covets the prayers of the people, indeed has requested them in earnest, and that we still live in a country where we are free to pray and worship as we wish. President Bush takes the freedom and well-being of our country seriously, as evidenced by his stepping up and urging the adoption of a Constitutional amendment establishing that marriage in the U.S. is only between one man and one woman. People advise him not to do it because they contend that it cannot pass, but clearly his criterion for supporting something is not whether it can successfully navigate the legislative labyrinth, but whether it is right! How refreshing and how unusual.

We have Congressmen and Senators who say they are not prepared to support the federal marriage amendment because they are not hearing from their constituents. Excuse me? We may be thankful that our Founding Fathers did not demand a poll of their constituents to determine whether or not to approve and submit the Constitution for ratification, or the Declaration of Independence, or the Bill of Rights. How different our history would have been if such self-serving dissembling had been the rule of the day back then. Recently I was with the President when he was talking with a handful of people. As he spoke about his attitudes toward the role of the President and the responsibility he feels toward our nation, I could not help but think that he exemplifies the qualities of leadership and public service set by the best of our Founding Fathers.

I am thankful our President is more concerned with the security of our country than the security of his party or his legacy. To paraphrase a great quote, there is no limit to what a man can do if he does not care too much about public opinion. We should all be grateful that our President cares not for our accolades, but for our well-being. I believe it is his passion, his unwavering commitment, and as I have said already, his sense of sacred duty to pursue what is best for "We the People." Having witnessed the damage wrought by the moral turpitude and weakness of character demonstrated by his predecessor, I am thankful God has called on a man like President Bush to lead us through these perilous times.

George W. Bush is steering our country through some very troubled waters as we embark on this new millennium, fighting elusive enemies in the form of terrorists abroad and creeping socialism within our own borders. Now more than ever, we must pray for our President and others in leadership: for wisdom, for insight, for endurance, and for courage to continue to make the difficult decisions because they are right, and not because they are expedient.

CHAPTER TWO

THE CHARACTER OF THE PRESIDENT

GOV. MIKE HUCKABEE

Mike Huckabee has served as Governor of Arkansas since 1996. He is vice chairman of the National Governors Association, a past president of the Council of State Governments, and a nationally-recognized leader on the issue of welfare reform. A former Southern Baptist pastor and president of the Arkansas Baptist State Convention, Gov. Huckabee is the author of several books including CHARACTER IS THE ISSUE.

We all remember those pictures from the classroom in Florida. We remember them as if they were taken yesterday. As President George W. Bush read to a group of schoolchildren, he was interrupted by Andy Card, the White House chief of staff. Card whispered something into the President's ear. A look of concern came over the President's face. The Sept. 11, 2001, attacks on our country were in progress, and the Commander-in-Chief had been notified. America was at war.

The scene most of us recall even more, however, occurred later that fateful week. Standing in the rubble where the Twin Towers of the World Trade Center had stood a few days before, the President grabbed a bullhorn and spoke to the rescue workers who were gathered there. He didn't work from a script. He didn't read from a TelePrompTer. He spoke from the heart. In that moment, the character of George W. Bush was on display for all to see.

Character and "American Exceptionalism"

Character. It defines the world in which we live. Our lives are shaped and directed according to it.

While some people are fond of saying you can't legislate morality, our laws are in fact a reflection of our moral values. We have laws against theft, murder and rape because we believe those acts to be wrong. When our moral values change, the laws change. At its heart, legislation is the codification in law of a particular moral concern. It is meant to ensure that the immorality of a few is not inflicted on the many. Murder is against the law because we recognize as a society that the premeditated killing of another human is a violation of a moral principle that most of us still cherish—the sanctity of human life. Theft is against the law because we recognize that taking someone else's belongings without permission is a breach of another of our fundamental ethical standards—the inviolability of private property.

President Bush came into office in January 2001 as a firm believer in the words of British writer G.K. Chesterton, who said, "America is the only nation in the world that is founded on a creed." Other nations find their identity in ethnicity, geography, cultural traditions or partisan ideology. The United States is an exception. It was and is the product of ideas—ideas about social responsibility, human dignity and freedom. The French politician and historian Alexis de Tocqueville called this "American

10

exceptionalism."

But this President also understands that "American exceptionalism" is not a given: it can be lost. A decline in moral
character in recent decades has produced an overall decline in
the character of our society. The blame for this has been laid on
everything from government policies to single-parent house-
holds. What it all comes down to, though, is that people of good,
godly character make good, godly laws. We need to elect more
people who have a God-centered worldview and aren't afraid to
act on it. The strength of our government institutions hinges on
the character of the men and women we choose to establish
public policies. That's why the most important aspect of this
President—any President—is his character. In the words of
former President Calvin Coolidge, "Character is the only secure
foundation of the state."

Character, Faith and the Danger of Moral Relativism

George W. Bush understands that you can live a God-
centered life of high moral character and still fight the political
wars.

A little background is in order so you will know where I'm
coming from. In the late 1980s and early 1990s, I was the pastor
of a growing church in Texarkana, Arkansas. We had an active
television ministry and a range of community outreach programs. But I felt God's call to leave the pulpit and take my
ministry into the political arena. I had no experience in politics. I
was a Republican in a heavily Democratic state. I discovered,
however, that people identified with my God-centered worldview, regardless of their party affiliation.

Please understand one thing. I don't believe that my views
make me better than others before God. But my views struck a
chord with people who were weary of a government that no
longer seemed to respect the things they thought were important. As Governor of Arkansas, I recognize the same moral

11

authority—God's authority—I recognized as a pastor, a student and even as a radio disc jockey in high school and college. God's standards never change. They are an unmoving goal toward which we can all travel.

President Bush also has a God-centered worldview that led him into public service late in life after a highly successful career in the private sector. He also recognizes God's ultimate authority. Since the day he took office, his critics have tried to use this against him. They claim he is a man who sees the world in black and white rather than shades of gray.

I believe most Americans understand there are indeed absolutes in this world. Those who argue against the existence of absolutes likely have never thought through the consequences of their positions. If there are no absolutes—if nothing can be defined as either always right or always wrong—then there is surely no God. If there is no God, then anything goes. Using this self-centered worldview, nothing is *always* right and nothing is *always* wrong. In this sort of society, right and wrong can only be determined by what a majority of people believe and accept at a certain time. Whatever the people consent to becomes "right."

In the absence of moral absolutes, the United States would have had no right to declare that Nazi Germany's annihilation of European Jews was wrong. We would also have no right to fight today's war on terrorism. You can see the slippery slope on which relativism rests. Where there are no absolutes, the leadership is free to set whatever standards it likes.

That's why I'm thankful to have a President who doesn't see everything in shades of gray.

I have visited on numerous occasions with George W. Bush—during his years as President and when he was Governor of the neighboring state of Texas. He is a man with a moral center. There are fixed reference points that guide his life and influence his decisions. He is not a man who will substitute his own standards of relative morality for true morality.

Faith in the Public Arena

Every day, President Bush puts his faith to work. I'm amazed by those who consider that a political liability. If political opponents want to use that against him, so be it. George W. Bush brings to mind these words from our first President, George Washington: "It is impossible to rightly govern without God and the Bible."

Thank goodness, too, that we have a man such as President Bush in the Oval Office at a time when the institutions that traditionally have provided stability and strength in our society—the churches, the community organizations, the civic clubs—have been so undermined. Many of these ethical institutions, such as the Boy Scouts, have been attacked in recent decades. Their methods have been challenged and their reputations have been distorted. The harm this has done to our society is incalculable.

The President realizes that many of the evils of our culture in this politically correct society fall in the domain of "victimless" crimes—at least superficially, no one is involved and no one is harmed except "consenting adults." The advocates of this approach believe that imposing community standards of ethics and decency is a violation of the spirit of American democracy and a contradiction of our most basic constitutional tenets. Any attempts to impose standards by the President and others in positions of power are labeled "intolerance," "bigotry," "zealotry," "insensitivity" and "religious fundamentalism." Too many well-meaning Americans have accepted this misguided version of tolerance. We've shied away from the biblical imperative to "do justice, love mercy and walk humbly" in our attempts not to offend anyone.

So, yes, President Bush has offended some people by bringing his deeply held religious beliefs into the public square. But I believe that his adherence to a God-centered worldview is why George W. Bush will go down with Ronald Reagan as one of the

THANK YOU, PRESIDENT BUSH

most important Presidents of the past 100 years. He is turning the tide in this country.

The Necessity of Public Virtue

We finally appear to be turning away from cavalier attitudes toward standards of goodness and morality. In the name of civil liberties, cultural diversity and political correctness, a radical agenda of moral corruption and ethical degeneration had pressed forward in this country until President Bush took office. This brazen disregard for any objective standard of decency actually threatened our liberties and diversity rather than strengthening them. That's because it threatened the foundations that made those things possible in the first place. George W. Bush has reminded us over and over that great privileges bring with them great responsibilities. The remarkable freedom we enjoy in this country was bought with a price: moral diligence, virtuous sacrifice and ethical uprightness. The pornographers, gay activists, abortionists and others of their ilk have confused liberty with license, at a tremendous cost to us all.

President Bush lives the words of John Jay, the first Chief Justice of the U.S. Supreme Court. Jay knew the necessity of having a standard of virtue for the maintenance of civil stability and order. He wrote, "No human society has ever been able to maintain both order and freedom, both cohesiveness and liberty apart from the moral precepts of the Christian religion applied and accepted by all the classes. Should our Republic ere forget this fundamental precept of governance, men are certain to shed their responsibilities for licentiousness and this great experiment will then surely be doomed."

The great Russian novelist and historian Aleksandr Solzhenitsyn had recognized the road this country was headed down when he wrote back in 1978: "Fifty years ago it would have seemed quite impossible in America that an individual be granted boundless freedom with no purpose but simply for the

14

satisfaction of his whims. The defense of individual rights has reached such extremes as to make society as a whole defenseless. It is time to defend, not so much human rights, as human obligations."

Moral absolutes matter. Ethical standards matter. Virtue matters. Right and wrong matter. Good and bad matter. Justice and injustice matter. They matter, especially in the current war on terrorism, because the destinies of people and nations hang on their determination. Crises such as the current war on terror provide a true test of character.

Character is the person you are when no one is looking. It is the person you are when the cameras are off, the witnesses are gone and there is no one to keep score. Those of us in politics are all performers to some extent, but the real person of character is the one who is the same behind closed doors as in the public eye. I've been with George Bush behind those closed doors. And I can assure you he is always the same.

There are, of course, many Americans who don't want to believe this. By finding character flaws in others, they affirm that their own inadequacies are not so abnormal. As the character of America plummeted during the final half of the previous century, many people wanted to justify their own lack of morality by trying to show that everyone else was just as bad. People who lie think everyone is a liar. Thieves think everyone steals. People who are insincere in their comments and actions think everyone else is insincere. People who are unethical think everyone is unethical, and they're determined to prove that our President is unethical. If you're not overtly flawed, you become a contrast and a threat to them. It's proof of the biblical statement that men are lovers of darkness rather than light because the light exposes their dark deeds. Some people are desperate to justify their own immoral attitudes by saying, "He's a failure, too, so I'm as good as he is."

President Bush challenges us to do better. He challenges the people of this country to return to the traditional standards of

15

integrity. We once recognized a common standard. This President is helping us reverse the trend that saw the United States move from a society with a shared, confident sense of what was right to a society of relativism and moral decay. President James Garfield once said, "It is a greater honor to be right than to be President—or popular ... for statesmanship consists rather in removing causes than in punishing or evading results—thus it is the rarest of qualities."

The President has not governed these past four years with his eyes only on the next election. He is grounded enough to realize that most of the headline-making political events of today will go down in the annals of history as mere backdrops to the real drama of everyday life. Columnist George Will once wrote, "There is hardly a page of American history that does not refute the insistence, so characteristic of the political class, on the primacy of politics in the making of history.... In a good society, politics is peripheral to much of the pulsing life of society."

George W. Bush comprehends this fact as well as any office-holder I have ever known. He knows that all of the campaigns, primaries, caucuses, conventions, elections, statutes, policy proposals, legislative initiatives, surveys, opinion polls and demographic trends ultimately are rather removed from the things that really matter. He realizes the strength of America is in the people who take their kids to school each morning, open their businesses on time and help the kids with homework at night. In the words of Chesterton, "The greatest political storm flutters only a fringe of humanity. But an ordinary man and an ordinary woman and their ordinary children literally alter the destiny of nations." How refreshing to have a President who recognizes the inherent strengths of this country.

That's not to imply that President Bush believes politics is irrelevant. Government is a necessary component in ordering a society. Unfortunately, politics for many officeholders takes on the illusion of something enticing and powerful rather than a serviceable function of government. I'm convinced that had

George W. Bush lost the election in 2000, he would have been content with his past accomplishments and the life he still had before him. Unlike President Lyndon Johnson, who once quipped "I seldom think of politics more than 18 hours a day," George W. Bush is a man who had a life before politics and will have a life once he leaves the White House. I'm comforted by the fact our country is being led by a man so grounded; a man who understands that faith, family and work are the components of the American spirit. He knows they are the cords that weave the fabric of our lives. He knows they are the essence of the Judeo-Christian tradition that has shaped Western civilization.

Like his father before him, George W. Bush is the epitome of a public servant. He is now working with good men and women in every state to bring about a long-needed reversal in the fortunes of our children and our nation. It is a struggle, but we again have the chance to prove to the doubters both within and outside this country that America will prevail because she stands for what is right and good. The President knows success doesn't happen overnight. Victory doesn't come in a day. Cultural trends aren't reversed on a whim. But under his leadership, we have at least finally started down that road.

The feelings about him are so strong—both pro and con—because he is trying to do bold things. Meek men do not arouse passions. Yes, there is polarization in our society. But one of the biggest faults of those with a God-centered worldview is trying to reconcile that view with a self-centered worldview. It is simply not possible. One worldview will prevail. Either by numbers or persuasion, one side will defeat the other in setting public policy. When two irreconcilable views emerge, one will dominate. Standards of right and wrong are either what we establish as human beings or they are what God has set in motion since the creation of the world. The winning worldview will dominate public policy, the laws we make and other details of our existence.

George W. Bush is not trying to impose his religion on anybody. Yet he understands we must shape our culture, our laws and our world by acting on the only worldview that has lasting value, the only one capable of supporting a culture of freedom. His spiritual light—his light of integrity, character and a God-centered worldview—shines just as brightly today as it did that day in September 2001 when he grabbed the bullhorn in New York City. The darker the world gets, the brighter that light shines.

CHAPTER THREE

THE RISE OF OPPORTU- NITY CONSERVATISM

TED CRUZ

Ted Cruz is the solicitor general for the state of Texas. He has previously served as domestic policy advisor to George W. Bush on the 2000 presidential campaign, as associate deputy attorney general at the U.S. Department of Justice, and as the director of policy planning at the Federal Trade Commission. He previously clerked for Chief Justice William Rehnquist on the Supreme Court.

The views expressed are those of the author, and do not necessarily represent those of the Office of the Texas Attorney General.

Republicans come in many stripes, with differing views that together comprise the American center-right. Conservatives and libertarians, social conservatives and economic conservatives, paleo-cons and neo-cons, country-club Republicans and movement conservatives—all represent flavors of the Republican Party. But one of the most important groups, whose efforts will determine the electoral success of the Republican Party in 2004 and beyond, is what I will call the "opportunity conservatives."

The vision of "opportunity conservatives" is simple and direct: they formulate and articulate conservative policies with the single-minded focus of easing the means of ascent for those on the bottom of the economic ladder. Opportunity conservatives consistently preach expanding the pathways for all Americans to have a chance to achieve the American dream.

Prominent opportunity conservatives include Ronald Reagan, Jack Kemp, and George W. Bush. Indeed, the patron saint, so to speak, of "opportunity conservatives" is Ronald Wilson Reagan. As President Reagan observed, "Government has an important role in helping develop a country's economic foundation. But the critical test is whether government is genuinely working to liberate individuals by creating incentives to work, save, invest, and succeed."

Reagan was not the first movement conservative atop a national ticket. Barry Goldwater, a few years before, espoused many principled positions. But, Goldwater could not fully communicate the message. Reagan could.

To communicate the message one must fully understand the message. And the message extends far beyond a bevy of policy positions and charts and pie-graphs. Conservative policies, properly conceived, expand opportunity for those at the bottom of the economic pile seeking to work their way up. In other words, contrary to conventional political thought, conservative policies inure dramatically to the benefit of the poor and disadvantaged, whereas "liberal" policies, in practice, often foreclose opportunity and make it harder for the economically disadvantaged to improve their position in life.

Far too few Republicans get that in their gut. As a result, far too few can explain it to anyone else. All too often, Republicans can be found in public fora defending their policies with a scowl. When the topic of race or poverty or failing education comes up, turn off the sound on the television and watch their body language. Far too many Republicans feel guilty about what they're saying, and that guilt comes through loud and clear.

That guilt is born of ignorance, because too many conservatives don't understand how and why the policies they're advancing are the policies of opportunity and hope.

Unless more Republicans begin to understand how conservative policies expand opportunity — are directly beneficial to the economically disadvantaged — the future of the party could be in serious doubt. Demographic changes and the rising tide of immigration necessitate Republicans learning how to articulate the message of opportunity. By 2030, the U.S. Census Bureau estimates, Hispanics and African-Americans will comprise over one third of all Americans; by 2050, nearly half. Today, many minority voters are not yet supporting Republicans; in 2000, CNN reports, 35 percent of Hispanics and only 9 percent of African-Americans supported President Bush.

Republicans must learn to better communicate to racial minorities, to express with sincerity and conviction the compassion and promise that their policies embody. That message, delivered from the heart, will in time reach those voters and will resonate with the many "swing" voters in the middle.

Immigrants — brave souls who, often at great personal peril, left behind everything to come to America and pursue the American dream — form a natural audience for the message of opportunity. "Americans by choice," as President Bush aptly describes them. Demographic realities mandate that more Republicans learn the opportunity message; the party's future depends on it.

President George W. Bush

President George W. Bush is an opportunity conservative. He regularly conceptualizes and articulates his policies in terms of their direct impact on expanding opportunity for the economically disadvantaged to move forward. As he explained repeat-

21

edly on the 2000 campaign trail, "Prosperity is not enough....
[G]overnment—active but limited government—can promote the
rewards of work. It can take the side of individual opportunity.
This is a higher and older tradition of my party. Abraham
Lincoln argued that 'every poor man should have a chance.' He
defended a 'clear path for all.'"

Some conservatives become uneasy at such language. But
focusing on expanding opportunity by no means entails aban-
doning conservative policies; to the contrary, the policies championed by President Bush that would expand opportunity the
most—school choice, Social Security private accounts—were
some of the most conservative.

Indeed, his domestic policy agenda reflects sound and consistent conservative principles, as robust as those enacted by any
U.S. President. To be sure, some fiscal conservatives have criticized President Bush because government spending has continued to grow over the past four years. But those concerns are
often overstated—not giving proper weight, for example, to the
enormous additional military and homeland security spending
required by September 11. Domestic discretionary spending
unrelated to defense or homeland security grew 15 percent in the
last year of the Clinton Administration; in the first three years of
the Bush Administration, that number dropped to 6 percent, then
5 percent, then 3 percent.

Nevertheless, there is much to be said for the lament that
government continues to grow too fast. But a President cannot
stop it alone. With a Congress seemingly addicted to spending—
"That's why they're called appropriators, because they appropriate," as President Bush memorably put it on the campaign trail—
rather than tilt at windmills the President has focused instead on
articulating and advancing the opportunity conservative message. As he led off a speech in the 2000 campaign, his purpose
was "to share with you my own vision of how—in every city,
and every barrio, and all across our country—we can make
opportunity not only a hope and a promise, but a living reality."

Opportunity conservatives (1) get it, understand the vision, and (2) can sell it, can explain with passion and conviction conservative principles to typical apolitical voters. Without that understanding, Republicans inevitably come across as mean and stingy misers. The Democrats' message is simple: government will give you more. Whatever ails you, additional government spending will solve it.

Unmoored from "opportunity conservatism," Republicans are consigned to saying "no," "too much," "let's spend less." And while fiscal prudence may be a virtue, bread and circuses are an easier sell. So, in practice, Republicans try to play "me too" instead. Democrats will give you $200 billion? We'll give you $100 billion instead! That's rarely a persuasive pitch.

Of course, reducing the size and reach of government is important. The more resources it consumes, citizens it employs, space it occupies, the less freedom and growth and markets prevail. Making that argument, however, has a green eyeshade character to it. Abstract political theory has a bit less salience in an era of reality TV. As President Bush put it in the 2000 campaign, when voters hear "Abolish the Department of Education," a lot of voters just hear "Abolish Education" and back away.

Faced with this political reality, most Republicans pitch instead the supply side of the story—tax cuts. Tax cuts sell, and Democrats are forced to sound like Republicans: "no," "too much," "let's reduce taxes less." Thus, in 2004, the parties are in an odd equilibrium: Republicans pitch tax cuts, and shift nervously when discussions turn to specific spending programs; Democrats pitch spending, and desperately try to avoid discussions of tax cuts.

Voters, in turn, choose both. Hence taxes fall, spending balloons, and deficits grow. Ultimately, in a Fabian conservative sort of way, that redounds to the good; falling revenues in effect starve the Leviathan and eventually deter new spending expansions.

23

But, in the meantime, Republicans have to find something to say about individual spending programs. Spending writ large, Republicans (and even some Democrats) happily decry, but when it comes to any particular program, the air is often silent.

The key to credibly addressing particular spending programs is to view them first through a Rawlsian lens. John Rawls, a liberal Harvard professor and one of the preeminent political theorists of the 20th century, posited a theory of justice whereby any social ordering should be measured behind a veil of ignorance, not knowing where one might fall in the economic hierarchy. Behind that veil, Rawls argued, rational decision-makers would seek to "maximize the welfare of society's worse-off members" and so structure society to enhance the ability of those at the bottom to move ahead.

Although Rawls' work has been used to justify a host of ill-advised liberal spending programs, his careful analytical focus on the least well-off provides a useful rubric for conservative policies and advocacy. Often, the fault in the liberal program lies not in the aspiration—to help the poor, the infirm, the elderly—but in the counter-productive means of ever-expanding government largesse and a consequential culture of hopelessness and dependency.

For the opportunity conservative, whatever the program, whatever the issue, ask first how it will affect those at the bottom of the economic ladder. And analyze that question through a sober and rigorous consideration of how it will affect incentives, ownership, and personal responsibility—the keys to genuine opportunity. Conservatives are and should be espousing programs that enhance opportunity, that promote responsibility, and that make it easier to climb the first few rungs of that ladder.

Modern Inversion

In 2004, the orthodox understanding of the political parties is flat wrong. Indeed, upon careful examination, reality directly contradicts the accepted view of each party. The conventional wisdom is that Democrats are the party of the little guy, of the poor and downtrodden; Republicans are the party of big business and the rich. But, in 2004, it is Republicans who are systematically advancing policy positions that, if enacted, would dramatically improve the condition of the economically disadvantaged, and it is the Democrats who, again systematically, are opposing that policy agenda. .

That bears repeating: in 2004, it is Republicans who are advocating policies that benefit the poor, and Democrats who are actively fighting those policies. Notably, President Bush's efforts to champion those ascending the economic ladder have not gone unnoticed. In the 2000 election, CNN concluded that Gore narrowly won "working class voters" by a 51-46 margin, while Bush won "middle class" voters 49-48, and also won "upper middle class" voters 54-43. In contrast—and precisely opposite from the conventional wisdom—self-described "upper class" voters overwhelmingly supported Gore over Bush, by 56 to 39. And the reason for that inversion is that Republicans, consistently, are fighting for policies to expand opportunity for all, while Democrats are opposing those policies. Take three examples: school choice; Social Security reform; and tax cuts and small business deregulation.

School Choice

School choice is in many ways the single most important domestic issue being debated today. For centuries, education has formed the most widespread and direct route to rising up the economic ladder. It is the path immigrants have followed for 200 years, and it is the greatest hope for economic advancement for underprivileged children in America.

The American education system provides world-class education for many or even most wealthy and middle-class children. But, for poor children, and for African-American and Hispanic children in particular, the system fails them miserably. Only 70 percent of all students in public high schools graduate; only 51 percent of all black students and 52 percent of all Hispanic students graduate. Even more distressingly, empirical studies suggest that only 20 percent of all black students and 16 percent of all Hispanic students leave high school with the basic skills to attend college. According to the National Assessment of Education Progress, 63 percent of black and 56 percent of Hispanic fourth graders are below basic proficiency levels in reading.

Drop-out rates and illiteracy intersect with crime and widespread substance abuse to destroy the educational prospects for many inner-city children. In just one city, Cleveland, a few years ago students were statistically more likely to fall victim to a crime *at school* than actually to graduate on time with 12th-grade-level proficiency.

For so many low-income children, the American dream is a myth. All Americans should be horrified and appalled at the tragedy these children face every day.

The fault does not lie with the teachers, most of whom are dedicated public servants undertaking personal sacrifice and even physical risk to do their best to reach and teach the kids. The fault lies with the broken system, that for over a generation has failed to educate. The policy responses of Democrats—more and more money, more teachers, smaller classrooms—are all fine in and of themselves; but they've been tried for four decades. For forty years, the Democrat establishment has run the public schools and their solutions, tragically, have not worked.

Minority parents are rightly demanding major change, and change today. Not more of the same that consigns yet another generation of children to life without a serious opportunity at education and a future.

In 1999, one private program, the Children's Scholarship Program, offered 40,000 scholarships to help low-income kids escape failing schools: *the families of over 1.25 million children applied for the scholarships.*

School choice has the potential both to provide disadvantaged children with the means to access a better education and to introduce competition into the system to improve public school education for all children. As President Bush observed, "school choice offers proven results of a better education, not only for children enrolled in the specific plan, but also for children whose public schools benefit from the competition."

The single most effective argument against school choice—that it will destroy the public schools—has now been resoundingly disproved. Fortunately, choice is no longer just a theory; successful programs in Milwaukee, Cleveland, San Antonio, Florida, and Arizona have yielded a wealth of data uniformly demonstrating (1) that students who use vouchers experience significant increases in test scores, and (2) that previously failing public schools *improve*, often substantially, when competition arises from the introduction of choice.

The importance of school choice for improving opportunity cannot be overstated: both because it systematically provides children today with hope and access to an educational future and because, in so doing, it can prevent a host of other social maladies, from crime to poverty to long-term heath problems. Education is antecedent to them all.

President Bush has been an outspoken defender of providing parents and children with options and choices. He championed the No Child Left Behind Act as his first major domestic achievement, which dramatically expanded testing, accountability, and choice. Some critics have objected to the increased federal money going to education, but the bill also requires testing of every child in third and eighth grades and requires schools to provide parents with detailed report cards of the school's performance. And it devotes greater resources to parents of children in schools that are failing, expanding their options to ensure an education for their children. The focus is on accountability and results, and by providing parents with real information and hard data about their schools' performance, No Child

Left Behind facilitates parental involvement and informed decision-making.

Al Gore almost certainly would have appointed—and John Kerry presumably would as well—federal judges as resolutely opposed to school choice as is their party. In contrast, when the U.S. Supreme Court, over the objection of both Clinton-appointed Justices, recently upheld the constitutionality of the Cleveland school choice program in *Zelman v. Simmons-Harris*, President Bush lauded the "landmark ruling [as] a victory for parents and children throughout America."

Education represents the most critical vanguard in the ongoing battle for civil rights, and President Bush's consistent leadership in attacking the "soft bigotry of low expectations" and in insisting upon reforms that actually produce results for low-income and minority children is emblematic of opportunity conservatism.

Moreover, African-American and Hispanic voters consistently support school choice in overwhelming numbers and, like other voters, respond that education is their top priority at the ballot box. And, the Democratic Party is irredeemably opposed to school choice; so long as union leaders remain aggressively opposed to choice, Democrat politicians will follow suit.

And so, on the issue that minority voters say matters most to them, it is only the Republicans who are advocating policies to actually make a difference and make it easier for them to begin to ascend the economic ladder.

Social Security Private Accounts

With the impending retirement of the Baby Boomers, there are sound and powerful arguments for shifting to Social Security private accounts as a means of addressing systemic insolvency in the trust fund. And many Republicans make those arguments, gladly donning the green eyeshade.

But those are not the arguments that enliven the opportunity conservative. Using the Rawlsian lens, one should instead ask: How will private accounts affect the least well-off in America?

As a starting point, reforms proposed by conservatives all typically maintain (1) no alteration of benefits for those at or near retirement and (2) a guarantee of security and minimum benefits administered through the current system. Despite the rhetorical bogeyman of "Social Security privatization," no reform being seriously proposed comes close to such a radical result.

The reforms usually devote a small portion of the current 12.4 percent tax stream—typically 2 percent—to a private account owned by the beneficiary. Those private accounts would allow all Americans the ability to realize the markedly higher long-term returns of the stock market—from 1926 to 1997, an average of 7.2 percent—rather than the anemic returns of 1.9 percent in the current Social Security system (even assuming future solvency). But, even more importantly, each American would *own* his or her own account. And that's where the excitement of the reform comes in.

Right now, a person can work his or her entire life, as a maid or a janitor or a migrant worker, pay into the system for fifty years, and then, when he dies, have absolutely nothing. The moment a retiree dies, his or her children get nothing. Even with a very modest income—say $20,000 per year—a 22-year-old paying into a 2% account could retire with an account of over $100,000, even with the most conservative of returns. Another worker, making $30,000 a year, would retire with more than $150,000. And, when they pass on, their children could inherit that asset.

Thus, that same menial worker could labor all those years, still have security in retirement, and when he dies leave the $100,000 account to his children to help them get started in life. And, standing on the shoulders of their hard-working parents, those children could begin several rungs higher on the economic

29

ladder, using the money for education or to buy a home or to start a business.

As the late Senator Daniel Patrick Moynihan put it—in a phrasing that may not be endearing to many Republicans, but should be embraced nonetheless—Social Security private accounts are the "grand culmination" of FDR's New Deal: "an estate" for every "doorman, as well as those living in the duplexes above."

Like school choice, Social Security private accounts are a potentially paradigm-shifting reform. If implemented, they could dramatically alter and improve the array of opportunities for those climbing the ladder.

Because of their ability to alter significantly the structural barriers that make it difficult for the disadvantaged to advance, these two reforms—school choice and Social Security private accounts—dwarf virtually every other domestic proposal in terms of importance and potential long-term impact.

In President Bush's first term, education was one of his signature domestic initiatives; in a second term, social security reform may well be his singular domestic legacy. As President, he has laid out seven principles and goals to guide social security reform: creating a society of stakeholders, expanding ownership of retirement assets, ensuring freedom of choice, minimizing risk through diversification, strengthening women's retirement security, helping future generations achieve the American dream, and spurring national savings and economic growth. In their focus, promise, and articulation, these goals bespeak opportunity conservatism.

Indeed, throughout the 2000 campaign, President Bush had the courage to speak out on the issue—to grab the "third rail" of politics and risk demagoguery—because reforming Social Security had the potential to make such a difference for so many Americans.

I'll never forget sitting with President Bush and a number of other advisors early in the campaign, in the summer of 1999, and

discussing Social Security reform. Many of the advisors coun-
seled caution, or even suggested avoiding the issue altogether. It
was too politically dangerous, they said. With a steel look in his
eye, Governor Bush literally pounded the table and said "I'm
running for a reason. It's the right thing to do, and I'm going to
fight for it."

That is the passion of the opportunity conservative. It is
worth emphasizing that both school choice and Social Security
reform benefit almost exclusively the economically disadvantaged. The "rich" — the alleged rhetorical recipients of Republican
largesse — are almost entirely unaffected by either reform. Virtually every school choice program is means tested, so that only
disadvantaged children are eligible, and a Social Security private
account would be a pittance to a Rockefeller. But, to a working-
class mother or father, it could be an enormous asset.

Indeed, if one were to imagine the issues a priori, or to try to
explain them to a visitor from another country who knew nothing whatsoever about American politics, the prevailing (but
false) stereotypes of the two parties—Democrats for the poor,
and Republicans for the rich—would yield a natural inference as
to where the parties would fall. Both school choice and Social
Security private accounts represent a potential transfer of tens of
billions of dollars directly to the most economically disadvantaged, but it is Democrats who are fighting with all their strength
to kill them, and Republicans who are advancing the reforms.

Tax Cuts and Small Business Deregulation

The average middle-class taxpayer pays 38 percent of his or
her wages in federal, state, and local taxes—more than food,
clothing, and housing combined. Before the Bush tax cuts, a
single working mother of two, earning between $21,000 and
$31,000 per year, faced a marginal *effective federal tax rate*—the
combined income taxes and loss of Earned Income Tax Credit

that she paid on each additional dollar of income earned—of over 36 percent.

That money, the price of our ever-expanding government, came directly from the dollars she would otherwise use to pay her rent, feed her children, purchase health care, or tend to the basic necessities of life. In 2001, 2002, and 2003, President Bush signed into law dramatic tax cuts, and as a result he lessened the tax burden on all Americans, especially those struggling to ascend the economic ladder. In 2003 alone, as a result of President Bush's tax cut:

- 91 million taxpayers saved an average of $1,126.
- 68 million women saved, on average, $1,338.
- 34 million families with children saved, on average, $1,549.
- 23 million small business owners saved, on average, $2,209.
- 12 million elderly taxpayers saved, on average, $1,401.
- 6 million single women with children saved, on average, $558.
- 3 million individuals and families had their income tax liability completely eliminated.

Reducing the burdens of government on those struggling to survive every day makes it easier for them to start to make economic progress. To do so, however, they need a job.

Small business employs more than half of all Americans. Yet, according to the Small Business Administration, in 2000 "federal regulations cost small firms (less than 20 employees) nearly $7,000 per employee annually." Every dollar unnecessarily sapped from small business is a dollar that cannot go to providing a job.

In addition to the debilitating effect of excessive regulation, expanding tort liability further drains the vitality of small business. One in four small business owners have either been sued or threatened with a suit, and the cost of defending those suits is estimated at $100,000—twice the average small business owner's salary.

Between regulation and litigation, modern society erects serious barriers to the success of small business. Yet it is small business that can be counted on to provide two-thirds of the new jobs in America. Without the entry-level jobs small business provides, those at the bottom of the economic ladder cannot begin to develop skills and experience to ascend. Already skilled workers, with training and advanced education, can most easily demand competitive wages and maintain their jobs despite the onslaught of regulation and litigation; unskilled workers—those at the bottom—are the most vulnerable to being driven out of the market.

Not only do the economically disadvantaged depend upon small business for immediate employment, but small business entrepreneurship provides one of the most reliable ways out of poverty for countless poor and immigrant families. For generations, those on the bottom have started small, with taxi services, and barbershops, and newspaper stands, only to see them grow into expanding and thriving businesses. Today, nearly 40 percent of small businesses are owned by women, and almost 15 percent—over 3 million—are owned by minorities.

But if regulations and the threat of litigation stifle those endeavors before they get off the ground—if protectionist ordinances impose unnecessary barriers to entry for new businesses—then the next generation of disadvantaged may never get a chance to continue the economic journey. Of course, lower taxes, decreased regulation, and tort reform are all themes that Republicans are comfortable championing, and that Democrats routinely oppose. But the opportunity conservative addresses the issues—formulates them, understands them, and articulates them—not in terms of the traditional business classes, but in terms of expanding opportunity for those at the bottom.

The opportunity conservative focuses on the incentive and deterrent effects upon those trying to rise into the middle class and on the need to encourage entrepreneurship and small business to ensure jobs for those most in need.

The opportunity conservative fights for the little guy and understands and explains that taxes, regulation, and litigation that place undue burdens on low-income workers and small business employers frustrate opportunity. The argument is always, always, always about that opportunity, and about ensuring each generation of Americans can climb the ladder and achieve success.

Conclusion

Our nation's birth was predicated on freedom and opportunity for all; America itself was forged as a commitment to expanding that promise: "We hold these truths to be self-evident, that all men are created equal, that they are endowed by their Creator with certain unalienable Rights, that among these are Life, Liberty and the pursuit of Happiness."

The opportunity conservative has a mantra: ownership, choice, and opportunity. He or she focuses on, as the proverb goes, teaching to fish, not just providing a fish; on enabling individual responsibility and potential to flourish.

This approach applies to virtually all policy areas, not just those discussed above. Crime policy can be expressed in terms of how incarcerating criminals, swiftly and surely, directly benefits the residents of the impoverished neighborhoods many of them terrorize. Excessive environmental regulation, stifling development of new residential neighborhoods, pulls up the "draw bridge" and denies lower-income Americans the ability to purchase an affordable first home. Nanny-state gun regulations, unnecessarily restricting ownership and driving up costs, make it all the harder for low-income minorities—those often at greatest risk of crime and violence—to protect themselves and their homes. Disability policy can be expressed in terms of expanding the ability of Americans with disabilities to be independent and self-sufficient, of supporting assistive technology and President Bush's New Freedom Initiative to increase the opportunity to learn and develop skills, engage in productive work, choose where to live, and participate in community life.

Likewise, President Bush's leadership on welfare reform—defending policies that promote work and responsibility and freedom from dependency—and on housing reform—encouraging home ownership—both demonstrate the bold promise of opportunity conservatism.

It is only fitting that the party of Abraham Lincoln—who heralded our nation, "conceived in Liberty, and dedicated to the proposition that all men are created equal"—would champion opportunity, and defend increased choice and freedom for all Americans.

Today President George W. Bush carries the mantle of Lincoln as an opportunity conservative, defending the promise of the Declaration and the vision of our great nation. And the future of the Grand Old Party depends upon ensuring that that vision comes to pass, that the policies we espouse facilitate the ability of every man, woman, and child to hope for and be able to realize the American dream.

FOREIGN

POLICY

CHAPTER FOUR

THE BUSH DOCTRINE: THE WAR ON TERRORISM AND AMERICA'S CHOICE

VICE PRESIDENT RICHARD CHENEY

Richard Cheney has served as Vice President of the United States since January 2001. His long career in public service has included time as Chief of Staff to President Gerald Ford, House minority whip, and Secretary of Defense under President George H.W. Bush.

The following is excerpted from a speech delivered by Mr. Cheney in Simi Valley, California, at the Ronald Reagan Presidential Library on March 17, 2004.

Last fall, some people with short memories were asking why on Earth California would want to put an actor in the Governor's office. The question brought to mind images of 1966, and all the great events that were set in motion by the election of Governor Ronald Reagan. From his first day in Sacramento to his last day in Washington, Ronald Reagan showed a certain kind of leadership. He had confidence in himself, and even deeper confidence in the United States and our place among nations. His principles were the product of a good heart, a sturdy Midwestern character, and years of disciplined preparation for the work that history gave him. He had a basic awareness of good and evil that made him a champion of human freedom, and the greatest foe of the greatest tyranny of his time. The Cold War ended as it did, not by chance, not by some inevitable progression of events: It ended because Ronald Reagan was President of the United States.

After the fall of Soviet communism, some observers confidently assumed that America would never again face such determined enemies, or an aggressive ideology, or the prospect of catastrophic violence. But standing here in 2004, we can see clearly how a new enemy was organizing and gathering strength over a period of years. And the struggle we are in today, against terrorist enemies intending violence on a massive scale, requires the same qualities of leadership that saw our nation to victory in the Cold War. We must build and maintain military strength capable of operating in different theaters of action with decisive force. We must not only have that power, but be willing to use it when required to defend our freedom and our security.

We must support those around the world who are taking risks to advance freedom, justice, and democracy, just as President Reagan did. American policy must be clear and consistent in its purposes. And American leaders—above all, the Commander-in-Chief—must be confident in our nation's cause, and unwavering until the danger to our people is fully and finally removed.

The Post-9/11 World and America's Response

The attacks of September 11th, 2001, signaled the arrival of an entirely different era. We suffered massive civilian casualties on our own soil. We awakened to dangers even more lethal—the possibility that terrorists could gain chemical, biological, or even nuclear weapons from outlaw regimes, and turn those weapons against the United States and our friends. We came to understand that for all the destruction and grief we saw that day, September 11th gave only the merest glimpse of the threat that international terrorism poses to this and other nations. If terrorists ever do acquire weapons of mass destruction—on their own or with help from a terror regime—they will use those weapons without the slightest constraint of reason or morality. Instead of losing thousands of lives, we might lose tens or even hundreds of thousands of lives in a single day of horror. Remembering what we saw on the morning of 9/11, and knowing the nature of these enemies, we have as clear a responsibility as could ever fall to government: We must do everything in our power to protect our people from terrorist attacks, and to keep terrorists from ever acquiring weapons of mass destruction.

This great and urgent responsibility has required a shift in national security policy. For many years prior to 9/11, we treated terror attacks against Americans as isolated incidents, and answered—if at all—on an ad hoc basis, and never in a systematic way. Even after an attack inside our own country—the 1993 bombing at the World Trade Center, in New York—there was a tendency to treat terrorist incidents as individual criminal acts, to be handled primarily through law enforcement. The man who perpetrated that attack in New York was tracked down, arrested, convicted, and sent off to serve a 240-year sentence. Yet behind that one man was a growing network with operatives inside and outside the United States, waging war against our country. For us, that war started on 9/11. For them, it started years before.

After the World Trade Center attack in 1993 came the murders at the Saudi Arabia National Guard Training Center in Riyadh, in 1995; the simultaneous bombings of American embassies in Kenya and Tanzania, in 1998; the attack on the *USS Cole*, in 2000. In 1996, Khalid Shaykh Muhammad—the mastermind of

9/11—first proposed to Osama bin Laden that they use hijacked airliners to attack targets in the U.S. During this period, thousands of terrorists were trained at Al Qaeda camps in Afghanistan. And we have seen the work of terrorists in many attacks since 9/11—in Riyadh, Casablanca, Istanbul, Mombasa, Bali, Jakarta, Najaf, Baghdad, and most recently, Madrid.

The Bush Doctrine

Against this kind of determined, organized, ruthless enemy, America requires a new strategy—not merely to prosecute a series of crimes, but to fight and win a global campaign against the terror network. Our strategy has several key elements. We have strengthened our defenses here at home, organizing the government to protect the homeland. But a good defense is not enough. The terrorist enemy holds no territory, defends no population, is unconstrained by rules of warfare, and respects no law of morality. Such an enemy cannot be deterred, contained, appeased, or negotiated with. It can only be destroyed—and that, ladies and gentlemen, is the business at hand.

We are dismantling the financial networks that have funded terror; we are going after the terrorists themselves wherever they plot and plan. Of those known to be directly involved in organizing the attacks of 9/11, most are now in custody or confirmed dead. The leadership of Al Qaeda has sustained heavy losses, and they will sustain more.

America is also working closely with intelligence services all over the globe. The best intelligence is necessary—not just to win the war on terror, but also to stop the proliferation of weapons of mass destruction. So we have enhanced our intelligence capabilities, in order to trace dangerous weapons activity. We have organized a proliferation security initiative, to interdict lethal materials and technologies in transit. We are aggressively pursuing another dangerous source of proliferation: black-market operatives who sell equipment and expertise related to weapons of mass destruction. The world recently learned of the network led by A.Q. Khan, the former head of Pakistan's nuclear weapons program. Khan and his associates sold nuclear technology and know-how to outlaw regimes around the world, including Iran and North Korea. Thanks to the tireless work of intelligence officers from the United States, the UK, Pakistan, and other nations, the Khan network is now being dismantled piece by piece.

And we are applying the Bush doctrine: Any person or government that supports, protects, or harbors terrorists is complicit in the murder of the innocent, and will be held to account.

The first to see this application were the Taliban, who ruled Afghanistan by violence while turning that country into a training camp for terrorists. America and our coalition took down the regime in a matter of weeks because of our superior technology, the unmatched skill of our armed forces, and, above all, because we came not as conquerors but as liberators. The Taliban are gone from the scene. The terrorist camps are closed. And our coalition's work there continues — confronting terrorist remnants, training a new Afghan army, and providing security as the new government takes shape. Under President Karzai's leadership, and with a new constitution, the Afghan people are reclaiming their own country and building a nation that is secure, independent, and free.

The Importance of Iraq

In Iraq, we took another essential step in the war on terror. Before using force, we tried every possible option to address the threat from Saddam Hussein. Despite 12 years of diplomacy, more than a dozen UN Security Council resolutions, hundreds of UN weapons inspectors, thousands of flights to enforce the no-fly zones, and even strikes against military targets in Iraq Saddam Hussein refused to comply with the terms of the 1991 Gulf War cease-fire. All of these measures failed. In October of 2002, the United States Congress voted overwhelmingly to authorize the use of force in Iraq. The next month, the UN Security Council passed a unanimous resolution finding Iraq in material breach of its obligations, and vowing serious consequences in the event Saddam Hussein did not fully and immediately comply. When Saddam failed even then to comply, President Bush gave an ultimatum to the dictator: to leave Iraq or be forcibly removed from power.

That ultimatum came one year ago today—12 months in which Saddam went from palace, to bunker, to spider hole, to jail. A year ago, he was the all-powerful dictator of Iraq, controlling the lives and the future of almost 25 million people. Today, the people of Iraq know that the dictator and his sons will never torment them again. And we can be certain that they will never again threaten Iraq's neighbors or the United States of America.

From the beginning, America has sought—and received—international support for our operations in Iraq and Afghanistan. In the war on terror, we will always seek cooperation from our allies around the world. But as the President has made very clear, there is a difference between leading a coalition of many nations and submitting to the objections of a few. The United States will never seek a permission slip to defend the security of our country.

We still have work to do in Iraq, and we will see it through. Our forces are conducting swift, precision raids against the terrorists and regime holdouts who still remain. The thugs and assassins in Iraq are desperately trying to shake our will. Just this morning, they conducted a murderous attack on a hotel in Baghdad. Their goal is to prevent the rise of a democracy—but they will fail. Just last week, the Iraqi Governing Council approved a new fundamental law, an essential step toward building a free constitutional democracy in the heart of the Middle East. This great work is part of a forward strategy of freedom that we are pursuing throughout the greater Middle East. By helping nations to build the institutions of freedom, and turning the energies of men and women away from violence, we not only make that region more peaceful, we add to the security of our own region.

The recent bombing in Spain may well be evidence of how fearful the terrorists are of a free and democratic Iraq. But if the murderers of Madrid intended to undermine the transition to democracy in Iraq, they will ultimately fail. Our determination is unshakable. We will stand with the people of Iraq as they build a government based on democracy, tolerance, and freedom.

Our steady course has not escaped the attention of the leaders in other countries. Three months ago, after initiating talks with America and Britain, and five days after the capture of Saddam Hussein, the leader of Libya voluntarily committed to disclose and dismantle all of his weapons of mass destruction programs. As we meet today, the dismantling of those programs is underway. I do not believe that Colonel Ghadafi just happened to make this very wise decision after many years of pursuing secretive, intensive efforts to develop the world's most dangerous weapons. He was responding to the new realities of the world. Leaders elsewhere are learning that weapons of mass destruction do not bring influence, or prestige, or security—they only invite isolation, and carry other costs. In the post-9/11 world, the United States and our allies will not live at the mercy of terrorists or regimes that could arm them with chemical, biological, or nuclear weapons. By whatever means are necessary—whether diplomatic or military—we will act to protect the lives and security of the American people.

Bush, Kerry and America's Future

These past three years, as our country experienced war and national emergency, I have watched our Commander-in-Chief make the decisions and set the strategy. I have seen a man who is calm and deliberate—comfortable with responsibility—consistent in his objectives, and resolute in his actions. These

45

times have tested the character of our nation, and they have tested the character of our nation's leader. When he makes a commitment, there is no doubt he will follow through. As a result, America's friends know they can trust—and America's enemies know they can fear—the decisive leadership of President George W. Bush.

The President's conduct in leading America through a time of unprecedented danger—his ability to make decisions and stand by them—is a measure that must be applied to the candidate who now opposes him in the election of 2004.

In one of Senator Kerry's recent observations about foreign policy, he informed his listeners that his ideas have gained strong support, at least among unnamed foreigners he's been spending time with. Senator Kerry said that he has met with foreign leaders, and I quote, " who can't go out and say this publicly, but boy they look at you and say, 'You've got to win this, you've got to beat this guy, we need a new policy,' things like that."

A few days ago in Pennsylvania, a voter asked Senator Kerry directly who these foreign leaders are. Senator Kerry said, "That's none of your business." But it is our business when a candidate for President claims the political endorsement of foreign leaders. At the very least, we have a right to know what he is saying to foreign leaders that makes them so supportive of his candidacy. American voters are the ones charged with determining the outcome of this election—not unnamed foreign leaders.

Senator Kerry's voting record on national security raises some important questions all by itself. Let's begin with the matter of how Iraq and Saddam Hussein should have been dealt with. Senator Kerry was in the minority of Senators who voted against the Persian Gulf War in 1991. At the time, he expressed the view that our international coalition consisted of "shadow battlefield allies who barely carry a burden." Last year, as we prepared to liberate Iraq, he recalled the Persian Gulf coalition a little differently. He said it was a "strong coalition," and a model to be followed.

Six years after the Gulf War, in 1997, Saddam Hussein was still defying the terms of the cease-fire. And as President Bill Clinton considered military action against Iraq, he found a true believer in John Kerry. The Senator from Massachusetts said, "Should the resolve of our allies wane, the United States must not lose its resolve to take action." He further warned that if Saddam Hussein were not held to account for violation of UN resolutions, some future conflict would have "greater consequence." In 1998, Senator Kerry indicated his support for regime change, with ground troops if necessary. And, of course, when Congress voted in October of 2002, Senator Kerry voted to authorize military action if Saddam refused to comply with UN demands.

A neutral observer, looking at these elements of Senator Kerry's record, would assume that Senator Kerry supported military action against Saddam Hussein. The Senator himself now tells us otherwise. In January he was asked on TV if he was "one of the anti-war candidates." He replied, "I am." He now says he was voting only to "threaten the use of force," not actually to use force.

Even if we set aside these inconsistencies and changing rationales, at least this much is clear: Had the decision belonged to Senator Kerry, Saddam Hussein would still be in power, today, in Iraq. In fact, Saddam Hussein would almost certainly still be in control of Kuwait.

Senator Kerry speaks often about the need for international cooperation, and has vowed to usher in a "golden age of American diplomacy." He is fond of mentioning that some countries did not support America's actions in Iraq. Yet of the many nations that have joined our coalition—allies and friends of the United States—Senator Kerry speaks with open contempt. Great Britain, Australia, Italy, Spain, Poland, and more than 20 other nations have contributed and sacrificed for the freedom of the

Iraqi people. Senator Kerry calls these countries "window dressing." They are, in his words, "a coalition of the coerced and the bribed."

Many questions come to mind, but the first is this: How would Senator Kerry describe Great Britain—coerced, or bribed? Or Italy, which recently lost 19 citizens, killed by terrorists in Najaf? Was Italy's contribution just window dressing? If such dismissive terms are the vernacular of the golden age of diplomacy Senator Kerry promises, we are left to wonder which nations would care to join any future coalition. He speaks as if only those who openly oppose America's objectives have a chance of earning his respect. Senator Kerry's characterization of our good allies is ungrateful to nations that have withstood danger, hardship, and insult for standing with America in the cause of freedom.

Senator Kerry has also had a few things to say about support for our troops now on the ground in Iraq. Among other criticisms, he has asserted that those troops are not receiving the material support they need. Just this morning, he again gave the example of body armor, which he said our Administration failed to supply. May I remind the Senator that last November, at the President's request, Congress passed an $87 billion supplemental appropriation. This legislation was essential to our ongoing operations in Iraq and Afghanistan providing funding for body armor and other vital equipment; hazard pay; health benefits; ammunition; fuel, and spare parts for our military. The legislation passed overwhelmingly, with a vote in the Senate of 87 to 12. Senator Kerry voted no. I note that yesterday, attempting to clarify the matter, Senator Kerry said, "I actually did vote for the $87 billion, before I voted against it."

On national security, the Senator has shown at least one measure of consistency. Over the years, he has repeatedly voted against weapons systems for the military. He voted against the Apache helicopter, against the Tomahawk cruise missile, against even the Bradley Fighting Vehicle. He has also been a reliable vote against military pay increases—opposing them no fewer than 12 times.

Many of these very weapons systems have been used by our forces in Iraq and Afghanistan, and are proving to be valuable assets in the war on terror. In his defense, of course, Senator Kerry has questioned whether the war on terror is really a war at all. Recently he said, "I don't want to use that terminology." In his view, opposing terrorism is far less of a military operation and far more of an intelligence-gathering, law enforcement operation. As we have seen, however, that approach was tried before, and proved entirely inadequate to protecting the American people from the terrorists who are quite certain they are at war with us—and are comfortable using that terminology.

I leave it for Senator Kerry to explain, or explain away, his votes and his statements about the war on terror, our cause in Iraq, the allies who serve with us, and the needs of our military. Whatever the explanation, whatever nuances he might fault us for neglecting, it is not an impressive record for someone who aspires to become Commander-in-Chief in this time of testing for our country. In his years in Washington, Senator Kerry has been one vote of a hundred in the United States Senate—and fortunately on matters of national security, he was very often in the minority. But the presidency is an entirely different proposition. The President always casts the deciding vote. And the Senator from Massachusetts has given us ample doubts about his judgment and the attitude he brings to bear on vital issues of national security.

The American people will have a clear choice in the election of 2004, at least as clear as any since the election of 1984. In more than three years as President, George W. Bush has built a national security record of his own. America has come to know the President after one of the worst days in our history. He saw America through tragedy. He has kept the nation's enemies in desperate flight, and under his leadership, our country has once again led the armies of liberation, freeing 50 million souls from tyranny, and making our nation and the world more secure.

All Americans, regardless of political party, can be proud of what our nation has achieved in this historic time, when so many depended on us, and all the world was watching. And I have been very proud to work with a President who—like other Presidents we have known—has shown, in his own conduct, the optimism, and strength, and decency of the great nation he serves.

CHAPTER FIVE

A CHANGED WORLD

GEORGE SHULTZ

George P. Shultz is the Thomas and Susan Ford Distinguished Fellow at the Hoover Institution. He served as Secretary of State under President Ronald Reagan, from 1982 to 1989, and as Secretary of the Treasury under President Richard Nixon from 1972 to 1974.

The following was delivered as the Kissinger Lecture at the Library of Congress, in Washington, D.C., on February 11, 2004. It appears with the permission of THE HOOVER DIGEST, *which ran this article in its Spring 2004 issue, and with the permission of the author.*

We are at one of those special moments in history. The topic of the day is Iraq and weapons not accounted for, but the implications of action in Iraq for the world and for our future go far beyond this immediate case. So I will put Iraq into context, give my view of developments there, and then set out a few of the important implications, including those for Israeli-Palestinian issues and for our own dangerous dependence on imported oil.

The Problem of Terrorism

We have struggled with terrorism for a long time. In the Reagan Administration, I was a hawk on the subject. I said terrorism is a big problem, a different problem, and we have to take forceful action against it. Fortunately, Ronald Reagan agreed with me, but not many others did. (Don Rumsfeld was an outspoken exception.) I argued long and hard against those who said that "one man's terrorist is another man's freedom fighter." Some people are still saying this; they are wrong, dreadfully wrong.

In those days we focused on how to defend against terrorism. We reinforced our embassies and increased our intelligence efforts. We thought we made some progress. We established the legal basis for holding states responsible for using terrorists to attack Americans anywhere. Through intelligence, we did abort many potential terrorist acts. But we didn't really understand what motivated the terrorists or what they were out to do.

In the 1990s, the problem began to appear even more menacing. Osama bin Laden and Al Qaeda were well known; but the nature of the terrorist threat was not yet comprehended, and our efforts to combat it were ineffective. Diplomacy without much force was tried. Terrorism was regarded as a law enforcement problem and terrorists as criminals. Some were arrested and put on trial. Early last year, a judge finally allowed the verdict to stand for one of those convicted in the 1993 World Trade Center bombing. It took ten years! Terrorism is not a matter that can be left just to law enforcement, with its deliberative process, built-in delays, and safeguards that may let prisoners go free on procedural grounds.

Today, looking back on the past quarter century of terrorism, we can see that it is the method of choice of an extensive, internationally connected ideological movement dedicated to the destruction of our international system of cooperation and progress. We can see that the 1981 assassination of President Sadat, the 1993 bombing of the World Trade Center, the 2001 destruction of the Twin Towers, and scores of other terrorist attacks were carried out by one part or another of this movement. And the movement is connected to states that develop awesome weaponry—with some of it, or expertise, for sale.

What Should We Do?

First and foremost, shore up the state system.

The world has worked for three centuries with the sovereign state as the basic operating entity, presumably accountable to its citizens and responsible for their well-being. In this system, states also interact with one another—bilaterally or multilaterally—to accomplish ends that transcend their borders. They create international organizations to serve their ends, not govern them.

Increasingly, the state system has been eroding. Terrorists have exploited this weakness by burrowing into the state system in order to attack it. As the state system weakens, no replacement in sight can perform the essential functions of establishing an orderly and lawful society, protecting essential freedoms, providing a framework for fruitful economic activity, contributing to effective international cooperation, and providing for the common defense.

I see our great task as restoring the vitality of the state system within the framework of a world of opportunity and with aspirations for a world of states that recognize accountability for human freedom and dignity.

All established states should stand up to their responsibilities in the fight against terror, our common enemy, by being a helpful partner in economic and political development, and taking care that international organizations work for their member states, not the other way around. When they do, they deserve respect and help to make them work successfully.

Then we need to remind ourselves and our partners of the Great Seal of our Republic, which carries a message as clear and relevant to these times as to our early days. The central figure is an eagle holding in one talon an olive branch and in the other, 13 arrows. As President Harry Truman insisted at the end of World War II, the eagle will always face the olive branch to show that the United States will always seek peace. But the eagle will forever hold onto the arrows to show that, to be effective in seeking peace, you must have strength and the willingness to use it.

Strength and diplomacy go together. They are not alternatives; they are complements. As President Bush put it in his State of the Union address:

> "Nine months of intense negotiations involving the United States and Great Britain succeeded with Libya, while 12 years of diplomacy with Iraq did not. And one reason is clear: For diplomacy to be effective, words must be credible, and no one can now doubt the word of America."

The civilized world has a common stake in defeating the terrorists. We now call this what it is: a war on terrorism. In war, you have to act on both offense and defense. You have to hit the enemy before the enemy hits you. The diplomacy of incentives, containment, deterrence, and prevention is all made more effective by the demonstrated possibility of forceful preemption. Diplomacy and strength must work together on a grand and strategic scale and on an operational and tactical level. But if you deny yourself the option of forceful preemption, you diminish the effectiveness of your diplomatic moves. And, with the consequences of a terrorist attack as hideous as they are, the United States must be ready to preempt identified threats, not at the last moment, when an attack is imminent and more difficult to stop, but before the terrorist gets in position to do irreparable harm.

Over the last decade we have seen large areas of the world where there is no longer any state authority at all, an ideal environment in which terrorists can plan and train. In the early 1990s we came to realize the significance of a "failed state." Earlier, people allowed themselves to think that, for example, an African colony could gain its independence, be admitted to the United Nations as a member state, and thereafter remain a sovereign state. Then came Somalia. All government disappeared—no more sovereignty, no more state. The same was true in Afghanistan. And who took over? Islamic extremists, who soon made it clear that they regarded the concept of the state as an abomination. To them, the very idea of the "state" was un-Islamic. They talked about reviving traditional forms of pan-Islamic rule with no place for the state. They were fundamentally, and violently, opposed to the way the world works, to the international state system.

The United States launched a military campaign to eliminate the Taliban and Al Qaeda's rule over Afghanistan. Now we and our allies are trying to help Afghanistan become a true state again and a viable member of the international state system. Yet there are many other parts of the world where state authority has collapsed or, within some states, large areas where the state's authority does not operate.

That's one area of danger: places where the state has vanished. A second area of danger is found in places where the state has been taken over by criminals, gangsters, or warlords. Saddam Hussein was one example. Kim Jong Il of North Korea is another.

They seize control of state power and use that power to enhance their wealth, consolidate their rule, and develop their weaponry. As they do this, violating the laws and principles of the international system, they at the same time claim its privileges and immunities, such as the principle of nonintervention in the internal affairs of a legitimate sovereign state. For decades these thugs have gotten away with it. And the leading nations of the world have let them get away with it.

This is why the case of Saddam Hussein and Iraq is so significant. Let me just stay on this point for a moment. Because of its importance, a careful review is in order.

The War Against Iraq Was Necessary

After Saddam Hussein consolidated power, he started a war against one of his neighbors, Iran, and in the course of that war he committed war crimes, including the use of chemical weapons, even against his own people.

About ten years later he started another war against another one of his neighbors, Kuwait. In the course of doing so, he committed war crimes. He took hostages. He launched missiles against a third and then a fourth country in the region.

That war was unique in modern times because Saddam totally eradicated another state and turned it into "Province 19" of Iraq. The aggressors in wars might typically seize some territory or occupy the defeated country or install a puppet regime, but Saddam sought to wipe out Kuwait, to erase it from the map of the world.

That got the world's attention. That's why, at the United Nations, the votes were wholly in favor of a U.S.-led military operation—Desert Storm—to throw Saddam out of Kuwait and to restore Kuwait to its place as a legitimate state in the international system. There was virtually universal recognition that those responsible for the international system of states could not let a state simply be rubbed out, as Saddam had done to Kuwait.

When Saddam was defeated, in 1991, a cease-fire was put in place. Then the UN Security Council decided that, in order to prevent Saddam from continuing to start wars and commit crimes against his own people, he must give up his arsenal of "weapons of mass destruction."

Recall the way it was to work. If Saddam cooperated with UN inspectors, produced his weapons, and facilitated their destruction, then the cease-fire would be transformed into a peace agreement, ending the state of war between the international system and Iraq. But if Saddam did not cooperate, and materially breached his obligations regarding his weapons of mass destruction, then the original UN Security Council authorization for the use of "all necessary force" against Iraq—an authorization that at the end of Desert Storm had been suspended but not canceled—would be reactivated and Saddam would face another round of the U.S.-led military action against him. Saddam agreed to this arrangement.

In the early 1990s, UN inspectors found plenty of material in the category of weapons of mass destruction and dismantled a lot of them. They kept on finding such weapons, but as the presence of force declined, Saddam's cooperation declined. He began to play games and to obstruct and undermine the inspection effort.

By 1998 the situation was untenable. Saddam had made inspections impossible. President Clinton, in February 1998, declared that Saddam would have to comply with the UN resolutions or face American military force. UN Secretary General Kofi Annan flew to Baghdad and returned with a new promise of cooperation from Saddam. But Saddam did not cooperate. The U.S. Congress then passed the Iraq Liberation Act by a vote of 360 to 38 in the House of Representatives; the Senate gave its unanimous consent. Signed into law on October 31, H.R. 4655 supported the renewed use of force against Saddam with the objective of changing the regime. By this time Saddam had openly and utterly rejected the inspections and the UN Security Council resolutions.

In November 1998 the Security Council passed a resolution declaring Saddam to be in "flagrant violation" of all the UN resolutions going back to 1991. That meant that the cease-fire was terminated and that the original authorization for the use of force against Saddam was reactivated. President Clinton ordered American forces into action in December 1998.

But the U.S. military operation was called off after only four days—apparently because President Clinton did not feel able to lead the country into war at a time when he was facing impeachment.

So inspections stopped. The United States ceased to take the lead. But the inspectors reported that, as of the end of 1998, Saddam possessed major quantities of weapons of mass destruction across a range of categories, particularly in chemical and biological weapons, and the means of delivering them by missiles. All the intelligence services of the world agreed on this.

From that time until late 2002, Saddam was left undisturbed to do what he wished with this arsenal of weapons. The international system had given up its ability to monitor and deal with this threat. All through the years between 1998 and 2002, Saddam continued to rule Iraq as a rogue state.

President Bush made it clear by 2002, against the background of 9/11, that Saddam must be brought into compliance. It was obvious that the world could not leave this situation as it was. The United States made the decision to continue to work within the scope of the UN Security Council resolutions—a long line of them—to deal with Saddam Hussein. After an extended and excruciating diplomatic effort at the United Nations in New York and in capitals around the world, the UN Security Council late in 2002 passed Resolution 1441, which gave Saddam one final chance to comply or face military force. When, on December 8, 2002, Iraq produced its required report, it was clear that Saddam was continuing to play games and to reject his obligations under international law. His report, thousands of pages long, did not in any way account for the remaining weapons of mass destruction that the UN inspectors had reported to be in existence as of the end of 1998. That assessment was widely agreed upon.

That should have been that. But the debate at the United Nations went on—and on. And as it went on it deteriorated. Instead

58

of the focus being on Iraq and Saddam, France induced others to regard the problem as one of restraining the United States—a position that seemed to emerge from France's aspirations for greater influence in Europe and elsewhere. By March 2003 it was clear that French diplomacy had resulted in splitting NATO, the European Union, and the UN Security Council and probably convincing Saddam that he would not face the use of force. The French position, in effect, was to say that Saddam had begun to show signs of cooperation with the UN resolutions because more than 200,000 American troops were poised on Iraq's borders ready to strike him; the United States should thus just keep its troops poised there for an indeterminate time, until France would presumably instruct us that we could either withdraw or go into action. This of course was impossible militarily, politically, and financially.

Where do we stand now? These key points need to be understood:

- There has never been a clearer case of a rogue state using its privileges of statehood to advance its dictator's interests in ways that defy and endanger the international state system.

- The international legal case against Saddam— 17 resolutions—was unprecedented.

- The intelligence services of all involved nations and the UN inspectors during more than a decade all agreed that Saddam possessed weapons of mass destruction that posed a threat to international peace and security.

- Saddam had four undisturbed years to augment, conceal, disperse, or otherwise deal with his arsenal.

- He used every means to avoid cooperating or explaining what he had done with them. This refusal in itself was, under the UN resolutions, adequate grounds for resuming the military operation against him that had been put in abeyance in 1991, pending his compliance.

President Bush, in ordering U.S. forces into action, stated that we were doing so under UN Security Council Resolutions 678 and 687, the original bases for military action against Saddam Hussein in 1991. Those who criticize the United States for unilateralism should recognize that no nation in the history of the United Nations has ever engaged in such a sustained and committed multilateral diplomatic effort to adhere to the principles of international law and international organization within the international system. In the end, it was the United States that upheld and acted in accordance with the UN resolutions on Iraq, not those on the Security Council who tried to stop us.

The question of weapons of mass destruction is just that: a question that remains to be answered, a mystery that must be solved—just as we also must solve the mystery of how Libya and Iran developed menacing nuclear capability without detection, of how we were caught unaware of a large and flourishing black market in nuclear material, and of how we discovered these developments before they got completely out of hand and have put in place promising corrective processes. The question of Iraq's presumed stockpile of weapons will be answered, but that answer, however it comes out, will not affect the fully justifiable and necessary action that the coalition has undertaken to bring an end to Saddam Hussein's rule over Iraq. As arms inspector David Kay put it in a February 1 interview with Chris Wallace:

> **Kay:** We know there were terrorist groups in state still seeking WMD capability. Iraq, although I found no weapons, had tremendous capabilities in this area. A marketplace phenomena was about to oc-

cur, if it did not occur; sellers meeting buyers. And I think that would have been very dangerous if the war had not intervened.

Wallace: But what could the sellers have sold, if they didn't have actual weapons?

Kay: The knowledge of how to make them, the knowledge of how to make small amounts, which is, after all, mostly what terrorists want. They don't want battlefield amounts of weapons. No, Iraq remained a very dangerous place in terms of WMD capabilities, even though we found no large stockpiles of weapons.

Above all, and in the long run, the most important aspect of the Iraq war will be what it means for the integrity of the international system and for the effort to deal effectively with terrorism. The stakes are huge, and the terrorists know that as well as we do, which is the reason for their tactic of violence in Iraq. And that is why, for us and for our allies, failure is not an option. The message is that the United States and others in the world who recognize the need to sustain our international system will no longer quietly acquiesce in the takeover of states by lawless dictators who then carry on their depredations—including the development of awesome weapons for threats, use, or sale— behind the shield of protection that statehood provides. As one of these criminals in charge of a state, you should no longer expect to be allowed to be inside the system at the same time that you are a deadly enemy of it.

North Korea is such a case. The circumstances do not parallel those of Iraq, so our approach is adjusted accordingly. China, Japan, Russia, and South Korea must labor with us. One way or another, that regime will undergo radical change or will come to an end. Iran is another very different case, where the interplay of strength and diplomacy is producing tentative results and where internal turmoil may change the complexion of the state.

The Middle East

The Middle East is an area where the population is exploding out of control, where youth is by far the largest group, and where these young people have little or nothing to do because governance has failed them. In many countries, oil has produced wealth without connecting people to reality, a problem reinforced by the fact that in some of them the hard physical work is often done by imported labor. The submissive role forced on women has led to the population explosion. Generations of young people have grown up in these societies with a surplus of time on their hands and a deficit of productive and honorable occupations. Since they are disconnected from reality, they can live in a world of fantasy. Denied opportunity, many have turned to a destructive, terror-using ideology. Islamism is the name most specialists have settled on. Yet these young people can see on their TV screens that a better life is possible in a great many places in the world. Whether or not they like what they see, their frustration is immense. A disproportionate share of the world's many violent conflicts is in this area.

Many Muslim regimes in the Middle East have finally realized that the radical variant of Islam is violently opposed to the modern age, to globalization, to secular governance, and to those Muslim regimes themselves, their primary target. Saudi Arabia, Egypt, and Pakistan top the target list. Years ago these regimes, and others, began a frantic search for ways to deflect the threat. Some tried to co-opt the Islamists into their governments. Some paid extortion money. Some pushed the Islamists into other countries and then subsidized them. Some of them pumped out huge volumes of propaganda to incite the Islamists to turn their attention from the "near enemy," such as Saudi Arabia, to the "far enemy," Israel and the United States. Some of these targeted regimes tried all these defensive tactics in an attempt to buy time.

Since September 11, 2001, some of these Muslim regimes have begun to realize that this approach only strengthens their

Islamist enemies, who will, sooner rather than later, turn against them directly. They have now had a reality check.

What we are witnessing is nothing short of a civil war in the Arab-Islamic world. On one side are those who, for reasons they ascribe to their version of Islam, reject the international system of states, reject international law and organization, reject international values and principles, such as human rights, and reject diplomacy as a means to work through problems. On this side are Al Qaeda and similar non-state terrorist groups that have spun a network running from West Africa to the East Indies, with outlying cells on every continent. Also on this side was the dictatorship of Saddam Hussein's Iraq, a pirate sailing under the false flag of legitimate statehood. And on this side as well are those Middle Eastern regimes, such as Syria, who have facilitated terrorism elsewhere in an attempt to keep it from home.

On the other side of the civil war are those regimes in the Arab-Islamic world that, however much they may have appeased, bought out, or propagandized the terrorists, have nonetheless now recognized that they are members of the international system of states and must find a way to reconcile their Islamic beliefs and practices to it. Saudi Arabia and others in the world of Islam must, in their own interests, recognize their responsibility to stop preaching hate and to start reforming their societies. Young people must have access to the world of opportunity. Women must be free to play substantial roles in their societies.

The United States, in our war with Iraq, has just intervened in this civil war in the Middle East. Because we have used our strength credibly and because we stand for good governance and for the right of Middle Eastern peoples to participate in the international system successfully, and as these peoples see that we will stay the course, we can expect attitudes in the region to shift in a positive way.

The Israeli-Palestinian Problem

And we have taken our long-standing role in the Israeli-Palestinian conflict to a new and deeper level, also because of a renewed recognition of the importance of the state.

In 1979 Egypt and Israel recognized each other as legitimate states and signed a peace treaty. At that time Egypt took on the role of state negotiator with Israel on behalf of the Palestinians, who did not have a state. This was in recognition that states can make peace only with other states within the context of the international state system.

But after Islamists murdered President Sadat, Egypt dropped its role as state negotiator. Jordan took up that role but dropped it in 1988. Since that time the negotiations have not made serious progress, despite some apparent high points, because there has been no state partner to sit across the table from the state of Israel.

But now the picture has some new possibilities. Yes, optimists should stand aside, but fatalists should, too. You do not work on probabilities in this area, just possibilities. But work we must—and with energy and timing—since the issues involved are vital in this dangerous world.

What are the possibilities? They are far more in evidence than is commonly assumed.

Security for the state of Israel is clearly an essential for fruitful negotiations. So far, nothing has worked. Those who seek to eliminate Israel have regarded efforts at Oslo or Camp David II and elsewhere as proof that terrorism works and that every Israeli step toward peace is really a sign of weakness.

Now a security barrier is under construction. Israel has stated that its path can be changed in the event of a negotiation. Israel seems ready to pull back some settlements beyond the new barrier, as in Gaza. If Israel, through these measures, gains security in its land, that will be a major step toward peace. Once again, Israel will have demonstrated that it cannot be beaten

64

militarily, this time by terrorist violence. The confirmation of this fact is essential. And when Palestinians face the fact that terrorism has become both ineffective and self-destructive, that realization may enable them to take a major step toward peace.

What else can we list as a basis for possibility?

The war in Iraq has eliminated a rogue state that repeatedly acted to disrupt progress toward peace. And Operation Iraqi Freedom has had an impact all across the region: as Iraq stabilizes, people in the Middle East will see that change for the better is possible.

For the first time in the history of the Israeli-Palestinian conflict, important Arab states have stated a willingness to promote peace between Israel and Palestine. Saudi Arabia, Egypt, and Jordan are the keystones of this structure. And remember the important initiative of Crown Prince Abdullah of Saudi Arabia. Under his initiative, in the event that a peace agreement is reached between the state of Israel and a state of Palestine, the Arab League states would recognize Israel as a permanent, legitimate state in the Middle East and in the international state system.

And there is a "road map" to work from. This document spells out the general directions for progress toward an Israeli-Palestinian peace. No document since the founding text of the peace process—the 1967 UN Security Council Resolution 242—has had such wide, if tentative, international support. Israelis and Palestinians, Egypt, Saudi Arabia, Jordan, and the "quartet"—the United States, the European Union, Russia, and the United Nations—all have indicated willingness to take this "road map" as a working paper of the parties to the conflict, and of the leading nations and organizations of the international state system itself.

This approach incorporates a way to fix the negotiating problems of the past 20 years. It provides for the establishment of a Palestinian state, not at the end of the negotiations but in the midst of the effort. Of course, there is much more to making a state than an announcement. But a structure of governance can be established, and if the states of Egypt and Jordan will help, violence can be suppressed and the emerging state can control the use of force. Then there would be a Palestinian state partner for the state of Israel to negotiate with. The Palestinians charged with governance will have more leverage, and the Israelis will have more confidence that their negotiating partner can deliver on the deal that is made—because it will be a state-to-state deal. Put some projects in the mix (water, for example) to energize those Palestinians who yearn for peace and a chance for a better life. Help them take the initiative from the extremists so that their state has a chance for decent governance. Who knows, possibility could become probability and then a new reality.

A World of Danger and a World of Opportunity

I cannot emphasize too strongly the danger and extent of the challenge we are facing. We are engaged in a long and bitter war. Our enemies will not simply sit back and watch as we make progress toward prosperity and peace in the world.

But September 11 forced us to comprehend the extent and danger of the challenge. We began to act before our enemy was able to extend and consolidate his network. If we put this in terms of World War II, we are now sometime around 1937. In the 1930s, the world failed to do what it needed to do to head off a world war. Appeasement never works. Today we are in action. We must not flinch. With a powerful interplay of strength and diplomacy, we can win this war.

We and our partners throughout the world can then work and live in a time of immense promise. Scientific and technological advances are breathtaking virtually across the board. The impact on the human condition and human possibilities is profound. New technologies are changing the way we live and work, globalizing access to an extraordinary range of information. People everywhere can see that economic advances have taken place in countries of every size, with great varieties of ethnic, religious, and cultural histories. So we should not be surprised—as Freedom House, the Heritage Foundation, and the *Wall Street Journal* carefully document—that open economic and political systems are becoming more common.

This new reality means that America's political-military-diplomatic policy must be joined by economic policy aimed at transforming the international energy picture. Our strength and our security are vitally affected by our dependence on oil coming from other countries and by the dependence of the world economy on oil from the most unstable part of the world: the Middle East. Presidents from Eisenhower on have called for energy independence. Ike, no stranger to issues of national security, thought that if foreign oil were more than 20 percent of our consumption, we were headed for trouble. The number is now pushing 60 percent and rising. What would be the impact of terrorist sabotage of key elements of the Saudi pipeline infrastructure?

I remember proposals for alternatives to oil from the time of the first big oil crisis in 1973. Pie in the sky, I thought. But now the situation is different.

Hybrid technology is on the road and increases gas mileage by at least 50 percent. Sequestration of effluent from use of coal may be possible. Maybe coal could be a benign source of hydrogen. Maybe hydrogen could be economically split out of water by electrolysis, perhaps using renewables such as wind power. An economy with a major hydrogen component would do wonders for both our security and our environment. With evident improvements in fuel cells, that combination could amount to a very big deal. Applications include stationary as well as mobile possibilities. Other ideas are in the air. Scientists, technologists, and commercial organizations in other countries are hard at work on these issues. The Administration is coordinating potentially significant developments. We should not be put off by experts who are forever saying that the possible is

67

improbable. Scientific advances in recent decades are a tribute to and validation of creative possibilities. Bet on them all. Sometimes long odds win.

Now is the time to push hard on research and development with augmented funds directed at identified targets such as sequestration, electrolysis, and fuel cells, and other money going to competent scientists with ideas about energy. You never know what bright people will come up with when resources and enthusiasm combine. We can enhance America's security and simultaneously improve our environment.

So an unprecedented age of opportunity is ahead, especially for low-income countries long in poverty. The United States and our allies can rally people all over the world. Don't let the terrorists take away our opportunities. We have the winning hand. We must play that hand with skill and confidence.

CHAPTER SIX

STANDING UP FOR AMERICAN SOVEREIGNTY

PHYLLIS SCHLAFLY

Phyllis Schlafly is president of Eagle Forum, an attorney, and the author or editor of 20 books, including: A CHOICE NOT AN ECHO *(1964),* FEMINIST FANTASIES *(2003) and* THE SUPREMACISTS: THE TYRANNY OF JUDGES AND HOW TO STOP IT *(2004).*

Thank you, President Bush, for standing up for American sovereignty against the globalists who are constantly devising plans to lock the United States into any kind of world government or global federation that erases national borders and diminishes national sovereignty.

The globalists want to induce America to join European political, military, economic, judicial, and governmental bureaucracies in which the United States has only one vote. Treaties are the major means of incrementally achieving this goal. Treaties play a significant role in inducing the United States to submit to international monitoring, regulations, and even rulings that override U.S. law. Every United Nations treaty would diminish U.S. sovereignty by interfering with self-government over some aspect of our lives.

President Bill Clinton was an enthusiastic advocate of this treaty process. On September 22, 1997 he told the United Nations that he wanted to put the United States into a "web of institutions and arrangements" for "the emerging international system." Clinton's chief foreign policy adviser, Strobe Talbott, famously wrote in the July 20, 1992 issue of *Time* magazine that "Nationhood as we know it will be obsolete, all states will recognize a single, global authority," and that "national sovereignty wasn't such a great idea after all."

Au contraire—American independence is the great idea that has enabled us to become the shining city on the hill, attracting people from all over the Earth. Clinton used his 78 days of bombing Yugoslavia, a sovereign state that had never attacked another country, to promote the rhetoric that "human rights" should trump national sovereignty. Czech leader Vaclav Havel called the Yugoslav war "an important precedent for the future" in which "state sovereignty must inevitably dissolve."

Clinton eagerly supported the UN Convention on the Rights of the Child and the UN Convention on the Elimination of All Discrimination Against Women, which fortunately the U.S. Senate has never ratified. We thank President Bush for not reviving those dangerous treaties.

The International Criminal Court Treaty

The International Criminal Court (ICC), which ties countries into a global judicial system, is the centerpiece of these persistent treaty plans to erase the borders of national sovereignty. President Clinton supported this treaty enthusiastically during its five years of formation, and then signed it as one of his last official acts near midnight on New Year's Eve, 2000, but the U.S. Senate never ratified it.

In May 2002 President George W. Bush caused our State Department to send a letter to UN Secretary General Kofi Annan stating that "the United States does not intend to become a party to the treaty" and "has no legal obligations arising from its [Clinton's] signature on December 31, 2000." This is colloquially referred to as "unsigning" the treaty. This unprecedented action served notice on the world that we are not going to allow American sovereignty to be submerged in the clutches of a global court.

However, ratified by 66 other nations, this treaty went into effect on July 1, 2002. The Court has started functioning in The Hague, and the pompous bureaucrats there claim the authority to detain and try U.S. citizens anyway—military personnel as well as current and future public officials—even though we didn't ratify the treaty. The ICC plans to prosecute individuals for war crimes, genocide and "crimes against humanity" whose definition is still evolving, using procedures that violate U.S. constitutional safeguards. The ICC is accountable to no one, not even to the United Nations where we have our Security Council veto.

Those who think that the ICC would limit itself to the really bad thugs of the world—the Pol Pots, the Foday Sankohs and the Idi Amins—have their heads in the sand. The expansive jurisdiction claimed by the ICC would put every U.S. serviceman and woman, and even U.S. travelers, especially if they are or have been public officials, at risk of being grabbed for trial by judges from Sierra Leone, Sudan, Iran, and other nations hostile to the rule of law. The ICC would be an enticing venue for anti-American sentiment, of which there seems to be plenty among the governments that have joined the ICC.

The globalists try to tell us that the ICC really "supports American values" and "mirrors the Constitution." That is false. U.S. constitutional protections against unfair prosecutions that are violated by the ICC include: (1) the right to trial by jury of

71

one's peers (the most important protection), (2) the trial must be in the jurisdiction of the offense, (3) proof must be beyond reasonable doubt, (4) verdict for capital offenses must be unanimous, (5) warrants are necessary to seize and use evidence, (6) the state must provide exculpatory evidence, (7) *compulsory* process to obtain defense witnesses, and (8) the protection against double jeopardy (the ICC language is full of loopholes).

Thank you, President Bush, for *un*signing the International Criminal Court Treaty.

The ABM Treaty

In one of the memorable highlights of President George W. Bush's presidency, on December 13, 2001, President Bush gave formal notice to Russia that the United States was withdrawing from the 30-year-old Anti-Ballistic Missile (ABM) Treaty.

This infamous treaty was signed by President Richard Nixon and Leonid Brezhnev in Moscow as part of the 1972 SALT I agreements. In the ABM Treaty, President Nixon signed away our right to build an anti-missile defense system because of the theory called Mutual Assured Destruction, known by its acronym MAD. Each of the superpowers was supposedly deterred from launching a nuclear attack on the other because of the knowledge that a launch by one side would be followed by massive retaliation that would assure the destruction of both sides. The ABM Treaty should have been immediately judged unconstitutional because it reneged on our government's constitutional duty to "provide for the common defense."

John Newhouse's 1973 book *Cold Dawn: The Story of SALT* confirmed that every substantive provision of the 1972 U.S.-Soviet agreements was dictated secretly to Henry Kissinger by the Kremlin without the knowledge of our U.S. negotiating team, was accepted by Kissinger, and was then rationalized by Kissinger to the President and Congress. Newhouse's book showed how Kissinger was personally and solely responsible for promising the Soviets that we would not build an anti-missile defense, even though the offensive-weapons provisions of the SALT I agreements guaranteed the Soviet Union superiority in numbers of missiles. In testimony to the Senate Foreign Relations Committee, Kissinger personally endorsed Newhouse, called his book "outstanding," thereby making Newhouse's book the authentic account of the Moscow agreements.

President Reagan exposed the fallacy in the ABM Treaty and in MAD when he asked the crucial question on March 23, 1983, "Would it not be better to save lives than to avenge them?" Reagan had no qualms about criticizing the mistaken policies of his predecessors.

We now know that President Reagan's determination to build a U.S. anti-missile system—which he enunciated in meetings with Mikhail Gorbachev at Geneva and Reykjavik—was the fundamental reason that Lady Margaret Thatcher was able to boast that Reagan won the Cold War without firing a shot.

Even though we worry less about Russia using its still-existing 6,000 nuclear warheads against us, the danger of attack or blackmail from other nuclear arsenals is real. China has 300 nuclear warheads deployed on ballistic missiles and 13 ICBMs targeting U.S. cities. The list of Third World countries developing nuclear, biological and chemical weapons, plus ballistic missile delivery systems, includes North Korea and Iran. The risk comes not only from intentional use but from accidental or unauthorized launches.

Thank you, President Bush, for officially withdrawing from the dangerous ABM treaty and for making the defense of the American people, including the building of an anti-missile system, our nation's priority.

The Global Warming Treaty

President George W. Bush deserves our thanks for resisting pressures to ratify Al Gore's favorite treaty, the global warming treaty known as the Kyoto Protocol. When Bush made his first trip to Europe as President in June 2001, he stood firm on his Kyoto decision despite daily hammering from big media in the United States to try to get him to change his mind.

The worldwide push for this fraudulent treaty got off the ground at the 1992 UN Earth Summit in Rio de Janeiro, which produced several international agreements including the United Nations Framework Convention on Climate Change. This called on countries to take "voluntary actions" to reduce greenhouse gas emissions (principally carbon dioxide, CO_2) to their 1990 levels. This agreement was, unfortunately, signed by the first President George Bush and ratified by the Senate in 1992.

This agreement should teach us the folly of signing UN treaties that are called voluntary. Any treaty called voluntary will surely morph into Other Countries' Great Expectations, which in turn will morph into demands by foreigners abroad and globalists at home that we meet our alleged "obligations."

Buried in the treaty's verbiage was this sentence: "The developed country parties should take the lead in combating climate change and the adverse effects thereof." Now the UN propagandists are asserting that this alleged "international law" binds the United States not only to actually do what was called "voluntary" (dramatically reduce our CO_2 emissions), but to do it immediately regardless of when, if ever, other countries do anything to conform to the treaty's goals.

UN bureaucrats and Non-Governmental Organizations (NGOs) have been working for years to turn this voluntary Rio agreement into a legally binding agreement called the Global Warming Treaty. The new treaty was agreed to by Vice President Al Gore in Kyoto, Japan in 1997 and signed in New York in 1998. Ever since, it's been called the Kyoto Protocol. Fortunately, treaties do not bind the United States unless ratified by two-thirds of the Senate.

The Kyoto Protocol would require the United States to reduce our greenhouse gas emissions to 7% below our 1990 levels, a tremendous reduction in our energy consumption (our use of electricity, gas, oil, and gasoline) and therefore in our standard of living. However, Kyoto would impose no limitations on 130 developing nations, including China (the world's second largest emitter of greenhouse gases), India, Mexico and Brazil, and would allow Europeans to evade reductions by averaging among the European Union (EU) countries.

Kyoto is so manifestly unfair to the United States that the U.S. Senate went on record against it in 1997 by passing the Byrd-Hagel Resolution 95-0 to warn our President that the treaty would not be ratified. President Bush reflected American views when he withdrew from negotiations.

Who is behind Kyoto? Kyoto is an issue that brings together many different anti-American interests, all of which enjoy wide access to the media:

- The anti-growth socialists, particularly the European countries that have moved left in recent years. The socialist mindset opposes economic growth and instead welcomes a scarcity of resources so that big government can apportion or ration the scarce resources. The private enterprise system, on the other hand, produces abundance so that a rising tide lifts all boats. It is clear that the Kyoto restrictions would impede economic growth.

- The foreign dictators in the United Nations who look upon the UN as a forum where they can demand that the United States redistribute our wealth to them. Our foreign aid never gets to the poor people who need it; it is gobbled up by the ruling tyrants.

- The cult of radical environmentalists who believe we should subordinate our standard of living to the supremacy of global ecology or, as Al Gore said in the title of his book, force us to put "Earth in the Balance." These groups have great sums of money available through the UN NGOs and tax-exempt foundations. But there's nothing balanced about the ideology or the treaty. The ideology of these radicals is the new religion of worshipping Mother Earth and elevating non-human life over human life.

- The leftist radicals who formerly demonstrated for the Communists but are now using their street skills for the radical environmentalists. When George W. Bush made his five-nation European tour in 2001, demonstrators carried Bush in effigy, shouted "Toxic Texan, Go Home," carried pictures of has-been Communists Mao Zedong and Che Guevara, and shouted typical Communist slogans such as "For a World Without Imperialism."

- The Democrats who use any available issue to attack George W. Bush. This issue is so attractive because big media chatter about it all the time. The Kyoto goals demand more federal regulations and higher taxes, both favorite Democratic Party goals.

The latest leftist attack on Bush's refusal to cooperate in Kyoto is this year's propaganda movie *The Day After Tomorrow.* Its thesis is that since the Bush Administration has failed to protect us from global warming, carbon dioxide emissions will melt the ice at the North Pole, which will then disrupt the Atlantic current, making northern hemisphere temperature drop precipitously and within hours bringing about a new Ice Age in which most of us will die. This climate disaster might be tomorrow, 100 years or 1,000 years from now, but regardless, it's all the fault of our insensitive, out-of-touch President who refuses to ratify the Kyoto Protocol. The movie's special effects are entertaining, but their utter improbability defeats the propaganda message.

The Kyoto Protocol is based on the assumption that all countries have a community of interest in cutting CO_2 emissions in order to reduce global warming. However, The Hague Conference in December 2000 displayed the hopelessness of this venture and the passionate demands of countries with diametrically opposed interests. In some nations the climate is too hot and they don't want it any hotter, while other nations hope global warming will make their crops more abundant.

Regulations are opposed by countries that are completely dependent on coal or oil and would be devastated by the new regulations. Regulations are favored by low-lying countries that worry about the rising of the seas that is predicted if the Earth warms and ocean ice melts. Some countries have already subjected their industries to heavy socialistic regulations and taxes and want to impose the same on the rest of the world. Other countries value their freedom from regulations.

The United States could actually go halfway toward meeting Kyoto's emission-reduction goals because our large forests function as a "sink" to naturally absorb the main greenhouse gas, which is CO_2 coming from our tailpipes and smokestacks. Our vast forests absorb up to 300 million tons a year of carbon dioxide. But other countries reject this as a "free ride" for the America they envy.

Nuclear power, which produces energy without greenhouse emissions, is another sticking point. The environmentalists have prevented the construction of modern nuclear plants in the United States, but other countries have no such restrictions and France relies heavily on nuclear plants for its electricity.

Kyoto advocates use a report of the National Academy of Sciences (NAS) to sell this thesis and clobber George W. Bush. But the Kyoto propagandists have maliciously misrepresented this report. The full report makes clear that there is no scientific consensus about long-term climate trends or what causes them. Yes, climate is constantly changing and the Earth is warmer than it used to be; we are grateful we don't live in any Ice Age. But scientists do not agree that past climate change was caused by CO_2 and they cannot forecast what the climate will be in the future.

The NAS report absolutely does not prove the need for the Kyoto Protocol. It documents the lack of consensus on the whole issue. More than 17,000 American scientists (two-thirds with advanced degrees) have signed a petition that reads as follows:

> We urge the United States government to reject the global warming agreement that was written in Kyoto, Japan in December 1997, and any other similar proposals. The proposed limits on greenhouse gases would harm the environment, hinder the advance of science and technology, and damage the health and welfare of mankind.... There is no convincing scientific evidence that human release of carbon dioxide, methane, or other greenhouse gases is causing or will, in the foreseeable future, cause catastrophic heating of the Earth's atmosphere and disruption of the Earth's climate. Moreover, there is substantial scientific evidence that increases in atmospheric carbon dioxide produce many beneficial effects upon the natural plant and animal environments of the Earth.

In May 2004, a team from Harvard University concluded the most comprehensive study ever made of global temperature over the last 1,000 years. The team reported that the world was much warmer during the Medieval Warm Period between the 9th and 14th centuries than it is today. Global warming isn't science; it's leftist propaganda to promote global regulation of our economy.

Kyoto is part of a web of UN treaties that attack American sovereignty. Each of the pending and proposed UN treaties sets up an international commission for monitoring and enforcement, on which the United States typically has just one vote (the same as Haiti and Cuba). Other countries form coalitions to oppose the United States.

Thank you, President Bush, for telling the world that the United States does not accept the Kyoto Protocol.

UN Attack on Gun Ownership

The Democrats' political gurus have figured out that Al Gore's pro-gun-control stance in the 2000 campaign was the reason he did not carry several crucial states. So the anti-gun activists have moved to a less democratic venue: the United Nations.

On July 9-20, 2001, New York City hosted the United Nations Conference on Illicit Trade in Small Arms and Light Weapons in All Its Aspects. The purpose of this conference was to demonize the private ownership of guns and get governments to confiscate all privately owned guns.

Don't be misled by the term "small arms." UN documents define small arms as weapons "designed for personal use" (such as your Browning pistol, your Ruger rifle, or your Winchester shotgun), while light weapons are for use by several persons as a crew. Don't be misled by the term "illicit" trade. UN documents make it clear that, since most illegal guns start out as legal purchases, illicit trade must be stopped by clamping down on legal gun owners.

Don't think that this UN conference was just a talkfest. The UN hopes to produce a legally binding treaty to require governments to mark, number, register, record, license, confiscate, and destroy all guns except those in the hands of the military and the police.

The 18-page Draft Programme of Action presented to this UN conference set forth the rationale plus the mechanisms for eliminating the "wide availability" of guns. It was obvious that the United States is the target because we are the only country with a Second Amendment, and other democracies such as

England, Canada and Australia have either banned or severely restricted private gun ownership.

The Draft Programme wrapped its gun-confiscation message in typical UN semantics, but made little attempt to conceal the mailed fist in the velvet glove. It states: "In order to promote peace, security, stability and sustainable development in the world, we commit ourselves to addressing this problem in a comprehensive, integrated, sustainable, efficient and urgent manner." Indeed, the plan was comprehensive and integrated. According to the Draft Programme, "Preventing and reducing the illicit trade in small arms and light weapons consists of two sets of measures: the national control of manufacture and the proper marking of small arms and light weapons, coupled with accurate, sustained recordkeeping and exchanges of information."

Government "marking" and recordkeeping would be "an integral part" of the process. The UN is demanding that governments build a national electronic database of all guns and their owners, and then facilitate "an information exchange" (i.e., share the database with the UN). Through the Department for Disarmament Affairs, the UN promises to "develop an international mechanism that will facilitate the exchange of information on all aspects" of guns, i.e., a global gun registry.

To wipe out private gun ownership, the UN demands that all governments enforce "adequate laws, regulations and administrative procedures to exercise effective control over the legal manufacture and possession of small arms and light weapons." And the UN demands that governments criminally prosecute all those who don't comply.

The UN plans to develop "model national legislation" so that Congress will pass laws that conform to the treaty's requirements. The UN plans to guide Congress by publishing "best practices" for legislation and procedures.

All unmarked or inadequately marked small arms and light weapons are to be confiscated and "expeditiously destroyed."

The government is to assure that "no retransfer of small arms and light weapons takes place without prior authorization" by the government because the UN disapproves of the possession of guns by civilians who are "not part of responsible military and police forces."

The UN even has a plan to propagandize Americans to accept this global ban on private gun ownership. The Draft Programme calls for "seminars, conferences, consultations and workshops conducted by the United Nations" for the purpose of "promoting the Action Plan." As part of its "awareness-training" to induce Americans to accept the new ban-the-guns policy, the UN wants government to pledge to destroy guns in "public destruction events."

We thank President George W. Bush for letting it be known that the UN anti-gun activists were whistling in the wind and the United States will never be a party to such a treaty.

We also thank President Bush for Attorney General John Ashcroft's excellent Statement on the Second Amendment, issued May 17, 2001, that said in part:

> Let me state unequivocally my view that the text and the original intent of the Second Amendment clearly protect the right of individuals to keep and bear firearms.... Just as the First and Fourth Amendments secure individual rights of speech and security respectively, the Second Amendment protects an individual right to keep and bear arms.... It is clear that the Constitution protects the private ownership of firearms for lawful purposes....

Thank you, President George W. Bush, for rejecting the International Criminal Court Treaty, the ABM Treaty, the Kyoto Protocol, and all UN anti-gun-ownership treaties. We expect you to continue to stand tall for American sovereignty and reject the coming attempt by the globalists to diminish American sovereignty through the Free Trade Area of the Americas (FTAA).

CHAPTER SEVEN

PRESIDENT BUSH, TER- RORISM, AND JUSTICE

ABRAHAM SOFAER

Dr. Abraham Sofaer is the George P. Shultz Senior Fellow at the Hoover Institution, a public policy think tank located on Stanford University's campus in Palo Alto, California. A veteran of the United States Air force, Dr. Sofaer received the Distinguished Service Award in 1989, the highest state department award given to a non-civil servant.

Thank you, Mr. President, for defending America, and for establishing the moral basis—rooted firmly in international law—for securing justice for all in the long-standing conflict in the Middle East. These achievements have assured your place in history and make your re-election essential for the continued protection of the American people at home and abroad.

Less than one year into your first term in office, Mr. President, you were forced to deal with the fruits of years of weakness and self-delusion. On September 11, 2001, America suffered its most severe domestic attack in modern history. That attack was part of a war that had been openly declared and waged against our country for over eight years. Until you acted in response, nothing had been done to deal seriously with the group that had declared that war, despite their having repeatedly attacked Americans, killing hundreds and destroying buildings, warships, and embassies.

Not surprisingly, until you became President, the U.S. government had done no more to protect its allies against the war waged by Muslim extremists throughout the world than it had done to protect itself. Thanks to your efforts, and to the principles that have guided your policies, many areas of the world that were headed for catastrophe have been stabilized and hope has been restored.

The record of American efforts against terrorism prior to your election is very clear and simply pathetic. The sophisticates that controlled American foreign policy during that period succeeded in one thing above all others: in talking themselves out of acting against our enemies. The results were disastrous, and led to the September 11 attacks. Our avowed enemies attacked us repeatedly and accurately predicted that we would fail to act effectively to stop them. President Clinton and his team threatened that they would "bring every terrorist to justice," but what they meant was that they would indict them for crimes. Preventing terrorist attacks became a game in which national security experts, the FBI, prosecutors, and intelligence personnel attempted to learn where and when attacks were to occur before they actually happened, so they could do their best to prevent them.

Defending America

We had known for many years prior to 9/11 that this approach to fighting terrorism was doomed to fail. Secretary of State George P. Shultz said in 1983 that the U.S. must adopt a policy of "active defense" against terrorism. "Fighting terrorism will not be a clean or pleasant contest," he said, "but we have no choice ... We must reach a consensus in this country that our responses should go beyond passive defense to consider means of active prevention, preemption, and retaliation. Our goal must be to prevent and deter future terrorist attacks."

By the end of the Reagan Administration, the Shultz Doctrine had become national policy, as reflected in the bombing of Libya in 1987 for arranging terrorist attacks on Americans. But under the Clinton Administration, the U.S. returned to a passive defense, based on law enforcement, against an enemy over whom we could not assert jurisdiction without force of arms.

Osama bin Laden fashioned his strategy on the basis of this passive policy. He became convinced the U.S. could be forced to leave Muslim countries, and to abandon Israel, if he launched attacks that shed American blood. Nothing that happened prior to September 11, 2001 gave bin Laden reason to doubt his assumption. Al Qaeda was responsible for several, successful attacks on U.S. targets prior to September 11; and throughout this onslaught we responded precisely as bin Laden anticipated.

In early 1993, Al Qaeda operatives began training Somali fighters to attack UN forces, and in October they participated in attacks that killed 18 U.S. Marines. We had boisterously arranged for the Security Council to issue a warrant to arrest Mohammed Aideed. But after suffering these casualties, we ignominiously withdrew from Somalia.

On February 26, 1993, a car bomb exploded under the World Trade Center, killing eight people and injuring over a thousand. We convicted most of the perpetrators, but left the organizations from which they came unscathed, and their leaders free to continue planning attacks.

On June 26, 1996, car bombs killed 19 American servicemen in Dhahran, Saudi Arabia, and injured over two hundred. The U.S. suspected bin Laden and Al Qaeda. All we did, however, was open a criminal investigation. Bin Laden was not intimidated; on October 12, he issued a "Declaration of War" against the US, calling on Muslims "to fight jihad and cleanse the land from these Crusader occupiers."

In November 1996, bombings in Riyadh and at the Khobar Towers barracks killed 19 American servicemen and injured 109. Bin Laden called these attacks "praiseworthy terrorism," and promised more would follow. Once again we sent in the FBI.

In February 1998, bin Laden put his war into the form of a religious order declaring "the killing of Americans and their civilian and military allies is a religious duty for each and every Muslim."

On August 7, 1998, Al Qaeda terrorists car-bombed the U.S. embassies in Kenya and Tanzania, killing 224 people and injuring almost 5,000. The U.S. launched a single, ineffectual strike on an Al Qaeda camp in Afghanistan, and on a pharmaceutical plant in Sudan. When it came to legal action, though, the Clinton Administration pulled out the stops. They indicted bin Laden on 224 counts of murder. Characteristically, he failed to show up for his trial. We settled for prosecuting four Al Qaeda operatives, after which prosecutors triumphantly declared that they would continue to investigate Al Qaeda until bin Laden and his cohorts were all "brought to justice." This so terrified bin Laden that he told *Time* magazine: "The U.S. knows that I have attacked it, by the grace of God, for more than ten years now."

On October 12, 2000, a suicide boat bombing of the *USS Cole* in Aden harbor killed 17 American sailors and injured 40, in addition to causing over $100 million in damages. We knew it was Al Qaeda's work, but the Clinton Administration did not bother to engage in even a symbolic use of force. Instead, it launched—once again—a massive invasion of aggressive FBI investigators.

At the turn of the millennium, we had some good luck. An attack planned for the Los Angeles Airport was aborted when a perpetrator panicked on his way into the U.S. from Canada.

Shamelessly, Clinton Administration witnesses at the 9/11 Commission hearings claimed credit for "preventing" this attack.

Given this history of passivity, it is small surprise that, after the attacks of September 11, bin Laden was triumphant. He was a hero. His strategy had worked. The U.S. had been unwilling to adopt the measures necessary to stop him.

Three Principles of American Strategy

The horrors of September 11 finally galvanized the nation into action. Mr. President, you adopted three principles to guide U.S. policy: first, that serious terrorist attacks should be treated as acts of war, not merely as crimes; second, that states are responsible for terrorism from within their borders; and third, that we must preempt attacks where possible.

Mr. President, these principles are strategically necessary, morally sound, and legally defensible. Ambiguity is no substitute for your forthright and essential strategic posture. We need a President that clearly confirms the need to adopt active measures of defense where grave threats are present, state responsibility exists, and the need for the use of preemptive force is demonstrable, even if not imminent. The notion that criminal prosecution could bring a terrorist group like Al Qaeda to justice is absurd. As for preemption, our nation cannot safely adhere to a position that would preclude the U.S. from acting in its self-defense merely because a real, terrible, and certain threat is not also imminent.

The need for preemptive actions to defend the U.S. stems ultimately from the conditions of modern life and the nature of radical terrorism. The U.S. is a target-rich, vast, and open society. In every area of potential weaponry—from the mundane and conventional to the sophisticated and unconventional—the U.S. is vulnerable. The nation's entire critical infrastructure will remain vulnerable to most types of attacks for many years to come.

The area of intelligence is no less subject to this reality. Many improvements should be made to enhance capacities, and especially to improve our ability to predict future attacks. It is illusory to believe, though, that intelligence—even combined with all presently conceivable advances in technology—will enable us to know in advance of all the attacks we will have to foil through passive measures to achieve an adequate level of security. We must, therefore, be able and willing when necessary to resort to active measures, and necessity must be determined on the basis of all relevant factors, not just imminence. No national security policy against terrorism can be regarded as sound if it fails to include preemptive action as an essential part.

The importance of preemption should not be underestimated. The historical record indicates that many terrorist attacks on the U.S. can be anticipated and prevented before they occur. Most recent attacks on the U.S. were by a single organization, Al Qaeda, led by a man who announced his intentions to kill Americans in advance and who demonstrated his capacity to do so over and over again before he was stopped. Other groups likely to attack us are also well known.

It is true that any war carries risks, and the "war" on terrorism is no exception. But the risks of using force must always be weighed against the risk of inaction. Mr. President, you have truly accepted this reality, as reflected in your speech at the National War College espousing this doctrine.

This profound insight is at the heart of the historic and successful effort to overthrow Saddam Hussein, one of the most evil and remorseless tyrants in human history. After sixteen UN Security Council resolutions, two wars of aggression, missile attacks on Saudi Arabia and Israel, an effort to use a terrorist group to kill a former President of the United States, years of providing safe haven to many notorious terrorists, and his open issuance of $25,000 rewards to the families of suicide bombers who killed Israeli civilians, you and the strong alliance you put together brought an end to his cruelty and madness. America and our allies have paid a great price for replacing Saddam Hussein. But the price is small compared to the horror and continuing danger that his leadership entailed. And Iraq, like Afghanistan, will soon be a free country, with a democratically elected leadership, providing stability and prosperity, rather than sanctuaries for terror and aggression.

The American people have recently heard President Clinton and his national security officials testify that they, too, would have pursued and destroyed the sanctuaries of Al Qaeda in Afghanistan if the attacks of September 11 had occurred during their time in office. We can never know whether this claim is accurate. The Clinton team had ample cause and opportunity to respond to Al Qaeda attacks, but apart from a limited missile attack on a single encampment, they did nothing but threaten and indict. Who is to say they would not have yet again talked themselves into a passive response, dressed up with threats that scared no one?

Many members of the Clinton team explained their failure to respond militarily to Al Qaeda attacks on the ground that President Clinton's personal conduct in office led many in Congress to claim he would be making war to divert attention from the political difficulties caused by his sexual antics. Regrettably, this claim seems to have been correct. But it hardly excuses the failure to protect America.

What it demonstrates, rather, is that the American people have even more to be thankful for with regard to the Bush presidency. Mr. President, you did not permit your conduct as Chief Executive of the nation to become a source of weakness. Improper conduct, even in the personal sphere, can make a President vulnerable to claims that weaken his authority, however sincere his motives. Thanks to the high standard of personal morality that guides your conduct as President, you are able to lead the nation in defending itself without fear of any credible claim that you are acting from any motive other than your genuine perception of the national interest.

Terrorism and Justice

Thank you also, Mr. President, for your unparalleled solidarity with others who are suffering from the war that terrorists have launched against civilization. You have used the diplomatic and other resources of the U.S. to persuade Pakistan to reign in the terrorist groups that have killed thousands of innocent Kashmiris and Indians. You have worked with the governments of many friendly countries to assist them in dealing with terrorists groups. You have persuaded Saudi Arabia to attack the sources of terrorist funding that come from that country, to attack terrorists attempting to undermine the safety and economic well being of the Saudi people, and to de-legitimize the extremist ideologies that have spread from there around the world, wreaking havoc and destroying the minds and lives of impressionable youth. Your strong leadership, and your success in overthrowing Saddam Hussein, no doubt account in part for the stunning success in having Moammar Gadhafi of Libya agree to renounce weapons of mass destruction. His cooperation has uncovered invaluable evidence of a market for nuclear materials and technology that the international community is continuing to evaluate with a view toward eliminating other grave threats, especially in North Korea and Iran.

Your leadership, Mr. President, has been especially significant with regard to Israel, and its effort to confront the continuing assault by its enemies aimed at destroying its existence. Fueled by hatred, weapons, and financial support, the PLO leadership that controls the Palestinian people has launched a terrorist war against the Israeli civilian population. In an historic decision, you rejected totally and unqualifiedly the use of terror as a proper means for achieving the aspirations of the Palestinian people. You said openly what others have long known but been unable to muster the courage to express: Yasser Arafat is unfit to govern. He is a man that had a chance to lead his people to safe and productive lives, and he squandered that opportunity, opting instead for a program of murder and lunacy, in which Palestinians have been urged to honor suicide and the murder of noncombatants. He has allowed and encouraged other terrorist groups to grow and take control of territory turned over to the Palestinian Authority by Israel in an effort to bring peace. Those groups have made a nightmare of the lives of innocent Israelis, and done even worse damage to the lives of their own people. But Arafat has been unwilling to take any steps to end attacks by these groups.

It was absolutely essential, Mr. President, in the face of the existential threat posed by Palestinian terrorism, that Israel be recognized to have the right to adopt measures of self-defense that America has adopted to protect itself. You have insisted, despite the chorus of anti-Israel rhetoric, that Israel has the right to defend itself against terrorists who are arranging for attacks against Israeli civilians and soldiers, including suicide bombings. You have given Israeli lives the same value you attribute to American lives, or the lives of other innocents. While this seems elementary justice, it is in fact a significant and essential change from prior policy. Even more significant, you have refused to continue the phony and destructive policy of insisting on Israeli negotiations and withdrawals while Palestinians continue to engage in terrorist attacks. No more, you said. Israel must negotiate, you declared, but not without a sincere and effective effort by Palestinians to end the violence they have instigated among their people.

Finally, Mr. President, and most impressively, you have defended America and its allies against vicious and inhumane actions without losing sight of the need to ensure justice. Despite the fact that virtually all the terrorists active today are Muslims, you have refused to blame Islam for the perverse use to which it has been put by the extremists who claim to rely on its doctrine in committing inhuman acts. These extremists, as you have said, have hijacked a great religion, the vast majority of whose adherents are decent human beings, deeply offended by what is being done in the name of their system of belief. Every religion, Mr. President, has been abused by extremists, claiming the right to do evil in God's Name. You have justly refused to blame the great majority of Muslims for the acts of a vicious minority.

Your policies in Iraq also demonstrate your commitment to justice and freedom for all peoples, including especially the Muslim victims of the Saddam Hussein regime. You have made the lie of claims that the U.S. has any long-term ambition in Iraq beyond restoring the nation to peace and providing its people with an opportunity for freedom and prosperity. You declared your intention to surrender occupying power status on June 30, 2004, and you stood firmly behind that commitment. You also brought the UN Security Council into the process and provided it with a robust role in negotiating and arranging the transition. Once again, you demonstrated that the U.S. is ready to act with the Security Council's approval, when possible, in defending America's most fundamental interests.

You also demonstrated another important American commitment: to bring even Americans to justice for wrongful conduct. When American investigations uncovered the abuse of prisoners at Iraqi prisons, you condemned that conduct in the strongest terms and committed America to punish all illegal actions. Experience has shown that wars inevitably involve some degree of improper behavior. In this war, by far the worst behavior has been by the terrorist groups deliberately targeting civilians, murdering prisoners in cold blood, and destroying the offices and personnel of the United Nations. But the behavior of American interrogators was enough to disgust and dishearten us all. You spoke for all Americans, Mr. President, when you condemned this conduct, and promised that all those responsible will be punished. Thank you, Mr. President, for insisting that America must meet the highest standards of behavior, even in the face of the brutal and inhuman conduct of our enemies.

In the same spirit of decency and humanity, Mr. President, you have committed this great nation for the first time to the creation of a Palestinian state. When the madness of the second *intifada* is over, and a new, responsible Palestinian leadership is prepared to assume the responsibilities of sovereignty, you will be there, as President, to ensure that Palestine becomes a reality, and a homeland for a talented people whose suffering has been unconscionably exploited in the long and bitter effort to destroy the State of Israel. Mr. President, you have placed the Israeli and Palestinian people on the path to a peaceful and just resolution of their conflict, not through conducting negotiations over mere words, but through deeds and principled conduct. The nation could ask no more of any leader.

Thank you, Mr. President, for these and the many other achievements of your Administration.

CHAPTER EIGHT

AESCHYLUS
AND AMERICA

JACK WHEELER

Dr. Jack Wheeler has been hailed as the architect of the Reagan Doctrine (and condemned in the Soviet press as an "intellectual gangster"). He received his Ph.D. in Philosophy from the University of Southern California, where he lectured on Aristotelian ethics. He later served as an "unofficial" liaison between the Reagan White House and anti-Soviet freedom fighters and insurgents around the world, in Nicaragua, Angola, Mozambique, Ethiopia, Cambodia, Laos, Afghanistan, throughout Eastern Europe and even in the Soviet Union itself. He was the youngest Eagle Scout in history; climbed the Matterhorn at 14; swam the Hellespont and lived with Amazon headhunters at 16; has retraced Hannibal's route over the Alps with elephants; and has made first contact with three previously unknown tribes in Africa and New Guinea. His writings are online at www.tothepointnews.com.

The founding culture of western civilization is that of Hellenic Greece—starting with Homer about the time of the first

Olympiad in 776 B.C. to the death of Aristotle in 322 B.C. (one year after that of his student, Alexander the Great).

Aeschylus and Homer

The singular invention of the ancient Hellenes—the foundation upon which western civilization has been built—is an idea unique in history: The individual human being, and not just the tribe to which he or she belongs, has an intrinsic value and thus a legitimate claim to exist for his or her own sake.

No other culture had ever had the courage to think this before, suffused as they were with fear of their gods and rulers. We owe our cultural existence to the moral audacity of the Hellenic Greeks. The Bible of the Hellenes was Homer's *Iliad* and *Odyssey*, which as one scholar puts it, was "the source of all instruction in ethics." Homer sings of individual heroes—Achilles, Hector, Ajax, Diomedes, Glaucus, Odysseus—whose motto was, in the words of Glaucus, "I lead. Strive your best." They were the role models for the Hellenes.

Homer's *Iliad* is a paean to the right of the individual to his existence. The scene that most dramatically expresses this is in Book V where the God of War Ares (the Roman Mars) takes human form and fights on the side of the Trojans. Outraged at the unfairness of a god taking sides, Diomedes, "tamer of wild stallions," thrusts his bronze spear "deep into Ares' bowels where the belt cinched him tight."

Here is a human physically attacking and wounding a god—and there is no retribution. When Ares, "the fresh immortal blood gushing from his wound," demands that Zeus punish this wretched mortal for his audacity, Zeus tells Ares to shut up and stop whining. In the *Odyssey*, Homer tells us that after the war, Diomedes returned safely home.

Yet for all their moral worship of individual heroism, the ancient Greeks suffered an existential crisis, a spiritual catharsis of fear and doubt, in the wake of their seemingly superhuman victories over the superpower of the Ancient World, the Persian Empire.

The Greeks looked upon Persia as an anthill society, whose king was an absolute ruler wielding total sway over subjects indistinguishable from chattels. The Greeks looked upon themselves as citizens possessing rights their leaders could not violate.

When the tiny, insignificant city-states were attacked by the gigantic Persian army, there seemed little hope. But on the fields of Marathon in 490 B.C., they defeated the hordes of Darius. Ten years later, Darius's son Xerxes invaded Greece again bent on revenge. On September 28, 480 B.C., in perhaps the most momentous naval battle in history, the 1,200 massive war galleys of the Persian navy were lured into the bay of Salamis by the Greek commander, Themistocles of Athens, where the 370 quick little Greek *trireme* ships cut the Persians to ribbons.

Xerxes ordered a throne chair placed on a mountain top so he could watch the battle. The Great King had come to gloat, to contemptuously snuff out these insolent Hellenes who had dared oppose him. He witnessed instead the destruction of his fleet, the most awesome naval force the world had ever seen, and had to retreat in humiliation through the snows of Thrace in winter with the remnants of his once-mighty army.

The Greeks, particularly the Athenians, had done the impossible. Rather than taking Homeric pride in their incredible victory of the Persians, they experienced instead a profound failure of nerve—a panicky self-abnegation to avoid the envy of the gods for such an astounding achievement.

The problem was that their victory over the Persians was *too* astounding—it seemed superhuman. Thus Aeschylus, the greatest of all Greek playwrights who had personally fought at both Marathon and Salamis, interpreted the victory not as a triumph of Hellenic valor, but as punishment for Persian *hubris*.

"Behold this vengeance," Aeschylus has the ghost of Darius warn in his play *The Persians*. "Curb that pride which calls down destruction from the gods upon our heads." The primitive fear of *phthonos*—the envy of the gods for the success of men—had arisen from the subterranean depths of the Hellenic soul to triumph over Homeric fearless optimism.

Aeschylus and Neal Armstrong

On July 20, 1969, as I sat with a group of friends around a television in Honolulu, Hawaii, watching with awe a human being place his foot on the moon, I commented, "Neal Armstrong will be the most famous man of the 20th century." Obviously, I turned out to be very wrong.

America's landing a man on the moon is the single greatest accomplishment in the history of the human race. It was an act of the purest Homeric fearless optimism. And yet after it, America—like Aeschylus and Ancient Athens—had a failure of nerve. Landing a man on the moon was epic heroism on a scale far beyond anything to which any other culture on Earth could aspire. It was a pinnacle that left the rest of the human race too far below. Landing a man on the moon, like the defeat of the Persians, was too unbelievably astonishing. It was a feat that placed Americans too far beyond the rest of humanity. The primordial anxiety that the gods would punish us for our succeeding too much caused us to give up.

We gave up going to the moon after the inertia of scheduled Apollo landings ran out in 1972. We gave up in Vietnam. We gave up in the Arab oil embargo. We gave up against the Soviets and let them colonize South Yemen (1971), Benin (1972), Angola (1975), Mozambique (1975), Ethiopia (1977), Seychelles (1977), Nicaragua (1979), Suriname (1979), Afghanistan (1979), and Grenada (1980). We gave up when the Communist Khmer Rouge committed genocide in Cambodia. We gave up and let Khomeini overthrow the Shah and gave up again when his thugs took American hostages at our embassy in Tehran. We gave up and let our economy collapse in a malaise of inflation and unemployment. We gave up and elected a pathetic nebbish for our President, Jimmy Carter.

The American retreat of the 1970s is attributed to the "Vietnam Syndrome," as if defeat in Vietnam was its cause. But the cause of America's defeat in Vietnam was a *prior* failure of nerve in the face of the envy of the gods—i.e., the rest of humanity—for the greatest achievement of mankind.

This defeat and subsequent retreat was a monumental disaster for humanity. Communist tyrants perpetrated mass slaughter in the millions and doomed scores of millions more to lives of hideous oppression and poverty from Ethiopia to Afghanistan to Cambodia and Vietnam itself. The Arab oil money financing a war by Muslim terrorists on western civilization was made possible only by America's capitulating to the Arab oil embargo. The end of the 1970s saw a clueless President whining about an American "malaise"—never comprehending that he was elected as an expression of America's prostrate self-image—and Henry Kissinger asserting that the Soviet Union was so close to winning the Cold War that the real question was how America could negotiate the best terms of surrender.

Getting Drunk

Ronald Reagan came to our rescue. He restored our pride in ourselves and our country. He resurrected America's economy and won the Cold War. Ronald Reagan is America's Homeric hero of the 20th century. So what did we Americans do in response to our defeating the Evil Empire of the Soviet Superpower? We got drunk.

To celebrate victory in the Cold War culminating in the disintegration of the Soviet Empire and the Soviet Union, America went on a bacchanalian bender of social, economic, and political irresponsibility. The most memorable line of the 1980s was: "Mr. Gorbachev, tear down this wall!" The most memorable line of the 1990s was: "It depends on what the meaning of 'is' is."

The Clinton bacchanal ended as all frenzies do, morphing into the morning-after Clinton hangover recession. The barest of electoral majorities voted to put the social wreckage of the Clintonistas behind us—but what finally sobered America up was the horror of September 11.

Getting Sober

Ten months earlier, in November 2000, Americans still couldn't decide if they wanted to end their binge of moral delinquency. The slightest breath of bad karma could have tipped the scales against a George W. Bush presidency. That whiff of bad breath would have installed people in the White House totally incapable of preventing what Osama bin Laden tried to achieve: America's will to protect itself collapsing like the Twin Towers of New York.

If the atrocity of September 11, 2001 had been committed under a Gore presidency, a few ineffectual Monica missiles would have been lobbed in Osama's general direction, the Gore White House would have sat around wringing its hands afraid to do anything serious lest "the whole Muslim world be against us," while the rest of America would have sat cowering in fear of the next terrorist assault.

The voices of the Left would have risen unchecked to claim America somehow deserved it, we would have sunk into a quicksand of demoralized gloom, the economy would have never recovered from the Clinton hangover, and the thousands of human beings slaughtered at the World Trade Center and the Pentagon would have died in vain.

This is what Osama bin Laden expected of us. Thus the pivotal event of our time is not the attack on America of September 11, but America's reaction to it. Nothing shocked the Al Qaeda terrorists more than to see in response to their attack not an emasculated America but an enraged America, not an America cringing in fear but an America actually attacking back.

Once again in a moment of direst need, at a mortal fork in America's road, one single individual had come, like Ronald Reagan, to his country's rescue: George W. Bush.

And the liberals hated him for it. To understand why, we must journey to the jungles of the Amazon.

The Evil Eye

Among the Yanomamo and other tribes deep in the Amazon rain forests still adhering to the ancient hunting-gathering lifestyle practiced by our Paleolithic ancestors, it is an accepted practice that when a woman gives birth, she tearfully proclaims her child to be ugly.

In a loud mortified lament that the entire tribe can hear, she asks why the gods have cursed her with such a pathetically repulsive infant. She does this to ward off the envious black magic of the evil eye, the *mal ojo*, which would be directed at her by her fellow tribespeople if they knew how happy she was with her beautiful baby. Anthropologists observe that for most primitive and traditional cultures, "every individual lives in constant fear of the magical aggression of others.... There is only one explanation for unforeseen events: the envious black magic of another villager."

Reflect for a moment on the extent to which tribespeople in a tribal, "primitive" culture suffuse their lives with superstition, witchcraft, sorcery, voodoo, "black magic," and the "evil eye." The world for them is teeming with demons, spirits, ghosts, and gods, all of whom are malicious and dangerous—in a word, *envious*.

Envy is the source of tribal and traditional cultures' belief in black magic, the fear of the envious evil eye. The fundamental reason why certain cultures remain static and never evolve (like present-day villages in Egypt or India that have pretty much stayed the same for a thousand years) is the overwhelming extent to which the entire lives of the people within them are dominated by envy and envy-avoidance—what anthropologists call the "envy-barrier."

There is one and only one way to combat envy and envious rage, and that it is to show no fear of it. For many, this is extraordinarily hard to do. Fear of the evil eye is ancient, deep-rooted in the human psyche. For those so afraid, nothing infuriates them more than a man who does not possess their fear. A man such as George W. Bush.

Terrorism as a Pathology of Envy

The crux understanding of terrorism is that it is a form of *envious rage*.

All three of the great barbarisms of modern times have been pathologies of envy: Nazism, preaching race-envy toward "rich exploitative Jews"; Communism preaching class-envy toward "rich exploitative capitalists"; and Muslim terrorism preaching culture-envy toward "rich exploitative America."

All forms of rage against success and prosperity—from the leftist university professor who considers himself to be in the progressive vanguard of sophisticated contemporary thought to the terrorist in a cave wanting to take us all back to the Dark Ages—are nothing but an atavism, a regression to a primitive tribal belief in black magic.

Take for example the primitive atavism of left-wing bromides like "the rich get richer while the poor get poorer." By the same logic, one can be healthy only at the expense of others. To be in superior health, bursting with energy and vitality, one has to make someone else sick or in poor health—just like to be rich you have to make others poor. The healthy are healthy because they unjustly exploited and ripped off the sick, spiriting away the sick's fair share of health with black magic. In fact, the sick *are* sick *because* the healthy are healthy. If this is absurd, then claiming the poor are poor because they have been exploited by the rich is equally so.

Terrorism is an expression of envious black magic. Nowhere is this more clear than the Nazi-type hatred Arabs have for Israel. The root cause of the Arab-Israeli conflict is envy. The Jews created a civilization out of the wilderness and a garden out of the desert, while the Arabs—even with their centibillions of petrodollars—continued to mire themselves in medieval tyranny and poverty.

Israel is a fount of creativity and achievement, a bastion of western civilization built by scratch out of a desiccated waste-land, sparsely populated by Arab nomads herding sheep, goats, and camels. And that is why the descendants of those nomads hate and envy it so much.

It is also why they hate America so much. Muslim terrorists do not hate America for its vices but for its virtues, its freedom, its prosperity, and its cultural success. Just as Nazis hate Jews for their success, just as Marxists hate capitalists for their success, so Muslim terrorists hate America, western civilization, and Christianity for their success. The hate is justified in all three cases by the claim that the success is due to "exploitation." In all three cases, the belief in exploitation is a primitive belief in voodoo black magic.

Liberalism as a Fear of the Evil Eye

What gives envy its enormous destructive capacity is the fear of the evil eye. It is envy which makes a Nazi, Communist, or Muslim terrorist. It is the fear of being envied which makes a liberal.

This is most easily seen in the children of wealthy parents. Successful businessmen, for example, who have made it on their own normally have a respect for the effort and the economic system that makes success possible. Their children, who have not had to work for it, are easier targets for guilt-mongering by the envious. So they assume a posture of liberal compassion as an envy-deflection device: "Please don't envy me for my father's money—look at all the liberal causes and government social programs I advocate!" Senator Ted Kennedy is the archetype of this phenomenon.

Then there are those who are terrified of envy even though they have earned success themselves. Many Jews are liberals because such lethal envy has been directed at Jews for so many centuries that it is little wonder they consider avoiding envy to be a necessity of life.

Envy-appeasement explains why Hollywood is so liberal. The vast amounts of money entertainment stars make is so grossly disproportionate to the effort it took them to make it that they feel it is unearned. So they apologize for it. The liberal strategy is to apologize for his success, his country's success, and his civilization's success to appease the envious.

Liberalism is thus not a political ideology or set of beliefs. It is an envy-deflection device, a psychological strategy to avoid being envied. It is the politicization of envy-appeasement.

One definitive characteristic of both envy and the fear of it is masochism. Envy is not simply hatred of someone for having something you don't—it is the willingness to masochistically hurt or deprive yourself as long as the person you are envious of is also hurt or deprived. The ultimate example is the Palestinian suicide-bomber.

Similarly, the more one fears being envied, the more one is driven to masochistic self-humiliation in attempts at envy appeasement.

The Masochism of Liberals

The lethality of liberal envy-appeasement is that personally felt guilt is projected onto the various social or tribal collectives to which the liberal belongs and are a part of his self-identity. Self-loathing is transformed into a loathing of one's society or race.

White male liberals become *auto-sexist*, sexist toward their own sex. White liberals become *auto-racist*: racist toward their own race (such as white writer Susan Sontag who denounces her own race as "the cancer of human history"). Dime-store demagogues like eco-fascist environmentalists, feminazis, People for the Ethical Treatment of Animals fanatics, homosexual marriage promoters, and race hustlers like Jesse Jackson and Al Sharpton all get their strength from the liberals' fear of their evil eyes.

All the passions of the Left are frenzies of masochism. What could be more idiotic and masochistic than to oppose missile defense? This opposition cannot be understood unless one dispenses with its rhetoric and rationales and realizes that such folks at their emotional core do not want their country defended. The "global warming" hoax cannot be comprehended other than that its masochistic advocates do not want their civilization to prosper. The entire political correctness movement is nothing but masochistic envy-appeasement advocated by those who do not want their culture to survive. The pro-abortionists' crazed determination to prevent the halt of mothers murdering their children by the millions, or the equally crazed mission of the environmentalists to prevent DDT from saving millions of children from dying of malaria, means that they do not want their species to exist.

As the Amazon tribeswoman who says her baby is ugly, so the white male liberal says his gender, his race, his country, his civilization, and even his entire species is ugly.

The Pathology of Bush Hatred

Today we—America and western civilization—are up against an enemy far more dangerous than the Soviet Union. We are up against an enemy that will actually use nuclear or biochemical weapons to destroy us if they have the chance, an enemy that will commit suicide in an attempt to destroy civilization as we know it.

Yet the liberal elite that controls the Democratic Party and mainstream media hate President Bush more than they hate the terrorists—just as they were more outraged at the humiliation of Baathist thugs in Iraq's Abu Ghraib prison than they were over the murder, mutilation, burning, and hanging of four Americans in Fallujah.

They—just like the Old Europeans and the "international community" to whom they always kowtow—hate George Bush precisely because he refuses to appease the envy of the terrorists, precisely because he is defending America without apology. Just as the terrorists hate America for her virtues and not her vices, the liberal elite hate President Bush for his virtues, not his vices.

This is a tragedy for the Democratic Party. "Patriotic Democrats" were once commonplace. Now they are an anomaly. The Democrats were once riddled with patriots like Scoop Jackson and George Meany. Now they are a rarity, like Joe Lieberman and Zell Miller. The process of McGovernization of the Democrats began in 1972, a consequence of America's failure of nerve after reaching the moon.

Today in 2004, the process has reached an apotheosis in the Democrats' hatred for a President that is not, like they, embarrassed to be American, a President who thinks that, unlike they, America is worth defending.

Once again, America has achieved another pinnacle in world history and accomplishment. America today stands alone as the sole superpower on Earth, far and away the richest nation in man's history, possessing the most powerful—and most morally humane—military force our planet has ever seen. There is no nation or group of nations remotely capable of challenging her.

And again, the liberals are terrified of the envy of the gods, and pathologically angry that America won't apologize to the world, won't appease those who hate us, won't beg and grovel for forgiveness for the sin of historically singular success.

Aeschylus and George Bush

Aeschylus wrote his ode to pessimism, *The Persians*, in 473 B.C., seven short years after Salamis. Over the ensuing decades he and his fellow Athenians regained their Homeric heritage. They elected Pericles to be their *Strategos* (i.e. their overall leader), inaugurating that magnificent moment in history known as The Glory That Was Greece, culminating in their building of the Parthenon and Aeschylus writing *Prometheus Bound*.

Prometheus, in giving fire to man in defiance of Zeus's command not to, has committed the ultimate sin, the super-hubris of *pleonexia*, rebellion against the gods—yet Aeschylus portrays him as nobly heroic precisely because of his hubris. Under the ghastly torture designed by Zeus, chained to a rock and his liver eaten by an eagle, Prometheus remains proud of his gift to humanity and refuses to submit: "There is no wrong however shameful, no malice of Zeus, whereby he can persuade me to unlock my lips … and bend my will."

The liberal intellectual elite of America and Old Europe are dominated by primitive fears, fear of *pleonexia*, fear of the evil eye. This is why their primary appeals to voters are based on negative emotions—anger, bitterness, angst, and dismay. Perhaps someday, years hence, they will be able to cast these fears aside as did Aeschylus—but for now their archaic fears are too deeply embedded in their psyches.

America cannot win the war on Muslim terrorism if she is tortured by fear of the world's evil eyes. The single greatest hope America's enemies have at this moment is that Americans will capitulate to this fear and defeat George W. Bush for the presidency in November 2004.

When Americans went to the polls in November 2000, they did not know the stakes history was about to create. When they go to the polls in November 2004, the stakes will be clear, with no fog of the future obscuring them. Will Americans surrender, retreat, and appease their enemies by electing the epitome of the

Vietnam Syndrome, of "blame America first" defeatism—or will they cast aside the fear of envy and strive for triumph?

The calamitous consequences of the former choice will far exceed those of America's retreat in the 1970s. The consequences of the latter will be America's standing on the pinnacle of history proud and unafraid, proclaiming without fear: "I lead. Strive your best."

CHAPTER NINE

THE KYOTO PROTOCOL: ONE OF THE WORLD'S GREAT RELIGIONS

ALEC RAWLS

Alec Rawls is a professional writer and columnist. He studied in Stanford University's Ph.D. program in economics where he focused on combining economics with moral theory to analyze the ideal structure of liberty. Mr. Rawls previously edited two opinion journals at Stanford and his upcoming book on the revival of republicanism is scheduled for release in 2005.

President Bush's first major policy decision—rejection of the United Nation's Kyoto Treaty on the reduction of carbon dioxide emissions—saved the United States from certain economic ruin. Carbon dioxide, or CO_2, is an unavoidable byproduct of burning fossil fuels, which is an unavoidable concomitant of productivity and prosperity, at least until new energy sources come on line. Enforcement of the Kyoto limit on CO_2 emissions—reducing them to 1990 levels for every first world nation—would place a very restrictive cap on the size of every first world economy.

With the Kyoto protocol, radical environmentalism was on the verge of an astounding coup. It was one step away from transferring the sovereignty of every Western nation on matters of energy policy over to the United Nations, then forcing every Western nation to commit economic suicide. Thank you, President Bush—many times over—for renouncing Kyoto. After a mere two months in office, "Mission Accomplished!" The mopping up exercises will take years, but the initial victory changes the world.

To get a taste of the irrationality of Kyoto, understand that even if one accepts alarmist assumptions about the threat of global warming, Kyoto does virtually nothing to reduce that threat. Using UN assumptions about the sensitivity of climate to CO_2, complete compliance with Kyoto by every nation would reduce global temperatures by about .15 degrees centigrade a hundred years from now. The price tag for this utter futility starts out at about 1 percent of economic output per year for each first world nation and rises as economic growth struggles against the cap on emissions.[1]

How can such a loser be the object of environmentalist passion? Here one must look at what Kyoto *would* accomplish. It might not do anything to affect global climate, but it would achieve the ultimate environmentalist ambition: it would profoundly suppress human activity. This, as the environmentalists see it, leaves more of the planet to the natural world. What a normal cost-benefit analysis would count as a cost—the suppression of economic growth—is counted by environmentalists as a

---

1.   The .15 degrees-centigrade estimate is based on the assumption that the Kyoto emission limits are left in place permanently. See Bjørn Lomborg, *The Skeptical Environmentalist* (Cambridge: Cambridge University Press, 2001): 302. Cost estimates vary with economic assumptions. Id, 303.

benefit. That is why they do not need to see benefits on the global warming issue to be fervent for Kyoto. Environmentalism is not about science—it is about values.

Environmental Religion

The environmentalist vision of conflict between man and environment was stated succinctly by leading environmentalist Paul Ehrlich over 30 years ago: "Western society is in the process of completing the rape and murder of the planet for economic gain."[2] In his 1992 book *Earth in the Balance*, Al Gore pinpointed technological advance as the particular danger because it has, "completely transformed our cumulative ability to exploit the Earth for sustenance—making the consequences of unrestrained exploitation every bit as unthinkable as the consequences of unrestrained nuclear war."[3] Absent is the economist's understanding that progress allows us to use resources more efficiently, treading lighter as we get richer. Poor countries chop down their forests for firewood. Rich countries use fossil fuels, nuclear power and photovoltaics. The environmentalist story is not a logical one. It is a morality tale, unhinged from reality.

Author Michael Crichton suggests that environmentalism has become "the religion of choice for urban atheists." To account for its appeal, he notes that it mimics the founding mythology of Judeo-Christian religion:

> There's an initial Eden, a paradise, a state of grace and unity with nature, there's a fall from grace into a state of pollution as a result of eating from the tree of knowledge, and as a result of our actions there is a judgment day coming for us all. We are all energy sinners, doomed to die, unless we seek salvation.[4]

---

2. From the nonfiction addendum to the Ehrlich's fictional prognostication, "Ecotastrophe," *Ramparts Magazine* (1969; reprint *Best SF: 1969*, Berkeley: Medallion, 1970): 82.

3. Albert Gore, *Earth in the Balance* (New York: Plume, 1992), 31.

4. Michael Crichton, "Environmentalism is Really Urban Atheism," speech delivered at the Commonwealth Club (San Francisco, Calif., September 2003).

Crichton urges environmentalists to focus on science and purge environmentalism of its religious element, but that defines the problem too broadly. We need values and probably would not be able to develop effective science without them. The problem is not religion but irrational religion.

Alaskan Drilling and California Wildfires

With Middle East oil supplies under threat, America has a strong national security interest in uncorking domestic reserves, yet the environmental movement was powerful enough to block oil drilling in the Arctic National Wildlife Refuge (ANWR) on the north coast of Alaska. President Bush wanted to allow a sprinkling of drilling outposts, occupying a total of about 2,000 acres out of ANWR's 1.5 million acres of costal plain (itself only 8 percent of ANWR's 19 million acres). The environmentalist objection to even this tiny footprint is that ANWR would no longer be "pristine." The explicit ideal is one of zero human impact, of pure nonuse.

An ideal of "pristine" wilderness has nothing to do with measuring actual environmental impacts. It is all or nothing. The counting and weighing of actual impacts is rejected in favor of a human aesthetic ideal. Line-item objections to human impact in ANWR maintain this same irrational quality. Concern is expressed for the caribou that breed on the coastal plain; but like our local deer, caribou quickly become oblivious to human presence, as revealed by the growth of caribou herds around the oil fields of Prudhoe Bay. A drilling platform a hundred miles away, or a hundred feet away, won't bother a caribou in the least. It is only environmentalists who are discomfited by this proximity. The ideology of untouched wilderness is not pro-environment. It is just anti-human.

The negative environmental consequences of anti-use environmentalism were on high-profile display during the disastrous wildfire seasons of 2002 and 2003. Timber is the archetypical renewable resource. Use of this resource is not only consistent with healthy forests but is *necessary* for healthy forests. Without thinning, forests build up dangerous fuel loads that cause wildfires to be unnecessarily destructive. With the Sierra Club, the Natural Resources Defense Council, and other powerful environmental groups fixated on the ideology of non-use, this is exactly what happened. Decades of hostility to rational forest management exploded into extraordinarily destructive conflagrations. The environmentalists would rather see the forests be destroyed than allow human use of forest growth.

Rational Environmentalism

When the 2003 wildfire debacle temporarily set the environmentalists back on their heels, President Bush adroitly pushed his Healthy Forests initiative through Congress. The environmentalists will fight implementation every step of the way, but at least now there can be some progress on thinning our dangerously overloaded forests. On ANWR the Bush Administration took rational environmentalism a step further, not only looking at actual impacts on the environment but weighing them against competing human concerns. The highest expression of rational environmentalism is President Bush's answer to Kyoto.

In what many people see as a strategic mistake, the Administration concedes the global warming alarmists their scientific presumptions before rejecting their solution. This actually allows President Bush to take the strongest possible policy position: In no circumstance does it make sense to chop the legs off of our economy. Go ahead, the President is saying, suppose that an infinitesimally thicker jacket of greenhouse gases will actually warm the Earth significantly. Pretend also that we have any idea how warm a jacket we will want to be wearing 50 or 100 years from now. Curtailing economic growth is still the worst thing we could possibly do.

Economic growth is not the problem. It is the answer. The richer we are, the faster we can make the technological progress necessary to create a clean energy future and the faster we can afford to implement advances. If current technologies have harmful effects, the worst mistake would be to put on the economic brakes and hamper our ability to move forward. Thus the Bush Administration's official policy position on CO_2 is to focus on technological change by aiming for reductions in CO_2 *intensity* (the amount of CO_2 produced per dollar of economic output). The Kyoto approach, focusing on the *level* of greenhouse gas emissions, only forestalls the economic growth necessary to make the transition to cleaner technologies. Reducing greenhouse gas intensity points the economy in the right direction, and so long as we are going in the right direction, economic growth is exactly what we want.

Overstating CO_2 Sensitivity

The case against Kyoto becomes even more powerful once the weakness and dishonesty of global warming science is accounted. Everyone agrees that adding CO_2 to the atmosphere will have some warming effect. CO_2 acts like the glass of a greenhouse, letting shortwave radiation from the Sun pass through to warm the Earth, then trapping some of the infrared radiation that the warm Earth directs back towards space. The question is how strong the warming effect of additional CO_2 will be. Carbon dioxide itself traps only a very small amount of heat. To predict a significant warming effect, alarmists have to assume that heat trapped by CO_2 gets multiplied several times by its effect on water vapor.

Water vapor is the Earth's main greenhouse gas. It does about 94 percent of the heat-trapping work that makes our planet livable. It is also volatile. When water vapor traps heat, the temperature increase causes additional evaporation of surface water. This additional water vapor traps yet more heat, evaporating more water, and so on. If this positive feedback effect is strong, then the small amount of additional heat trapped by CO_2 could end up causing global temperature to rise substantially. But there were clear indications from the beginning that models used to predict several degrees of global warming over the next 50 or 100 years had much too strong a water vapor feedback effect. When historic levels of CO_2 were fed in, the models significantly over-predicted current temperatures.

NASA climate modeler Dr. James Hansen ignited the public furor over global warming in 1988 when he told Al Gore's Senate Committee on Science, Technology and Space that he was "99 percent certain" that global warming was taking place. But global warming science was anything but certain. As Reid Bryson, professor of meteorology at the University of Wisconsin, fumed at the time of Hansen's testimony:

> [H]ere we have the new computer models, which neither back test nor explain contemporary weather patterns very well, being used by the researchers and the media to make 50-year weather forecasts. The models, in my estimation, are just mule muffins.[5]

Clouds and Rain

In addition to having positive temperature feedback effects, water vapor also has negative feedback effects that could make the net marginal feedback effect small or even negative (so that temperature forcings get damped down instead of multiplied up). The most obvious is clouds. If there were no water vapor there would be no clouds, and clouds are known to on average have a slight cooling effect, blocking more heat from reaching the Earth than they trap below. The question is how cloud formation behaves at the margin. Does a marginal increase in global temperature cause a marginal increase in cloudiness that tends to

---

5. Jonathan R. Laing, "Climate of Fear: The Greenhouse Effect May Be Mostly Hot Air," *Barron's* (February 27, 1989), 6.

offset the temperature increase? Cloud research by M.I.T. Meteorologist Richard Lindzen suggests that the answer is yes.[6]

Another negative temperature feedback effect of water vapor works through increased efficiency of the rain cycle. As the amount of water vapor in the atmosphere increases, condensation of clouds into rain becomes more complete, leaving less water vapor in the upper troposphere to trap heat below. The heat released by condensation (the opposite of the cooling effect of evaporation) can then radiate out into space. These cloud and rain effects give reason to think that the sensitivity of climate to CO_2 may be small, which complements the evidence for low sensitivity that comes from the failure of high sensitivity models to back test.

By assuming high water vapor feedback effects, climate modelers simply begged the question of whether human-induced global warming would be large. Here were these big impressive computer models, doing trillions upon trillions of calculations, and the alarmist answers they spat out were simply inserted at the beginning.

Other Global Warming Overstatements

Alarmists also overestimated the rate at which CO_2 is building up in the atmosphere by about 60 percent, thanks to their failure to properly account for the fact that carbon dioxide is plant food. According to horticulturist Sylvan Wittwer, the foremost researcher on the effects of CO_2 on plant growth, carbon dioxide is "nearly always limiting for photosynthesis."[7] Thus it is not surprising that the increase of atmospheric CO_2 over the last

---

6. More specifically, Lindzen found that when tropical temperatures rise, cirrus clouds decrease and cumulus clouds increase. Cirrus clouds trap more heat than they block while cumulus clouds block more than they trap, so this change has a cooling effect. See Richard Lindzen, Ming-Dah Chou, and Arthur Y. Hou, "Does the Earth Have an Adaptive Infrared Iris?" *Bulletin of the American Meteorological Society*, 82 (March 2001): 417–432.

7. Sylvan H. Wittwer, *Food, Climate, and Carbon Dioxide: The Global Environment and World Food Production* (Boca Raton, Fla.: CRC Press, 1995).

200 years—from about 260 parts per million (26 one-thousandths of one percent) to 370 parts per million (a 40 percent increase)—should coincide with a substantial increase in the rate at which CO_2 is extracted from the atmosphere. Plants are like animals that way. Whatever food we put out, they will eat.

Another mitigating factor is the decreasing marginal heat-trapping effect of CO_2. The fact that CO_2 emissions are increasing exponentially sounds scary, as if this must lead to an exponential increase in global warming, but it won't. Once most of the infrared that is of a wavelength to be trapped by CO_2 is getting trapped by the CO_2 already in the atmosphere, there isn't a lot more warming that additional CO_2 can do. Mathematically, the marginal warming effect of CO_2 decreases logarithmically. When combined with an exponential increase in CO_2 emissions, the total warming effect comes out approximately linear. Climatologists Patrick Michaels and Robert Balling call this "the law of climate models: despite exponential greenhouse forcing, *once greenhouse warming starts, it takes place at a constant rate.*"[8]

High-end measures put the slight warming trend since 1970 at about .15 degrees centigrade per decade. (Low-end temperature series show little or no warming.) If the high-end measurements are correct, and if warming is human-induced, as the alarmists claim, then this slight warming trend is about what we can expect to continue, *if* we keep burning exponentially more fossil fuel. This "skeptical" position has lately been adopted by Dr. Hansen, who started the whole foofaraw with his Senate testimony in 1988. "Future global warming can be predicted much more accurately than is generally realized," Hansen now says. "[W]e predict additional warming in the next 50 years of 0.75 ºC [plus or minus] 0.25ºC, a warming rate of 0.15ºC [plus or minus] 0.05ºC per decade."[9]

---

8.   Patrick Michaels and Robert Balling, *The Satanic Gases* (Washington, DC: Cato Institute, 2000), 104. Italics in original.
9.   See James E. Hansen and Makiko Sato, "Trends of Measured Climate Forcing Agents," *Proceedings of the National Academy of Sciences* 98 (December 18, 2001): 14778-14783.

The UN and the IPCC

Global warming alarmism has so far generated a total of about 18 billion dollars of American funding for a gigantic global warming industry, most of it spent as people like Al Gore have seen fit. Most egregiously, the religionists brought the United Nations in to orchestrate research, creating the Intergovernmental Panel on Climate Change (IPCC) that now presumes to speak for the climate field, and they used the United Nations to charge ahead on setting global warming policy.

When the IPCC produced its first global climate assessment report in 1990, it baldly misrepresented the accuracy of its models, claiming that: "When the latest atmospheric models are run with the current concentrations of greenhouse gases, their simulation of present climate is generally realistic on large scales." In fact, the models referred to were saying that the climate should have already warmed between 1.3 and 2.3 degrees Celsius, when actual global warming since the latter half of the 19th century had been about .6°C.[10] This false claim of accuracy for the alarmist models was then used to railroad policy makers into taking aggressive action against CO_2, starting with the first Earth Summit in Rio de Janeiro in 1992.

By the time the IPCC's Second Assessment Report came out in 1995, a lot of people knew that the 1990 report had badly misrepresented the science. In its technical portions, the '95 report acknowledged this mistake, then proceeded to repeat it, explaining away the failure of earlier models to back test by suggesting that powerful CO_2 warming effects were being masked by the cooling effect of sulfates. That is, the IPCC modified its climate models as necessary in order to preserve the assumption of high climate sensitivity to CO_2, which it had to do

---

10.   Dr. Patrick Michaels, "Testimony Before the House Subcommittee on Energy and Environment of the Committee on Science" (November 6, 1997), http://www.house.gov/science /michaels_11-6.htm.

if it wanted to maintain its call for draconian reductions in fossil fuel burning. But the indispensable Dr. Michaels had already investigated the sulfate cooling hypothesis and found that it has implications that are not borne out by the evidence.

Sulfates

Because sulfates come from coal burning, and because they fall out of the atmosphere fairly quickly, they are mostly found in the northern hemisphere. If they are causing cooling, they should be making the northern hemisphere cooler than the southern hemisphere. But actual temperature differences go the other direction, and this has been a continuing trend. Satellite data from the National Oceanic and Atmospheric Administration show the northern hemisphere warming at a rate of .155°C per decade between 1979 and 2004 while the southern hemisphere has been warming at the miniscule rate of .014°C per decade. There could well be some sulfate cooling effect. There is just no evidence that it is large, hence it cannot rescue the hypothesis that CO_2 sensitivity is large. "It is the sensitivity," argue Michaels and Balling, "not the sulfates, that was the problem."[11]

Global warming religionists are not about to let the facts stand in their way. Just before the United Nation's Geneva policy conference in 1996, one of the second assessment report's lead authors, Benjamin Santer, published an article in *Nature* claiming that sulfate augmented computer models were highly accurate in back tests and were showing rapid global warming in the southern hemisphere, as the sulfate hypothesis predicts. Michaels and another climatologist, Paul Knappenberger, quickly redid Santer's calculations and discovered that Santer had artificially lopped off both ends of his data set in a way that drastically misrepresented southern hemisphere temperature effects. It would seem that Santer adjusted the data in order to stampede

---

11.   Michaels and Balling, 194.

policymakers. Only the quick work of Michaels and Knappen-berger kept his ploy from being more successful.[12]

Natural Temperature Variation

The travesty in the IPCC's third and latest assessment report (2001) is its denial that natural temperature variation exists on the millennium scale. The report opens with what is popularly referred to as the "hockey stick" diagram. It depicts global temperature for the last 1,000 years as essentially a straight line until the 1900s, where it shoots up like the blade of a hockey stick. One obvious problem with the diagram is that it mixes apples and oranges. The pre-1900 temperature data is inferred from proxies, like tree rings, while the blade part of the data series pastes on modern thermometer readings. Another possible problem is the inability of other researchers to reconstruct the series using the same source data.[13] But what is astounding is the reaction of the UN scientists to contrary evidence.

Willie Soon and Sallie Baliunas of Harvard University col-lated the evidence from numerous studies and came to the conclusion that the Medieval Warm Period (800 A.D.-1400 A.D.) and the Little Ice Age (1400 A.D.-1900 A.D.) were global, not local phenomena (as the hockey stick diagram implies).[14] In response, the UN scientists went on the warpath. The author of the hockey stick diagram, University of Virginia Climatologist Michael Mann, waged a campaign along with his associates to fire the editor of the journal where the Soon and Baliunas paper had been published. Mann also testified before the U.S. Senate

12.   B.D. Santer, et al, "A Search for Human Influences on the Thermal Structure of the Atmosphere," *Nature*, 382 (1996), 46-45. P.J. Michaels and P.C. Knappenberger, "Human effect on Global Climate?" *Nature* 384 (1996): 522-23. Michaels and Balling recount the Geneva context of Santer's paper and their response in *Satanic Gases*, 93-99.

13.   Stephen McIntyre and Ross McKitrick, "Corrections to the Mann et al. (1999) Proxy Data Base and Northern Hemispheric Average Temperature Series," *Energy and Environment* 14 (2003): 751-771.

14.   Willie Soon and Sallie Baliunas, "Proxy Climactic and Environmental Changes of the Last 1000 Years," *Climate Research* 23 (January 31, 2003): 89-110.

Committee on Environment and Public Works as to the supposed incompetence of the Soon and Baliunas research, present-
ing his tale of no-known-natural-variation as the mainstream
view. "In truth," says climatologist David Legates from the
University of Delaware, "Mr. Mann's work is the scientific
outlier—the one study that does not fit with the wealth of
scientific evidence."[15]

Part of the conflict stems from the fact that the science of trying to reconstruct temperature history from proxy variables is
fraught with difficulty. The technical issues are far from resolved,
creating a normal process of correction and debate. But trying to
suppress contrary evidence by trying to have the people who
publish it fired is a perversion of this normal process.

Why would environmental religionists be hostile to the possibility of natural temperature variation? Because if natural
variation is in the cooling direction, then human-induced warming would be acting to stabilize temperature, which would seem
to be good. Conversely, if natural temperature variation is
headed in a warming direction, then human-induced cooling
would be beneficial. Most importantly, if we don't know *which*
way natural variation is headed, then we have no idea what
human effect will be desirable and no way to say that any
particular human impact is bad. For the religion of non-use, with
its goal of suppressing human impact, all of this is a disaster.

Orbits and Sunspots

There are some very long-time-scale sources of natural temperature change that can be predicted. Variations in the Earth's
orbit, which moves further from and closer to the Sun, have been
generating 100,000-year-long ice ages interrupted by 10,000- to
13,000-year-long interglacial periods, for the last 2.5 million

---

15. David Legates, "Global Warming Smear Targets," *The Washington Times* (August 26, 2003).

years. Given that the current interglacial period started about 12,500 years ago, this cycle gives some grounds for worry about impending cooling, but not much. Change in the Sun's intensity due to orbital change occurs very slowly, and the year-to-year change is infinitesimal. Still, there is evidence that, when climate change does occur, it can be abrupt. Thus as a general matter, we had better be prepared to adapt to the next ice age or to ward it off by artificially absorbing a bit more solar heat.

On shorter time scales, the great driver of natural temperature change seems to be sunspots. On the one hand, sunspots directly warm the Earth by slightly increasing the sun's energy output. (The spots themselves are cooler than the rest of the Sun's surface, but they coincide with super-hot "faculae" that cause the Sun's total luminescence to increase.) More importantly, sunspots blast storms of solar-magnetic flux into space that have the effect of puffing away the Earth's cloud cover. What they actually blow away is some of the cosmic radiation that would otherwise hit the Earth. Cosmic radiation turns out, through mechanisms that are not well understood, to be critical to cloud formation, especially the cumulus clouds that have the strongest cooling effect. Thus when sunspot activity is high, cosmic radiation and cloud cover are scarce, giving the Earth a sunburn.

Scientists have been able to trace the level of sunspot activity over the last 1,000 years by measuring the residue of cosmic radiation in ice cores. Initial results confirm the warming effect of sunspots. Sunspot activity was higher than average during the Medieval Warm Period and virtually disappeared at the onset of the Little Ice Age, providing strong evidence both that these episodes were indeed global events and that they were driven by sunspot activity.[16] The ice-core record also contains a startling revelation. The Sun has been, as the ice-core researchers put it,

16.   Ilya Usoskin, Sami Solanki, Manfred Schussler, Kalevi Mursula, and Katja Alanko, "Millenium Scale Sunspot Number Reconstruction: Evidence for an Unusually Active Sun Since the 1940's," *Physical Review Letters* (November 21, 2003): 91.

"in a frenzy since the 1940s." In the 1960s, solar activity shot above anything else in the 1,000-year-old record. Today the Sun is more than twice as active as at any other recorded time. Once sunspot warming effects are subtracted from observed temperature changes, the component of warming that might be attributable to human impact gets substantially smaller.

Choice Under Uncertainty

Unfortunately, the revelation that the Sun is in a state of frenzy tells us absolutely nothing about what kind of policies would be beneficial. There are some interesting theories about where sunspots come from, but science is far from being able to predict the level of sunspot activity 50 or 100 years from now. The current high level of solar activity could be the beginning of an upsurge that threatens to warm the Earth dangerously or it could be the end of an upsurge, the fall-off of from which will prompt the end of our current interglacial period. In short, we have no way of saying whether a modicum of human-induced global warming is more likely to cause a catastrophe or save us from a catastrophe. The only way to cast human-induced warming as a danger is to assume that natural temperature variation is benign and human effects are harmful. That is not science. That is anti-human ideology.

The likelihood of natural temperature change, and the uncertainty of its future direction, reveals the broader superiority of the Bush approach to global warming. Economic growth maximizes our ability to adapt to an uncertain future. Suppose we go ahead and hobble economic progress in order to put a lighter jacket on, as the Kyoto crowd wants, and the solar weather turns out to be cold. Not only will we have the wrong jacket on, but we will have fewer technological resources for adapting. President Bush's pro-growth answer to global warming is the correct answer, not just to one scenario, but to *every* possible scenario. That is the most important reason for embracing it. Where global

123

warming science is highly uncertain, economic science is un-equivocal. Don't chain Prometheus. His creative fire will always be wanted.

If not for a few hundred Florida voters in 2000, Kyoto would still be on track and might even be the law of the land by now. Does everyone understand how close the environmentalists came to putting a UN dog collar on the U.S. economy? Think of it as the Twin Towers attack that didn't happen. Thank you, President Bush for standing up to *both* the great moral irrationalities of our age. Radical Islam and mainstream environmentalism both use conflict-based world views (believer vs. infidel; man vs. environment) to discount those interests that they identify as being on the wrong side. Only by resolute insistence on the full accounting of value can we wrest these important religions from those who pervert them.

ECONOMIC

POLICY

CHAPTER TEN

THE BUSH TAX CUTS HAVE PAID DIVIDENDS

STEPHEN MOORE

Stephen Moore is president of the Club for Growth, and a contributing editor of NATIONAL REVIEW *magazine. He previously served as the Cato Institute's director of Fiscal Policy Studies, and is now a Cato senior fellow. He is the author of several books, including* IT'S GETTING BETTER ALL THE TIME *and* GOVERNMENT: AMERICA'S #1 GROWTH INDUSTRY.

The centerpiece of President Bush's domestic economic agenda has been a series of tax cuts oriented toward reviving economic growth, spurring investment, and reversing the catastrophic declines in the stock market that occurred in 1999 and 2000. By all accounts, those tax policies—especially the 2003 tax reduction plan, which reduced tax rates on labor income, capital gains, and dividends—have worked almost precisely as its supply-side proponents had predicted. Bush took a page out of Reaganomics by understanding that high tax rates deter economically productive activity and the economy has performed admirably just as it did in the 1980s after the Reagan-Kemp tax reductions.

The table below shows the reductions in tax rates that were implemented by the Bush tax cuts. The jewel of the President's plan was the reduction in the dividend tax rate from as high as 40 percent down to 15 percent.

Table 1
Bush Tax Cut Puts Money in America's Pockets

	Bush Tax Cut	Old Law
Capital Gains Tax	15%	20%
Dividend Tax	15%	40%
Income Tax Rate (highest)	35%	40%
Income Tax Rate (Middle)	25%	28%
Income Tax Rate (Lowest)	10%	15%
Per Child Credit	$1,000	$500
Marriage Penalty Tax	Eliminated	Reinstated
Death Tax in 2010	0%	55%

The capital gains tax was reduced from 20 percent to 15 percent, and the data so far confirms what 40 years of evidence has taught us: Every time the capital gains tax rate has been reduced, capital gains tax revenues have soared. In 2003 capital gains tax receipts exceeded the level of collections in 2002 and reversed a four-year slide in capital gains tax revenues even though the rate was chopped by a fifth. This is called a "Laffer Curve" effect, after the economist Arthur Laffer who described the possibility of rising tax receipts accompanying falling tax rates in the 1970s and 1980s. Once again the validity of the curve was borne out by real-world evidence.

The dividend tax cut was perhaps the most controversial of all of Bush's tax proposals. It was ridiculed during congressional debate as a tax relief plan for yacht owners and the billionaires' boys club. I and other proponents of the dividend tax cut argued that it would help the economy in two ways. First, by cutting the double tax on dividend income, the plan would boost the sagging stock market by lifting the after-tax rate of return on business earnings. Second, by chopping the tax barrier on dividends, the tax cut would induce firms to increase their dividend payments to shareholders. In the wake of corporate scandals, with scores of firms lying about the health of their balance sheets, this new incentive for firms to actually pay out profits to shareholders would have the added benefit of improving corporate governance by discouraging firms from cooking their books.

It is now beyond dispute that the stock market got a nice boost from the reduction in the dividend and capital gains taxes—just as predicted. Stock prices rose by roughly 20 percent after one year of the Bush tax plan's passage. That was the best year for stocks since the late 1990s. That created about $1.5 trillion in new shareholder wealth. One of the smart economists who predicted this market surge was Donald Luskin of Trend-Macrolytics. As Mr. Luskin puts it: "Cause and effect relationships are nearly impossible to conclusively prove when stock prices are involved. But considering that stock prices are so much higher since the tax cuts, the burden of proof is on the skeptics. We are satisfied we were right—because it happened."

What has been even more remarkable has been the dividend windfall that shareholders have enjoyed. It appears that the President's tax cut has reversed the whole corporate culture over dividend payments. In the go-go 1990s, when stock values soared, especially in the tech sector, paying dividends was interpreted as a sign of corporate weakness—a concession on the part of management that they had no higher value-added use of their profits. Until last year Microsoft never paid a dividend, even though the firm, like a plump mother hen, was sitting atop a golden egg of some $50 billion of cash reserves. Why? As Thomas Smith, president of Prescott Associates, a Connecticut investment firm, points out: "The tax code severely penalized a dividend payout because the corporation pays a 35 percent tax on the profits and then the shareholder pays an additional punitive 40 percent tax rate if the profits are passed through in dividends." Hence, paying a dividend under the old tax regime was not a "tax-rational option."

Now it is, and companies have responded. Standard & Poor's reports a "massive increase in dividends reversing a 20 year decline." My estimates are that Fortune 500 companies increased their dividend payouts by more than $10 billion in 2003. Several very large Fortune 500 firms that had not recently or in some cases *never* paid a dividend started sending out checks late last year. MGM recently announced it will pay an $8 per share dividend, which is worth about $2 billion to shareholders. Microsoft paid out more than $1 billion in dividends last year, something CEO Steve Ballmer has said the firm would not have done absent the Bush tax cut.

So what difference does it make to our economy that firms are paying dividends again? One obvious answer is that shareholders are better off because stock values have risen and they are receiving more of the cash. Moreover, it is worth repeating the conclusion by Mr. Luskin on the value of the dividend tax cut: "Now that firms are free to pay out money that had been previously held captive behind the dividend tax barrier, companies now can realize their own optimal payout rate and improve economy-wide resource allocation." This tax cut appears to have put America on a path toward greater economic efficiency in the corporate sector and therefore a path to longer term sustainable growth.

You wouldn't know that from listening to the Kerry Democrats. Early in 2004 John Kerry charged, "This is the worst job market since Herbert Hoover was President." A new liberal attack ad by the Hate-Bush coalition on the Left ridicules the Bush tax cut because, although it has created jobs and new businesses, they are all in China. And Moveon.org suggests that if the budget deficit keeps escalating, we will have to bring back child labor to pay off the bills.

But almost every economic indicator points in a bullish direction. The standard measure of economic growth, gross domestic product, has accelerated over the past nine months faster than at any time in the past 20 years. Since the Bush tax cuts took effect in May 2003, the economy has grown in annualized real terms at 8.2 percent in the third quarter of 2003, 4.0 percent in the fourth quarter of 2003, and 4.3 percent in the first quarter of 2004. Over that same time period labor productivity, which is the key ingredient to higher wages for workers, has grown at nearly 4 percent per year; business investment has climbed by 8 percent; corporate pre-tax profits rose by 12 percent in the fourth quarter of last year; and interest rates, despite the edge upward in recent months, are lower than they were under President Clinton. Arguably, the U.S. economy had a better year in 2003 than even Barry Bonds.

It may still be too early in this expansion to label what we are experiencing now the Bush Economic Boom. But at the very least the last year has brought what might be described as a Bush boomlet.

One indication of how rapidly the economy is growing is that Mr. Kerry has been forced to conjure up new statistics to try to cast a pessimistic pall over the economy. The Kerry camp has trotted out the new "George Bush misery index." What's wrong with the old "misery index"? The embarrassing problem for the Kerry Democrats is that if we use that misery index (inflation plus unemployment), things have seldom been finer. In fact, the misery index now stands at 8.2 percent (that's 5.7 percent unemployment and 2.5 percent inflation), which is actually lower than the 8.4 percent when Bill Clinton ran for re-election in 1996 all atwitter over the unprecedented American prosperity. So now Mr. Kerry has cooked up a concoction that includes items like college tuition costs, gasoline prices, and the trade deficit. Even the media, which has been mighty obliging to Mr. Kerry in trashing President Bush whenever possible, couldn't help snicker when the Democrats pulled this ploy.

The U.S. economy has beaten the stuffing out of the Europeans and the Japanese over the past three years. Our economic growth rate has been nearly twice what Europe and Japan has managed. On the jobs front, the nations of the new workers' paradise of Western Europe have an average unemployment rate of nearly 8 percent. That is fully 2 percentage points higher than the rate of joblessness in the United States. If the United States had German levels of unemployment, we would have a new army of unemployed workers the size of the entire population of Colorado. Best that we not try to imitate European style work rules, welfare policies, and high tax rates.

What is arguably most impressive of all about the U.S. economic performance is not that we are growing at a brisk pace, but that we are growing at all. Imagine that back in the summer of 2000 we knew what the next President was about to be bequeathed: a bubble-bursting stock market that would in the next 18 months liquidate $5 trillion in wealth; a corporate accounting scandal that would further shatter investor confidence; a global recession; a U.S. recession; a bloody terrorist attack on U.S. soil that would kill thousands of Americans and require massive new military expenditures; and a full-scale financial meltdown in the nation's largest state, California, which one in six Americans call home. Would a 5 percent growth rate in 2004 and a 5.7 percent unemployment rate have seemed at all achievable? Most economists (including this one) would have thought this kind of rebound inconceivable.

So where did the growth come from? More than any politician or policy change, the revitalization of the U.S. economy in the wake of all these crises is a testament to what George Gilder once described as "the pervasive spirit of capitalistic enterprise" that makes the U.S. economy the unique wealth creation machine in the world. The ability of the U.S. economy to get back on its feet so rapidly is especially impressive given that many of the

Bush Administration and congressional policies have actually been economically counterproductive. The surge in government spending and the flirtation with trade protectionism in areas like steel and agriculture have not been proud moments for this Republican regime.

But Bush got one giant thing absolutely right: the tax cuts, especially the 2003 tax plan, which lowered income, capital gains, and dividend tax rates. These reforms were a vitally necessary antibiotic injection through the veins of the economy when it was most needed. They helped lift the stock market by nearly 30 percent last year, just as supply-siders had predicted. This in turn helped raise the overall level of wealth in the U.S. economy to a record $44 trillion. It is no coincidence that the growth spurt of 2003 began in the very month the pro-investment tax cuts were enacted.

The tiresome mantra of the Kerry Democrats of late is that Bush's tax cuts were slanted to the super wealthy. Where is the fairness in cutting income tax rates for those in the highest tax brackets, "the people who need tax cuts the least?" the Democrat's economic guru Paul Krugman asks. But it is Mr. Krugman who is employing fuzzy math here. The percentage of all taxes paid by the richest 1 percent of tax filers actually rose after the Bush tax cut. But here is the more important point. Almost two of every three of these "undeserving rich" in the highest income tax bracket are small business owners, the Tax Foundation reports. That is to say, the Bush tax cut smartly reduced taxes on the wealth producers and job creators in the economy — and for that there is no need to apologize. If Mr. Kerry is hell bent on raising the taxes back up on these employers, how in the world is he going to entice these businesses to create more jobs?

All that seems to be holding back even more rapid growth of incomes and jobs is the reluctance of liberal Democrats in Congress to make the tax cuts a permanent fixture in the tax code (the investment tax cuts are scheduled to expire in 2008). The Kerry Democrats are pledging to repeal the tax cuts if they ever take back power in Washington. That's a frightening prospect for the financial markets.

The final and loudest objection to the Bush tax cuts is that they have caused the federal debt to soar. But the surge in the budget deficit from 2001 to 2003 was mostly attributable to the war on terrorism, runaway domestic spending, and the economic recession and stock market collapse that caused tax receipts to fall for four straight years. Remember that it was economic growth and a surging stock market that created the surpluses in the late Clinton years, not tax hikes.

Republicans need to impose spending discipline for the first time in years. The budget has been growing at an 8 percent clip over the past three years, not including the money for national defense. Senate Appropriations Committee Chairman Ted Stevens recently absurdly complained that "there just isn't enough money to go around." Wrong. There is just too much money being spent by appropriators. House Budget Committee Chairman Jim Nussle wants to freeze domestic spending—at least until the war in Iraq has been completed. That alone would cut the deficit in half in five years.

The Bush tax plan has pulled the United States out of a recession, helped us recover from the aftermath of 9/11, revived the sagging stock market, and brought the United States the highest rate of economic growth of virtually any other industrialized nation over the past two years. This is no Herbert Hoover economy. Bush's tax cut confirms decades of evidence that, when tax rates are reduced and impediments to private sector growth are removed, the economy performs as if on steroids. That was true when Calvin Coolidge cut taxes in the 1920s, when John F. Kennedy cut taxes in the 1960s, and when Ronald Reagan cut them in the 1980s. In each case, tax revenues rose, the industrial sectors surged, and the muscle was put back in the American economy. Bush's critics lambasted his tax policies as risky and reckless. But what now seems patently obvious is that repealing these tax cuts is what would be truly risky and reckless.

CHAPTER ELEVEN

A SUPPLY-SIDE
PERSPECTIVE ON
THE BUSH TAX CUTS

ARTHUR B. LAFFER

Arthur B. Laffer is widely recognized as the father of modern supply-side economics. He was a member of President Ronald Reagan's Economic Policy Advisory Board from 1981 to 1989, and he is the chairman of Laffer Associates, an economic research and consulting firm.

"The momentum of today's prosperity began in the 1980s—with sound money, deregulation, the opening of global trade, and a 25 percent tax cut. Along the way we have confirmed some truths and discarded some dogmas. Government can be an ally of enterprise—by creating an environment that rewards work and inspires investment. But government does not create wealth. Wealth is the economic measure of human creativity and enterprise."

President George W. Bush

The last 100 years are defined by a handful of Presidents whose policies made a difference. Looking back at the last four years of George W. Bush's presidency, it's clear he will join that exclusive list of economic greats whose supply-side, pro-growth agenda changed people's lives, and America, for the better. Economic and political history has taught this President a powerful lesson: People respond to positive incentives, and the government can provide those incentives by cutting taxes.

The broad-based tax cuts in the early 1980s ignited the industrialist spirit of innovation and prosperity that carried into the 1990s and sustained the Clinton-era boom. Republican or Democrat, we (nearly) are all supply-siders now. And for those not yet convinced, President Bush's pro-growth policies will make them believers. This is one of the most fiscally conservative Administrations I've seen in decades. And I have full faith in their economic agenda, and in their sincerity to implement it.

The President's economic plan has primarily aimed to create incentives to work, invest, employ and produce. The Economic Growth and Tax Relief Reconciliation Act (EGTRRA) of 2001 cut personal income tax rates, but it phased in those reductions over many years. The Jobs and Growth Tax Relief Reconciliation Act (JGTRRA) of 2003 accelerated the rate cuts to January 1, 2003.

Frankly, I was worried that the first act didn't go far enough. Phasing in tax cuts sends the wrong message about the right policy, encouraging Americans to postpone work, production and employment. This is not the effect that tax cuts should have on a sluggish economy. Tax cuts should entice individuals to work harder, be more productive, and push employment to converge toward full capacity.

In addition to making the previous cuts immediate, the dividends and capital gains tax rates were reduced, a 10 percent tax bracket was created and subsequently extended, the child credit was expanded, the alternative minimum tax (AMT) exemption was increased, the marriage penalty tax was assuaged, and relief was given to small business owners in the form of increased bonus first-year depreciation and expensing election. Now this President understood what it meant to have pro-growth reforms. He got the right tax cuts passed, and his ideas were a home run.

One of the fundamental tools a government has to increase its country's standard of living is its ability to cut taxes. People don't work to pay taxes, nor do they save to go bankrupt—they work to get paid in after-tax dollars, and save to maximize their after-tax rate of return on savings. Individual motivation in response to incentives is an essential tenet of economics: if you tax people who work, and pay people who don't work, don't be surprised if a lot of people stop working and a massive shift away from productivity occurs.

With the residual effects of Y2K, Sept. 11, the financial market scandals, the election debacle, and the Iraq War, it is a miracle that President Bush has not only survived, but has succeeded to implement his economic vision. His unwavering beliefs and the content of his character have revived the American people's faith in the marketplace and that a hard day at work will be rewarded.

In the Face of Adversity, Recovery

The two major tax acts of 2001 and 2003 represent a significant victory for supply-side economics and the country as a whole. Unfortunately, not enough time has elapsed to fairly evaluate the total effects of the two tax cuts. But so far, so good— from the onset of the first tax cuts, real GDP growth has skyrocketed back to levels not experienced since the late 1990s (see Figure 1).

In essence, the two separate tax acts are one giant tax cut phased in over three years. Naysayers point to the tax cuts as further exacerbating the budget deficit, but they are dead wrong.

Government revenues will increase once the effects of the tax cuts work their way though the system. There is nothing worse than a static forecast of such a dynamic system. Static revenue forecasts just look at the loss in the current period as if behavior will not change, but behavior does change in response to a change in incentives.

Figure 1
Real GDP Growth—Trailing Four Quarters

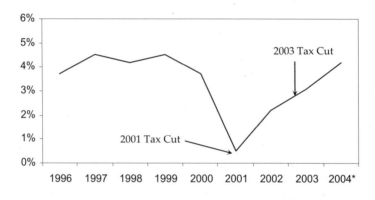

* Q1 only.

Tax cuts are an exceptionally positive force for the economy as a whole. Lower taxes lead to higher after-tax returns, which, in turn, make people save more, invest more and produce more. Higher savings and higher investment mean more capital (and more income to produce that capital). More capital means higher wages. Higher after-tax income and higher wages mean more work effort, more employment and higher total income. These effects are in addition to the income effects mentioned earlier.

And, of course, higher after-tax returns on capital mean higher stock prices and more profits, and, therefore, more capital gains, more dividends, and more taxes collected by both the federal and state governments. Not all of these effects will appear on day one, but they will appear. Bush's tax cuts will bring the economy back into shape, and the further out into the future you look, the greater its muscles and might will grow.

Why Cutting Taxes Works

The theory of supply-side economics, though often thought of as a recent phenomenon, is not a new concept. The Laffer Curve is a modern name applied to a fundamental idea. The Muslim philosopher, Ibn Khaldun, wrote in his 14th century work *The Muqaddimah*:

> It should be known that at the beginning of the dynasty, taxation yields a large revenue from small assessments. At the end of the dynasty, taxation yields a small revenue from large assessments.

A more recent version of incredible clarity was written by none other than John Maynard Keynes:

> When, on the contrary, I show, a little elaborately, as in the ensuing chapter, that to create wealth will increase the national income and that a large proportion of any increase in the national income will accrue to an Exchequer, amongst whose largest outgoings is the payment of incomes to those who are unemployed and whose receipts are a proportion of the incomes of those who are occupied, I hope the reader will feel, whether or not he thinks himself competent to criticize the argument in detail, that the answer is just what he would expect—that it agrees with the instinctive promptings of his common sense.
>
> Nor should the argument seem strange that taxation may be so high as to defeat its object, and that, given sufficient time to gather the fruits, a reduction of taxation will run a better chance than an increase of balancing the budget. For to take the opposite view today is to resemble a manufacturer who, running at a loss, decides to raise his price, and when his declining sales increase the loss, wrapping himself in the rectitude of plain arithmetic, decides that prudence requires him to raise the price still more—and who, when at last his account is balanced with naught on both sides, is still found righteously declaring that it would have been the act of a gambler to reduce the price when you were already making a loss.[17]

---

17. John Maynard Keynes, *The Collected Writings of John Maynard Keynes* (London: Macmillan Cambridge University Press, 1972).

Theory Basics

The basic idea behind the relationship between tax rates and tax revenues is that changes in tax rates have two effects on revenues: the arithmetic effect and the economic effect. The arithmetic effect is simply that if tax rates are lowered, tax revenues per dollar of tax base will be lowered by the amount of the decrease in the rate. And, the reverse is true for an increase in tax rates. The economic effect, however, recognizes the positive impact that lower tax rates have on work, output, and employment, and therefore the tax base, by providing incentives to increase these activities. Raising tax rates has the opposite economic effect by penalizing participation in the taxed activities. The arithmetic effect always works in the opposite direction from the economic effect. Therefore, when the economic and the arithmetic effects of tax rate changes are combined, the consequences of the change in tax rates on total tax revenues are no longer quite so obvious.

Figure 2 is a graphic illustration of the concept of the Laffer Curve. At a tax rate of 0%, the government would collect no tax revenues, no matter how large the tax base. Likewise, at a tax rate of 100%, the government would also collect no tax revenues because no one would be willing to work for an after-tax wage of zero—there would be no tax base. Between these two extremes there are two tax rates that will collect the same amount of revenue: A high tax rate on a small tax base and a low tax rate on a large tax base.

Figure 2

The Laffer Curve

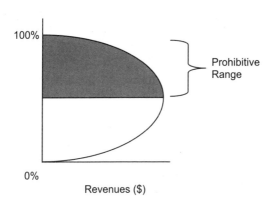

The Laffer Curve itself doesn't say whether a tax cut will raise or lower revenues. Revenue responses to a tax rate change will depend upon the tax system in place, the time period being considered, the ease of moving into underground activities, the level of tax rates already in place, the prevalence of legal and accounting-driven tax loopholes, and the proclivities of the productive factors. If the existing tax rate is too high—in the "prohibitive range" shown above—then a tax rate cut would result in increased tax revenues. The economic effect of the tax cut would outweigh the arithmetic effect of the tax cut.

Moving from total tax revenues to budgets, there is one expenditure effect in addition to the two effects tax rate changes have on revenues. Because tax cuts create an incentive to increase output, employment and production, tax cuts also help balance the budget by reducing means-tested government expenditures. A faster growing economy means lower unemployment and higher incomes, resulting in reduced unemployment benefits and other social welfare programs.

Over the past 100 years in the U.S., there have been three major periods of tax rate cuts: the Harding/Coolidge cuts of the mid-1920s, the Kennedy tax cuts of the mid-1960s, and the Reagan tax cuts of the early 1980s. Each of these periods of tax cuts was remarkably successful in terms of virtually any public policy metric.

Prior to discussing and measuring these three major periods of U.S. tax cuts, two critical points have to be made, one regarding the size of tax cuts, and another regarding their timing.

Size of Tax Cuts

People don't work, consume or invest to pay taxes. They work and invest to earn after-tax income and they consume to get the best buys — after-tax. Therefore, people are not concerned *per se* with taxes, but with after-tax results. Taxes and after-tax results are very similar but have crucial differences.

Using the Kennedy tax cuts of the mid-1960s as our example, it is easy to show that identical percentage tax cuts, when and where tax rates are high, loom far larger than when and where tax rates are low. When Kennedy took office in 1961, the highest federal marginal tax rate was 91 percent and the lowest rate was 20 percent. By earning a dollar pre-tax, the highest-bracket income earner would receive nine cents after-tax (the incentive), while the lowest-bracket income earner would receive 80 cents after-tax. These after-tax earnings were the relative after-tax incentives to earn the same amount (one dollar) pre-tax.

By 1965, after Kennedy's tax cuts were fully effective, the highest federal marginal tax rate had been lowered to 70 percent (a drop of 21 *percentage points* on a base of 91 percent, implying a 23 percent reduction) and the lowest tax rate was dropped to 14 percent (a 30 percent reduction). Now by earning a dollar pre-tax the person in the highest tax bracket would receive 30 cents after-tax, or a 233 percent increase from the nine cents of after-tax income when the tax rate was 91 percent; the person in the lowest tax bracket would receive 86 cents after-tax, or a 7.5 percent increase from the 80 cents earned when the tax rate was 20 percent.

Putting this all together, the increase in incentives in the highest tax bracket was a whopping 233 percent for a 23 percent cut in tax rates—a ten-to-one benefit-cost ratio—while the increase in incentives in the lowest tax bracket was a mere 7.5 percent for a 30 percent cut in rates—a one-to-four benefit-cost ratio. The lessons here are simple: The higher tax rates are, the greater will be the economic (supply-side) impact of a given percentage reduction in tax rates. Likewise, under a progressive tax structure, an equal across-the-board percentage reduction in tax rates should have its greatest impact in the highest tax bracket and its least impact in the lowest tax bracket.

Timing of Tax Cuts

The second and equally important concept of tax cuts concerns the timing of those cuts. People in their quest to earn what they can after-tax not only can change how much they work, but they also can change when they work, when they invest, and when they spend. Lower expected tax rates in the future will reduce taxable economic activity in the present as people try to shift activity out of the relatively higher taxed present period into the relatively lower taxed future period. People tend not to shop at a store a week before that store has its well-advertised discount sale. Likewise, in the periods before legislated tax cuts actually take effect, people will defer income and then realize that income when tax rates have fallen to their fullest extent. It has always amazed me how tax cuts don't work until they actually take effect. President Bush realized this as demonstrated by the tax act of 2003, as he accelerated all of the tax cuts set forth in 2001.

When assessing the impact of tax legislation, it is imperative to start the measurement of the tax cut period after all the tax cuts have been put into effect. As will be obvious when we look at the three major tax cut periods and even more so when we look at capital gains tax cuts, timing is of the essence.

The Harding/Coolidge Tax Cuts

President Bush's Administration is the fourth in the last 100 years to join my list of supply-side Presidents. This President understands what role the government should play when it comes to creating pro-growth, economic incentives. His name stands among a list of well regarded Presidents and, therefore, it is only fitting that we touch upon the stories of the other supply-side Presidents who have influenced and shaped our society over the last century.

In 1913, the federal progressive income tax was put into place with a top marginal rate of 7 percent. Thanks in part to World War I, this tax rate was quickly increased significantly and peaked at 77 percent in 1918. Then, through a series of tax rate reductions, the Harding/Coolidge tax cuts dropped the top personal marginal income tax rate to 25 percent in 1925.

While tax collection data for the National Income and Product Accounts (from the U.S. Bureau of Economic Analysis) don't exist for the 1920s, we do have total federal receipts from the U.S. budget tables. During the four years prior to 1925 (the year the tax cut was fully enacted), inflation-adjusted revenues declined by an average of 9.2 percent per year. Over the four years following the tax rate cuts, revenues remained volatile but averaged an inflation-adjusted gain of 0.1 percent per year. The economy responded strongly to the tax cuts, with output nearly doubling and unemployment falling sharply.

In the 1920s, tax rates on the highest income brackets were reduced the most, which is exactly what economic theory suggests should be done to spur the economy. But those income classes with lower tax rates were not left out in the cold: the Harding/Coolidge rate cuts did result in reduced tax rates on lower income brackets.

Figure 3
The Top Marginal Personal Income Tax Rate, 1913-2006
(when applicable, top rate on earned and/or unearned income)

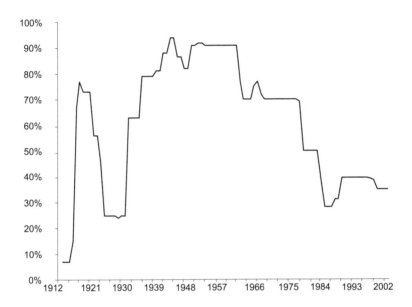

Internal Revenue Service data show that the dramatic tax cuts of the 1920s resulted in an increase in the share of total income taxes paid by those making more than $100,000 per year from 29.9 percent in 1920 to 62.2 percent in 1929 (Table 2). And keep in mind the significance of this increase, given that the 1920s was a decade of falling prices and therefore a $100,000 threshold in 1929 corresponds to a higher real income threshold than $100,000 did in 1920. The consumer price index fell a combined 14.5 percent from 1920 to 1929. In this case, the effects of bracket creep that existed prior to the federal income tax brackets being in-dexed for inflation (in 1985) worked in the opposite direction.

Table 1
Before and after the Harding/Coolidge tax cut

	1921-1924	1925-1929
Annual revenue growth (real)	-0.1%	9.2%
GDP growth (real)	2.0%	3.4%
Average unemployment	6.5%	3.1%

Table 2
**Percentage Share of Total Income Taxes Paid
By Income Class: 1920, 1925 and 1929**

Income Class	1920	1925	1929
Under $5,000	15.4%	1.9%	0.4%
$5,000-$10,000	9.1%	2.6%	0.9%
$10,000-$25,000	16.0%	10.1%	5.2%
$25,000-$100,000	29.6%	36.6%	27.4%
Over $100,000	29.9%	48.8%	62.2%

Source: Internal Revenue Service

The Kennedy Tax Cuts

During the Depression and World War II the top marginal income tax rate rose steadily, peaking at an incredible 94 percent in 1944 and 1945. The rate remained above 90 percent well into President John F. Kennedy's term in office, which began in 1961. Kennedy's fiscal policy stance made it clear he was a believer in pro-growth, supply-side tax measures. Kennedy said it all in January of 1963 in the Economic Report of the President:

> Tax reduction thus sets off a process that can bring gains for everyone, gains won by marshalling resources that would otherwise stand idle—workers without jobs and farm and factory capacity without markets. Yet many taxpayers seemed prepared to deny the nation the fruits of tax reduction because they question the financial soundness of reducing taxes when the federal budget is already in deficit. Let me make clear why, in today's economy, fiscal prudence and responsibility call for tax reduction even if it temporarily enlarged the federal

146

deficit—why reducing taxes is the best way open to us to increase revenues.

Kennedy reiterated his beliefs in his Tax Message to Congress on January 24, 1963:

> In short, this tax program will increase our wealth far more than it increases our public debt. The actual burden of that debt—as measured in relation to our total output—will decline. To continue to increase our debt as a result of inadequate earnings is a sign of weakness. But to borrow prudently in order to invest in a tax revision that will greatly increase our earning power can be a source of strength.

President Kennedy proposed massive tax rate reductions which passed Congress and went into law after he was assassinated. The 1964 tax cut reduced the top marginal personal income tax rate from 91 percent to 70 percent by 1965. The cut reduced lower-bracket rates as well. In the four years prior to the 1965 tax rate cuts, federal government income tax revenue, adjusted for inflation, had increased at an average annual rate of 2.1 percent, while total government income tax revenue (federal plus state and local) had increased 2.6 percent per year. In the four years following the tax cut these two measures of revenue growth rose to 8.6 percent and 9.0 percent, respectively. Government income tax revenue not only increased in the years following the tax cut, it increased at a much faster rate in spite of the tax cuts.

The Kennedy tax cut set the example that Reagan would follow some 17 years later. By increasing incentives to work, produce and invest, real GDP growth increased in the years following the tax cuts, more people worked and the tax base expanded. Additionally, the expenditure side of the budget benefited as well because the unemployment rate was significantly reduced.

Table 3
Before and after: the Kennedy Tax Cut

	1961-1964	1965-1969
Annual federal income tax revenue growth (real)	2.0%	8.6%
GDP growth (real)	4.6%	5.1%
Average unemployment	5.8%	3.9%

Using the Congressional Budget Office's revenue forecasts made with the full knowledge of, yet prior to, the tax cuts, revenues came in much higher than had been anticipated, even after the "cost" of the tax cut had been taken into account (Table 4).

Table 4
Actual vs. Forecasted Federal Budget Receipts, 1964-1967
(in $billions)

Fiscal Year	Actual Budget Receipts	Forecasted Budget Receipts	Difference	Percentage Actual Revenue Exceeded Forecasts
1964	$112.7	$109.3	+$3.4	3.1%
1965	$116.8	$115.9	+$0.9	0.7%
1966	$130.9	$119.8	+$11.1	9.3%
1967	$149.6	$141.4	+$8.2	5.8%

Source: Congressional Budget Office, A Review of the Accuracy of Treasury Revenue Forecasts, 1963-1978 (February, 1981), p. 4.

In addition, in 1965, one year following the tax cut, personal income tax revenue data exceeded expectations by the greatest amounts in the highest income classes (Table 5).

Table 5
Actual vs. Forecasted Personal Income Tax Revenue by Income Class, 1965
(calendar year, revenue in $millions)

Adjusted Gross Income Class	Actual Revenue Collected	Forecasted Revenue	Percentage Actual Revenue Exceeded Forecasts
$0 - $5,000	$4,337	$4,374	-0.8%
$5,000 - $10,000	$15,434	$13,213	16.8%
$10,000 - $15,000	$10,711	$6,845	56.5%
$15,000 - $20,000	$4,188	$2,474	69.3%
$20,000 - $50,000	$7,440	$5,104	45.8%
$50,000 - $100,000	$3,654	$2,311	58.1%
$100,000+	$3,764	$2,086	80.4%
Total	$49,530	$36,407	36.0%

Source: Estimated revenues calculated from Joseph A. Pechman, "Evaluation of Recent Tax Legislation: Individual Income Tax Provisions of the Revenue Act of 1964," *Journal of Finance*, vol. 20 (May 1965), 268. Actual revenues are from *Internal Revenue Service, Statistics of Income—1965, Individual Income Tax Returns*, 8.

Testifying before Congress in 1977, Walter Heller, President Kennedy's Chairman of the Council of Economic Advisors, summed it all up:

> What happened to the tax cut in 1965 is difficult to pin down, but insofar as we are able to isolate it, it did seem to have a tremendously stimulative effect, a multiplied effect on the economy. It was the major factor that led to our running a $3 billion surplus by the middle of 1965 before escalation in Vietnam struck us. It was a $12 billion tax cut, which would be about $33 or $34 billion in today's terms, and within one year the revenues into the Federal Treasury were already above what they had been before the tax cut.
>
> Did the tax cut pay for itself in increased revenues? I think the evidence is very strong that it did.[18]

---

18. Walter Heller, in testimony before the Joint Economic Committee of Congress, 1977, as quoted by Bruce Bartlett, *National Review* (October 17, 1978).

The Reagan Tax Cuts

In August of 1981, Ronald Reagan signed into law the Economic Recovery Tax Act (ERTA, also known as Kemp-Roth, after its legislative sponsors, Congressman Jack Kemp and Senator William Roth). ERTA slashed across-the-board marginal earned income tax rates by about 25 percent (i.e. by one-quarter), over a three-year period. The highest marginal tax rate on earned income dropped immediately from 70 percent to 50 percent (the Broadhead Amendment) and the tax rate on capital gains also fell immediately from 28 percent to 20 percent. Five percentage points of the 25 percent cut (i.e. one fifth of the total tax cut) went into effect on October 1, 1981. An additional 10 percentage points of the cut then went into effect on July 1, 1982, and the final 10 percentage points of the cut began on July 1, 1983. As a provision of ERTA, Reagan also saw to it that the tax brackets were indexed for inflation beginning in 1985.

To properly discern the effects of the tax rate cuts on the economy, I use the starting date of January 1, 1983, given that the bulk of the cuts were in place on that date. However, a case could be made for a start date of January 1, 1984, the date the full cut was in effect.

These across-the-board marginal tax rate cuts resulted in higher incentives to work, produce and invest, and the economy responded (Table 6). Between 1978 and 1982 the economy grew at a 0.9 percent rate in real terms, but from 1983 to 1986 this growth rate increased to 4.8 percent.

Prior to the tax cut the economy was choking on high inflation, high interest rates and high unemployment. All three of these economic bellwethers dropped sharply after the tax cuts. The unemployment rate, which had peaked at 9.7 percent in 1982, began a steady decline, reaching 7.0 percent by 1986 and 5.3 percent when Reagan left office in January 1989.

Inflation-adjusted revenue growth dramatically improved. Over the four years prior to 1983, federal income tax revenue declined at an average rate of 2.8 percent per year, and total government income tax revenue declined at an annual rate of 2.6 percent. Between 1983 and 1986 these figures were a positive 2.7 percent and 3.5 percent, respectively.

Table 6
Before and after: the Reagan Tax Cut

	1979-1982	1983-1986
Annual federal income tax revenue growth (real)	-2.8%	2.7%
GDP growth (real)	0.9%	4.8%
Average unemployment	7.6%	7.8%

The most controversial portion of Reagan's tax revolution was the big drop in the highest marginal income tax rate from 70 percent when he took office to 28 percent in 1988. However, Internal Revenue Service data reveal that tax collections from the wealthy, as measured by personal income taxes paid by top percentile earners, increased between 1980 and 1988 despite significantly lower tax rates (Table 7).

The Laffer Curve and the Capital Gains Tax

Changes in the capital gains maximum tax rate provide a unique opportunity to study the effects of taxation on taxpayer behavior. Taxation of capital gains is different from taxation of most other sources of income because people have more control over the timing of the realization of capital gains (i.e., when the gains are actually taxed).

The historical data on changes in the capital gains tax rate show an incredibly consistent pattern. Just after a capital gains tax rate cut, there is a surge in revenues; just after a capital gains tax rate increase, revenues take a dive. Also, as would be expected,

Table 7

Percentage of Total Personal Income Taxes Paid by Percentile of Adjusted Gross Income (AGI)

Calendar Year	Top 1% of AGI	Top 5% of AGI	Top 10% of AGI	Top 25% of AGI	Top 50% of AGI
1980	19.1%	36.8%	49.3%	73.0%	93.0%
1981	17.6%	35.1%	48.0%	72.3%	92.6%
1982	19.0%	36.1%	48.6%	72.5%	92.7%
1983	20.3%	37.3%	49.7%	73.1%	92.8%
1984	21.1%	38.0%	50.6%	73.5%	92.7%
1985	21.8%	38.8%	51.5%	74.1%	92.8%
1986	25.0%	41.8%	54.0%	75.6%	93.4%
1987	24.6%	43.1%	55.5%	76.8%	93.9%
1988	27.5%	45.5%	57.2%	77.8%	94.3%

Source: Internal Revenue Service

just before a capital gains tax rate cut there is a sharp decline in revenues, and just before a tax rate increase there is an increase in revenues. Timing really does matter.

This all makes total sense. If you could choose when to realize capital gains for tax purposes you would clearly realize your gains before tax rates are raised. No one wants to pay higher taxes.

In the 1960s and 1970s capital gains tax receipts averaged around 0.4 percent of GDP, with a nice surge in the mid-1960s following President Kennedy's tax cuts and another surge in 1978-79 after the Steiger-Hansen capital gains tax-cut legislation went into effect (Figure 4).

Following the 1981 capital gains cut from 28 percent to 20 percent, capital gains revenues leapt from $12.5 billion in 1980 to $18.7 billion by 1983—a 50 percent increase. During this period capital gains revenues rose to approximately 0.6 percent of GDP. Reducing income and capital gains tax rates in 1981 helped launch what we now appreciate as the greatest and longest period of wealth creation in world history. In 1981 the Dow Jones

Industrial Average troughed at about 1,000, compared to nearly 10,000 today (see Figure 5 for the broader market's performance during that period). As expected, the increase in the capital gains tax rate from 20 percent to 28 percent in 1986 led to a surge in capital gains realizations prior to the increase ($328 billion in 1986) and a collapse after the increase took effect ($112 billion in 1991).

The return of the capital gains tax rate from 28 percent back to 20 percent in 1997 was an unqualified success and every claim

Figure 4
Top Capital Gains Tax Rate and Inflation-Adjusted Revenue
(1960-2000, federal, billions of 2000 $)

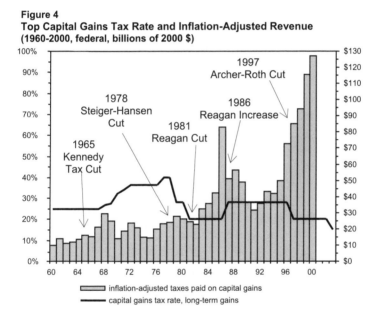

made by the critics was wrong. The tax cut, which went into effect in May of 1997, increased asset values and contributed to the largest gain in productivity and private sector capital investment in a decade. Also, the capital gains tax cut was not a revenue loser for the federal treasury.

In 1996, the year before the tax rate cut, total taxes paid on assets sold equaled $66.4 billion. A year later tax receipts jumped to $79.3 billion, and they jumped again one year later to $89.1 billion in 1998. The capital gains tax rate reduction played a big part in the 91 percent increase in tax receipts collected from capital gains between 1996 and 2000—a percentage far greater than the most ardent supply-siders expected (Table 8).

Seldom in economics does real life so conveniently conform to theory as capital gains revenues in the late 1990s did to the Laffer Curve. Lower tax rates change people's economic behavior and stimulate economic growth, which in turn creates higher tax revenues.

Figure 5
U.S. Stock Market: "Bull vs. Bear"
Nominal and Inflation-Adjusted Appreciation
(monthly, 12/31/59—1/6/04)

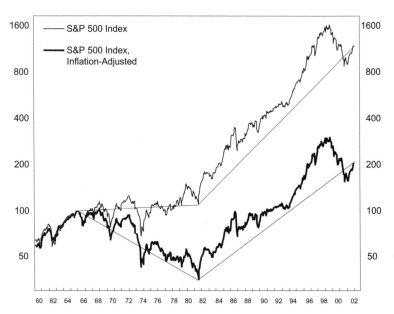

Table 8
1997 Capital Gains Tax Rate Cut: Actual Revenues vs. Government Forecast
(in $billions)

	1996	1997	1998	1999	2000
Long term capital gains rate	28%	20%	20%	20%	20%
Pre-tax cut CBO estimate					
Net capital gains	--	$205	$215	$228	na
Revenue	--	$ 55	$ 65	$ 75	na
Actual					
Net capital gains	$261	$365	$455	$553	$644
Revenue	$ 66	$ 79	$ 89	$112	$127

Source: Congressional Budget Office

The Bush Tax Cuts

Reduction in the Capital Gains and Dividends Tax Rates

In my opinion, the best part of Bush's tax policy has been the reduction in the taxation of dividends. Dividends—unlike interest paid on corporate debt—are not deductible from corporate income. Prior to the tax act of 2003, dividends were fully taxable to individuals at the same federal tax rates that apply to earned income (these rates vary from 15 percent to 40 percent). So dividend income was effectively double-taxed: first at the corporate level and then taxed *again* at the personal level.

Under the 2003 tax act, the tax rates applicable to dividend income fell to 5 and 15 percent. These rate reductions are fantastic. My only problem with them is that there is still a dividend tax at all—it should have been cut to zero. Hopefully in the near future we will see the rest of the task of eliminating double taxation of dividends completed.

The tax act of 2003 also reduced the tax rate on capital gains, from 10 or 20 percent to 5 or 15 percent. The 5 percent rate terminates on December 31, 2007 and falls to 0 percent for 2008.

These tax cuts have already provided a boon to the stock market, and will continue to provide a much needed boost in the future. Using a conservative set of assumptions, I have estimated the impact of the tax cut on the value of equity markets held in the United States. Assume the following:

i. Asset holders receive cash flows either as dividend payments or proceeds from the sale of the asset.
ii. Some 68 percent of companies pay dividends.
iii. Dividend-paying companies have a 52 percent pay-out ratio (i.e. dividends divided by after-tax reported earnings).
iv. Every dollar of retained earnings will increase a company's net worth (capital gains) by exactly one dollar.
v. 50 percent of dividends are paid to tax-exempt entities (such as pension funds, endowments and charities), who cannot take advantage of a dividend credit.
vi. All dividends paid are considered qualified dividends.

Now, let us examine how after-tax corporate earnings travel through the income stream. Currently, 35.36 percent (68 percent x 52 percent) of after-tax profits are paid out in dividends, or $35.36 of every $100 of after-tax corporate profits. Therefore, of every $100 of after-tax corporate profits, $64.64 is in the form of retained earnings, implying a capital gain. The current maximum capital gains rate is 29.3 percent, which is the 20 percent long-term federal rate plus a 9.3 percent effective state tax rate (let's use California's top rate in this example).

Half of all investors are tax exempt and half must pay this 29.3 percent tax, thus the total taxes on those capital gains will be $9.47 ($64.64 x 50 percent x 29.3 percent = $9.47). The after-tax return in the form of capital gains for $100 of after-tax corporate profits will be $55.17, which is the difference between the initial $64.64 and the $9.47 tax.

Out of $100 of after-tax corporate profits, $35.36 is paid as dividends and is subject to the highest personal federal and state income tax rate of 44.3 percent (35 percent federal and 9.3 percent in California). Since half of all dividends are paid to taxable entities, and half to tax exempt entities, the previous tax burden was $7.83 ($35.36 x 50 percent x 44.3 percent = $7.83).

Under the tax cuts of 2003, the capital gains tax rates were reduced, so that all qualified dividends are taxed at the maximum long-term capital gains rate, or 15 percent. Added to this percent is the relevant state personal income tax rate.

Using the same methodology as outlined above, 35.36 percent of after-tax profits are paid out in dividends. This still leaves $64.64 as corporate retained earnings out of $100 of after-tax profits. Using the new capital gains tax rate, and previous assumptions, the total taxes on the same value of capital gains are $7.85 ($64.64 x 50 percent x 24.3 percent = $7.85). This is a 17.1 percent reduction in the capital gains tax burden.

Dividends under the tax act of 2003 are taxed at an effective federal rate of, at most, 15 percent. The effective state personal income tax rate in California of 9.3 percent, so a combined tax rate on dividends is the same as on capital gains (24.3 percent). Again, since half of all dividends are paid to taxable entities, and half to exempt entities, the current tax burden on dividends received is $4.30 ($35.36 x 50 percent x 24.3 percent = $4.30).

Table 9

Previous Taxation System: Value of $100 of After-Tax Corporate Earnings

	% of profits	% taxable	Effective tax rate	Effective taxes paid	Value of $100 in earnings
Capital gain	64.64%	50.0%	29.3%	$ 9.47	$55.17
Dividend	35.36%	50.0%	44.3%	$ 7.83	$27.53
Total	100.00%	50.0%	34.6%	$ 17.30	$ 82.70

Table 10

Current Taxation System: Value of $100 of After-Tax Corporate Earnings

	% of profits	% taxable	Effective tax rate	Effective taxes paid	Value of $100 in earnings
Capital gain	64.64%	50.0%	24.3%	$ 7.85	$56.79
Dividend	35.36%	50.0%	24.3%	$ 4.30	$31.06
Total	100.00%	50.0%	24.3 %	$ 12.15	$ 87.85

Under the previous system, an after-tax $100 of earnings nets $82.70 in after-tax dividends and capital gains. Under the new system after the 2003 tax act, this number jumps to $87.85. Thus, the minimum gain that we should be observing in the market under the current system is 6.2 percent, and this number ignores all of the dynamic effects and only takes into account this one proposition. That's not chopped liver.

In a dynamic world, of course, this 6.2 percent number will do nothing but increase. For example:

i. With a tax rate cut on dividends, people will attempt to increase the share of net cash flows in dividends. Thus the 35.36 percent of net cash flows to shareholders currently paid out in dividends will increase.

ii.   In 1980, 94 percent of all S&P 500 companies paid dividends, and today that number has dropped to 68 percent. More companies are expected pay dividends as a result of the tax cut, and undo this trend. As more companies join the dividend ranks, the net effect of the Bush tax cuts will increase.

iii.   Companies will increase the dividends they pay. The S&P 500 has a payout ratio of 52 percent, but this will rise in response to the tax cut, amplifying the effects.

iv.   Individuals will enter the market and buy dividend-paying stocks, and new entrants would further boost the level of the market.

All in all, these dynamic affects will greatly increase the 6.2 percent estimate on the static effects of this tax cut. The order of magnitude of the increase is anybody's guess, but a doubling or tripling is not out of the question.

Also, the high tax on dividends may be a major reason that over the last decade investors have been lenient with managements' decisions to reinvest earnings in hopes of getting capital gains through stock price appreciation. This shift from dividends to retained earnings involved the tax code changes over the past few decades.

This gave individual investors incentive to take risks with management that they would not ordinarily take, and value stocks in irrational ways. A change in the tax treatment of dividends could potentially reduce accounting scandals and help rekindle investor faith. Not only can we expect an increase in the overall value of the stock market, we will likely see more transparency in accounting, and an end to the environment that spawned Enron, Tyco and other apparent miscreant managements.

The pre-2003 system also encouraged management to undertake more than the optimal amount of corporate debt financing. Due to the difference in the tax treatment of corporate interest payments and dividends, for each $100 of pre-tax corporate profits paid out in the form of interest, the asset holder receives $55.70 ($100—$44.30). Therefore, corporations previously found debt financing far more attractive than equity financing. Large amounts of debt increased the risk of bankruptcy, all in the name of greater interest deductions. With the tax code changed, the equity cost of capital decreased for the corporation. An equity issuance under the post-2003 tax cut system would demand a higher price for the stock than under the current system since its dividend is worth more to the investor; therefore, equity issuance would be more profitable to corporations.

One last effect of the Bush tax cuts is on stock turnover and capital gains tax revenues. Since more of each corporate dollar of profit is paid directly as dividends, after the initial boost from the tax change, less of total returns will occur through capital gains. The "locked in" phenomenon is diminished. With dividend payments comprising a higher proportion of total returns, investors are more willing to realize their capital gains and move on to the next investment. A steadier stream of capital gains revenues flows to the Treasury.

The Economics of Accelerating Bush's 2001 Personal Income Tax Cuts

The Jobs and Growth Tax Relief Reconciliation Act (JGTRRA) of 2003 accelerated all of the tax changes legislated in the Economic Growth and Tax Relief Reconciliation Act (EGTRRA) of 2001, and made them effective retroactive to January 1, 2003. These tax cuts were originally designed to be phased in, with some of the tax cuts not fully taking effect until 2006, and others not until 2010.

As a result of having accelerated the tax cuts, the average taxpayer should have realized about a 2 percent increase in static after-tax income. This increase provided both additional resources for investment and has and will continue to provide incentives for more economic growth. Once all the dynamics are accounted for, there's no telling what the full effects will be on output, employment and production, but they should be substantial.

The Creation and Expansion of the 10 Percent Tax Bracket

A new 10 percent tax bracket was created with the signing of the Economic Growth and Tax Relief Reconciliation Act (EGTRRA) of 2001. With the enactment of the Jobs and Growth Tax Relief Reconciliation Act (JGTRRA) of 2003, the 10 percent tax bracket was immediately expanded from $6,000 to $7,000 for single filers, and from $12,000 to $14,000 for married couples.

This is good news for everybody. By creating and then expanding the 10 percent bracket, all taxpayers regardless of their incomes paying taxes at a marginal rate higher than 10 percent will automatically save $50 for single filers and $100 for married filers. This additional injection into the economy has been the driving force behind increased employment, production, savings and investment.

Increase in the Child Tax Credit

With the signing of the Economic Growth and Tax Relief Reconciliation Act of 2001, the expansion of the child tax credit from $500 to $1,000 was put into motion and was to be phased in over 10 years. By 2010, and beyond, the child tax credit was to be maximized at $1,000. However, with the signing of the 2003 tax act (JGTRRA) the child tax credit was immediately extended to $1,000, up from $600 ($100 of the 2001 extension had already been phased in).

The immediate impact was that $400, per child, was due in the form of a refund to all individuals who met the child credit refundability threshold (for 2003 the threshold was $10,500). These refund checks were mailed out to all eligible individuals starting in July 2003 and represented a significant injection of spending into the economy.

Many individuals have criticized the refundability threshold, saying the extremely impoverished are simply being passed over. This is simply not true. While we all should do what we can to help those in need, it should be noted that these people who do not meet the threshold of $10,500 already get a significant refund in the form of negative tax liabilities, i.e. they pay no taxes. If we were to extend rebate checks to all of those individuals who have paid zero taxes, this would not only be bad economics, it would also be a poor use of the English language. Last time I checked, a rebate is defined as a return of money that has already been paid.

If Congress does not vote to make the current child credit of $1,000 permanent then it will revert to $700 and continue to be phased in up to $1,000 under the Economic Growth and Tax Relief Reconciliation Act of 2001.

Alternative Minimum Tax Exemption Boost

The alternative minimum tax (AMT) is an additional tax levied on some individuals in addition to regular income taxes. The original idea for creating such a tax is that the government wanted to prevent people with very high incomes from devising a way to avoid paying taxes by finding loopholes in our tax system. A flat tax would be much more fair and effective than the usurious AMT.

In 2001 under the EGTRRA, the AMT tax law was tweaked slightly because the AMT offset of refundable credits was repealed and the AMT exemption was increased $4,000 for joint filers and $2,000 for single filers. With the signing of JGTRRA in 2003, the AMT exemption was significantly increased again for both joint and single filers. For joint filers, the AMT exemption was increased $9,000, from $49,000 to $58,000, and for single filers the exemption was up $4,500, from $35,750 to $40,250.

Though the tax act of 2003 fell short of completely reforming the AMT, the increases in the exemption amounts are definitely a step in the right direction. However, some individuals may not be able to fully capitalize on the new lower tax rates on dividends and capital gains due to the AMT, so serious reform should be considered by President Bush and Congress alike in the future.

Easement of the Marriage Penalty Tax

Under the JGTRRA of 2003, the marriage penalty tax was not completely eliminated, but it was diminished. The standard deduction for married couples was immediately doubled to twice the amount of the standard deductions for single tax payers. The standard deduction has been increased from $7,950 to $9,500. The 15 percent tax bracket for married filers was made twice as wide as the 15 percent bracket for single filers.

Though these are definitely steps in the right direction, the easement of the marriage tax penalty is not permanent. The relief is only good for two years, 2003 and 2004. In 2005 the standard deduction for married couples will fall to 174 percent of the standard deduction for single filers and will gradually rise to double the amount by 2009. And, after 2004, the 15 percent bracket for married individuals falls to 180 percent of the maximum taxable income for unmarried individuals.

Ideally the marriage penalty tax would be completely eliminated. There is no reason that individuals filing as married should have to pay more than they would if they were to file as singles. Hopefully the President will add this to his "to do" list.

Tax Changes for Corporations and Small Businesses

One way to stimulate a struggling economy is to provide the appropriate incentives to companies in order to spur investment and employment. President Bush realized this and made sure to provide relief to small businesses and corporations in the form of increased bonus first-year depreciation and expensing election.

The 2003 tax act gradually increases expense election for small businesses in various ways. First, the maximum annual expensing amount was revised up to $100,000 from $25,000. Also, the act expanded the definition of property eligible for the expenses deduction, such as off-the-shelf computer software which was previously not included. The tax act also increased the expense phase-out threshold from $200,000 to $400,000, allowing slightly larger businesses to take advantage of the expensing election. These increases in dollar amounts from $200,000 to $400,000 are inflation-indexed for tax years beginning after 2003.

Included in the 2003 Bush tax cuts is an increase in the first year depreciation allowance for qualified property from 30 to 50 percent, although businesses can elect to pursue the smaller bonus if they want to.

These two provisions of the tax act have created an environment that has never been better for businesses to invest in themselves by purchasing new capital. By having made these expensing and depreciation changes immediate as of 2003, businesses have been enticed into purchasing new equipment in order to expand their production capacities. Corollary to the expansion of physical capital is the expansion of human capital (i.e. more workers), and as such the U.S. economy has been experiencing an increase in output, production, and employment. This is very good for us all.

Conclusion

By signing the 2001 and 2003 tax acts, President Bush has joined the ranks of only a few other Presidents who have understood the logically simplistic yet often misunderstood tenets of supply-side economics, and he clearly has a place in history with only a handful of growth oriented Presidents. By implementing the two tax cuts, President Bush has created a pro-growth economic environment full of positive incentives needed to sustain a flourishing economy and to augment the happiness, prosperity, and industriousness of the American people.

CHAPTER TWELVE

OF DEBT, DEFICITS, AND ECONOMIC GROWTH

AMAN VERJEE

Aman Verjee, CFA, is an entrepreneur who is currently the director of strategy for a Silicon Valley company. He is the founder of AMERICAN THUNDER, *one of the nation's leading magazines for NASCAR fans, and served as editor in chief and CFO of that publication. Mr. Verjee studied economics and public policy at Stanford University, where he graduated with distinction and with honors, and then worked as a bond trader at Lehman Brothers on Wall Street. He later attended Harvard University, where he studied at the law and business schools and taught economics to the University's underclassmen. He is now working on two new books: a biography of Governor Arnold Schwarzenegger and a quantitative analysis of the greatest sports arguments of all time.*

In 2003, the federal deficit was $375 million, which was the largest deficit that the United States had ever seen. The deficit is projected to reach $500 million in 2004. Federal tax revenues have stagnated since 1999, but federal spending has rocketed by 36 percent during that time.

Critics of George W. Bush's fiscal policies have argued that the rising deficits, and the consequently heavier national debt burden, are causing reduced national savings; this, in turn will push interest rates higher and economic growth lower. Are they right? Are the President's fiscal policies setting us up for a fall?

In this chapter I examine this view—which I will call the "deficit hawk" view—using a variety of analytical and statistical techniques. First, I review the historical evidence in the United States, comparing the performance of the economy in years when the federal debt was relatively high to years in which federal debt was relatively low.

Second, I analyze the relationship between budget deficits, the outstanding stock of national debt, and real interest rates.

Finally, I survey international industrialized economies for evidence of a relationship between public debt, budget deficits and real or nominal interest rates.

I conclude that neither budget deficits nor the level of out-standing public debt bear any relationship to real or nominal interest rates. Nor do they affect economic growth. There *is* evidence to suggest that a weak form of the "deficit hawk" view holds: that *changes* in deficits drive *changes* in real, long term interest rates. This has implications for economic policies, be-cause it suggests that the simple Keynesian prescription of expanding the deficit during recessions to stimulate economic growth may be self-defeating—it ultimately triggers higher interest rates, which in turn dampen prospects for economic growth. But even this relationship is a weak one; furthermore, even if correct, this argument implies that a series of short term, transient deficits that are eventually reversed will have no long term impact on either interest rates or on economic growth.

I am no fan of budget deficits, and I supported the balanced budget amendment proposed by House Republicans in 1995. But while balancing the budget is a commendable policy goal, support for it must be based on criteria other than concern over interest rates. Therefore, worries over interest rates should not stand in the way of tax rate reductions and the pro-growth tax reforms supported by President Bush.

The Critique of the Bush Economic Plan

Conventional left-wing Keynesian economics calls for fiscal deficits in response to a recessionary environment. That didn't stop a coterie of left-leaning economists, including 10 Nobel laureates, from taking out a full-page advertisement in the New York Times on February 11, 2003, attacking the President's tax cuts and deficit financing. They claimed that President Bush's policies would "worsen the long-term budget outlook, adding to the nation's chronic deficits."

The International Monetary Fund and the Organization for Economic Cooperation and Development have also weighed in, arguing that the willingness of the U.S. to run a large deficit reduces economic growth in the long run. In its semiannual World Economic Outlook in April, 2004, the IMF conceded that the fiscal stimulus had "provided important support" to the U.S. and world economic recoveries, and that it hadn't pushed up long-term interest rates. But, the IMF contended, in the long run deficits will soak up limited savings, driving up interest rates and "crowding out" investment. The OECD concurred, helpfully suggesting that the U.S. boost revenues by ending tax breaks for mortgage interest, charitable donations, and employer health-insurance premiums, while implementing a national sales tax.[19]

All else being equal, a budget deficit *will* reduce the pool of national savings, and *will* put upward pressure on interest rates. The problem, of course, is that all else is never equal: just because

---

19.   Greg Ip, "IMF, OECD See Economic Risks in Bush's Budget," *Wall Street Journal* (April 15, 2004), A1

economists can assume away other root causes of interest rate fluctuations doesn't mean that those causes don't exist.

In the real world, many factors besides budget deficits drive interest rates. These include (but are not limited to): actual and expected inflation; the attractiveness of the economic and political environment; perceived credit risk; incentives to work, save and invest, which in turn drive the *supply* of loanable funds; actual and prospective economic growth and the expected economic returns on productive assets, which in turn drive the *demand* for loanable funds; and the expected real and nominal returns on a nation's financial assets, including equities, convertible bonds, real estate and commodities.

In a world where capital may flow at little cost among dozens of open economies, the complex interplay of all of these factors on a global scale swamps the marginal impact of a budget deficit in any one country. In the end, it is easy to overstate the impact of deficits *per se*, because fiscal policy has to be understood to impact all of the various drivers of interest rates, not just total public savings.

The Current Situation

Like Chicken Little, who caviled because she mistook a tumbling acorn for a crashing sky, President Bush's critics are unjustified when they foretell of doom. Alarmists who worry about the historical heights to which deficits have climbed need to step back and review the historical data for context.

At the end of 2001, the federal debt of the United States that was held by the public stood at 33 percent of U.S. GDP, which was the lowest it had been in 18 years. At the end of 2003, federal debt stood at 36 percent of GDP, and was projected by the Congressional Budget Office to reach 40 percent of GDP by 2005 before beginning to decline again.[20]

---

20. *Economic Report of the President* (Feb. 2004), Table B-79.

Moreover, it is important to note that most of the deficit that has emerged in the past year has been the result of two temporary factors—a post-bubble recession, which reduced personal incomes, capital gains-related tax receipts, and corporate profits; and a 50-percent increase in national defense spending, which followed 9/11.

The relative increase in debt has been caused in equal parts by a reduction in federal tax receipts and an increase in federal expenditures. From 1998 to 2000, federal tax receipts were 20.0, 20.0 and 20.8 percent of GDP, respectively—these were the three highest numbers posted since 1945. In 2003, federal tax receipts declined to 16.5 percent of GDP, the lowest such number since 1959.[21] The reduction in federal tax receipts reflected two factors: the recession, and the large tax cut pushed by President George W. Bush in 2001. According to the CBO, the Bush tax cut contributed to a decline in federal tax receipts by roughly 2 percentage points of GDP, implying that the recession itself reduced revenues by about 2 percent of GDP.[22]

In large part, the historically high revenue numbers in 1999-2000 were caused by enormous capital gains tax collections (capital gains realizations do not count as part of GDP, but they *are* taxable). From 1998 to 2000, tax receipts from capital gains taxes alone comprised over 1.1 percent of GDP, up from an average of 0.5 percent for the previous two decades (see Figure 1). The reversion to mean in capital gains collections alone pushed federal receipts back to around 20 percent of GDP in the early part of the Bush presidency; the cyclical downturn in corporate profits and personal incomes did the rest.

---

21.   Ibid.

22.   Cost estimates for 2003 of the "Economic Growth and Tax Relief Reconciliation Act of 2001," the "Job Creation and Worker Assistance Act of 2002," and the "Marriage Penalty and Family Tax Relief Act of 2001" per the *Congressional Budget Office*.

Figure 1
Capital Gains Tax Receipts—Federal Government

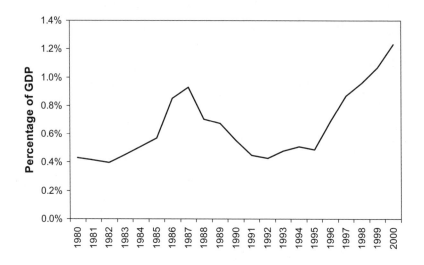

Source: Congressional Budget Office

The economy has turned around in 2004, so tax collections should move back to about 18-19 percent of GDP by 2005. This would be more than enough to balance the budget, if the federal government were to maintain its aggregate expenditures at the level of 1999-2001, when federal expenditures averaged 18.5 percent of GDP. That period marked a 40-year low in this metric—indeed, federal expenditures had fallen for nine straight years, from a high of 22.3 percent of GDP in 1991 to the low of 18.4 percent in 2000.

Between 2000 and 2004, federal expenditures rose from 18.4 percent of GDP to 19.9 percent of GDP, erasing about two-fifths of the reductions achieved since 1991. But of that spending increase, two-thirds came from higher national defense spending, which rose from 3.0 percent of GDP to 4.0 percent.[23] As the growth in this category of spending normalizes, pressure on the

---

23. *Economic Report of the President* (Feb. 2004), Table B-79.

deficit should ease, and federal expenditures should normalize back to between 19 and 20 percent of GDP.

If defense spending were to remain relatively constant as a percentage of GDP, then the United States appears to be headed towards a modest "cyclically adjusted" federal deficit of between 0 and 2 percent of GDP. This can be reduced further if domestic federal spending can be held to 4 percent growth or less, as President Bush has demanded.[24]

If the scenario sketched out above comes to pass—federal spending that remains around 19-20 percent of GDP; mean-reversion in tax collections that brings revenues to 18-19 percent of GDP; deficits of around 0-2 percent of GDP; and a federal debt that steadies around 40 percent of GDP in 2005 and then begins to fall gently—does the country have anything to worry about? Does this deficit and debt scenario portend a tumbling acorn or a crashing sky?

Economic Growth in High-Debt and Low-Debt Years

First of all, it is important to distinguish between the *deficit*, which is a *flow* of funds (it represents an imbalance between tax receipts and expenditures in any one fiscal year) and the *debt*, which is a *stock* (it represents the accumulated obligations of the federal government since the beginning of the republic).

A budget deficit *per se* should not be seen as a problem. After all, families and corporations frequently run deficits, when they obtain mortgages or take out loans to finance new operations. The public debt, on the other hand, *can* become an impediment to economic growth if the cost of servicing that debt becomes prohibitively high, or of the debt is rising faster than national incomes for an extended period of time.

---

24. George W. Bush, "Second State of the Union Address" (January 29, 2003), http://www.cnn.com/2003/ALLPOLITICS/01/28/sotu.transcript/.

Today, the total federal government debt held by the public is about 36 percent of GDP. This is quite low by historical standards. Since 1939, we have had 24 years when the federal debt has been below 36 percent of GDP and 41 years when it has been higher. A straightforward interpretation of the IMF-OECD-*New York Times* view suggests that economic growth should have been somewhat better in the low debt years than in the high debt years, because higher debt means higher actual or expected government borrowing, which in turn should drive out private borrowing via higher interest rates. In fact, real GDP growth averaged 4.44 percent in the high debt years and just 3.14 percent in the low debt years.

To some extent, this divergence in growth rates was a result of the war years, when debt piled up quickly and economic growth was relatively robust. But the story is the same over a more restricted time horizon. Indeed, we can look at only the years since 1963, which is when the debt fell to present-day levels for the first time since WWII. Since 1963, public debt fell to a low of 24 percent in 1974, rose to a high of 50 percent in 1993 and fell back to 33 percent in 2001. Economic growth was higher in the relatively high debt years during this period, averaging 3.47 percent versus 2.59 percent. Unemployment was also lower in the high debt years averaging 5.65 percent as opposed to 6.43 percent in the low debt years. And consumer price inflation was almost three times higher in the low debt years than in the high debt years—7.6 percent to 3.0 percent.

Based on this evidence, one must conclude that economic performance is not materially hampered by the level of public debt. Economic prosperity can continue even if the federal government maintains a debt burden that is much higher than it is today as a percentage of GDP.

Deficits, the Federal Debt, and Interest Rates in U.S. History

The belief that high tax rates increase national savings and reduce interest rates (call it Rubinomics, after former Treasury Secretary Robert Rubin) is not new. It dates back at least to 1932, when President Hoover and a Congress tripled tax rates to stem a ballooning budget deficit and "maintain the public confidence." Of course, we all know what happened then—the economy went into a deep tailspin and didn't recover until 1939. Ever since then, the deficit fighters (mostly Republicans) have tried to sell voters the idea that lower deficits—as opposed to incentive-based tax reductions—would spur economic growth. Yet time and again, the link between budget deficits, outstanding public debt and interest rates has proved to be very weak.

First, let's consider the link between deficits and interest rates. Figure 2 shows the historical relationship between the federal surplus or deficit as a percentage of GDP, and real long term interest rates. If the IMF-OECD-*New York Times*-Robert Rubin view was strictly correct, then the two lines in Figure 2 should be moving *consistently in opposite directions*—a deteriorating budget picture should be crowding out private investment and leading to *higher* real interest rates. In fact, there have been long periods in U.S. history when the lines are moving *together*. For instance, throughout most of the 1970s, a *deteriorating* budget outlook was accompanied by *falling* interest rates. At other periods, the budget outlook was *improving* dramatically but interest rates were steady or even *rising*—for instance, most of the 1950s and all of the 1990s.

A more refined expression of the critique is shown in Figure 3. This scatter plot shows *changes* in the federal surplus/deficit as a percentage of GDP, against *changes* in real long term interest rates. The argument expressed here is less robust than the straightforward, conventional view of the modern day deficit hawks. It suggests that variations in the budget picture—not the absolute magnitude of the deficit *per se*—drives movements in

175

interest rates. This is a much weaker argument than the IMF-OECD view, because it implies that a series of short term deficits that are reversed or corrected will have no long term impact on either interest rates or on economic growth.

Figure 2
Budget deficits versus real interest rates

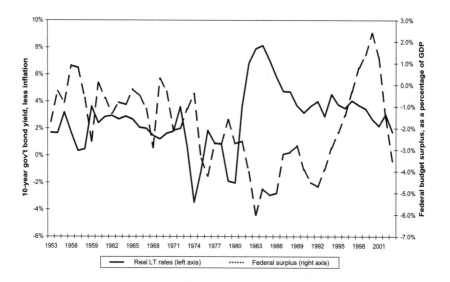

Source: Economic Report of the President, 2004

Points in the top-left and bottom-right quadrants are consistent with this view, because they either represent years in which the budget picture improved and real interest rates fell (the bottom right quadrant), or years in which the budget deficit deteriorated and the real interest rates rose (top left quadrant).

In fact, the scatter plot in Figure 3 *does* show that points fall in one of these two quadrants about 70 percent of the time, implying that there is indeed a relationship between rising deficits and rising interest rates. The "line of best fit" suggests that a 1 percentage point increase in the federal deficit, in relation to GDP, would increase real bond yields by about 50 basis points.

Figure 3
Changes in budget deficits versus changes real interest rates

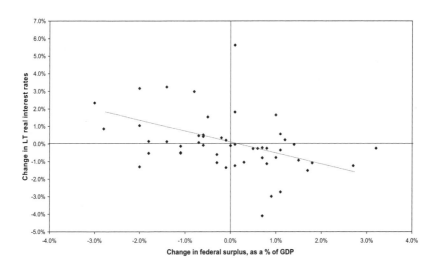

Source: Economic Report of the President, 2004

This simple scatter plot is a good, first order approximation of the impact of a rising deficit on long term interest rates. Using more sophisticated techniques, the economics literature has generated a number of different estimates of what this number actually is. Brookings Institution scholars Bill Gale and Peter Orszag have estimated that an increase in the deficit that amounts to 1 percent of GDP (roughly the impact of the Bush plan in the first year) would result in a 50 bp increase in long term interest rates immediately, rising to 100 bp over 10 years.[25] However, they used a misleading methodology, comparing unanticipated changes in deficits to the *steepness of the yield curve*, rather than to a level of absolute long term interest rates. In times of economic distress, when deficits are generally rising, the yield curve often gets steeper as the Federal Reserve brings down short-term interest rates faster than market forces can bring

---

25. William G. Gale and Peter G. Orszag, "The Economic Effects of Long Term Fiscal Discipline," *Urban-Brookings Tax Policy Center* (December 17, 2002).

down long-term yields—this scenario happened in each of the last four major recession-driven easing cycles (2001-2002, 1991-1992, 1982-1983, and 1974-1975). This steepening of the yield curve does not necessarily mean that rising deficits cause higher interest rates, as the authors suggest—it could just as easily mean that rising deficits often coincide with rapid Fed easings.

Separately, Gale has looked at the impact of the Bush tax plan, and estimated that it would raise interest rates by 20 basis points in the short term and by 40 basis points in the long term.[26]

But other economists have made much lower estimates. For instance, economists Gregory Mankiw of Harvard (now serving as the Chairman of President Bush's Council of Economic Advisers) and Douglas Elemendorf of the Federal Reserve estimated that an increase in the deficit amounting to 1 percent of GDP would raise rates by just 1 or 2 basis points.[27] Prof. Glenn Hubbard of Columbia University, and a former CEA Chairman, has estimated this impact at 10 bp.[28]

Part of the problem is that all of the statistical techniques used, from simple scatter plots to complex regressions that map deficits to interest rates, fail to show a close, tight relationship between these two variables. Figure 3 shows how varied the response of interest rates has been to changes in the budget outlook over the past fifty years—note the scattered nature of the points on the chart. In other words, none of these predictions can be made with a high degree of confidence.

This is what we should expect when so many variables go into determining interest rates. Indeed, the reason for the deficits is at least as important as the deficits themselves in determining what's driving interest rates—for instance, a pro-savings and investment tax cut should stimulate private savings, offsetting

26.   William G. Gale, "The President's Tax Proposal: First Impressions," *Urban-Brookings Tax Policy Center* (January 9, 2003), http://www.brook.edu/views/papers/gale/20030109.htm.

27.   Douglas W. Elmendorf and N. Gregory Mankiw, "Government Debt" (January 1998), http://www.federalreserve.gov/pubs/feds/1998/199809/199809pap.pdf.

28.   Glenn Hubbard, et al., "Do Budget Deficits Raise Long-Term Interest Rates?" *The International Economy* (Summer 2003), http://www.international-economy.com/TIE_SU03_Defic.pdf.

much of the decline in public savings and mitigating the effect on interest rates, while an expensive new retirement benefit may simultaneously decrease public savings and decrease the incentive to save and invest for retirement, compounding the problem.

While there appears to be a statistically significant link between changes in deficits and changes in interest rates, let me emphasize that the short-term impact of a budget deficit on current year interest rates is a poor guide to the long term effect on national wealth. Fluctuations in real interest rates from year to year might impact short-term economic growth, but ultimately the long term wealth of a nation depends upon the absolute, systemic level of real interest rates in the economy.

So let's consider the more important question—does the overall level of outstanding public debt affect the level of real interest rates? Figure 4 shows this historical relationship. If the level of debt had the effect on interest rates that the deficit hawks would posit, then the lines should be moving steadily *in the same direction*.

Importantly, the lines in Figure 4 don't seem to sustain a relationship at all, implying that the level of federal debt outstanding does not significantly drive real long term rates.

Impact of Fiscal Policy on Interest Rates

The impact of fiscal policy on interest rates can be analyzed more closely by examining five broad periods of post-war American

Figure 4
Federal debt versus long-term real interest rates

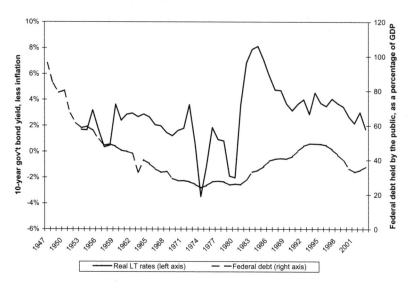

Source: Economic Report of the President, 2004

economic history where different approaches to fiscal policy were implemented. In only two of these five periods, the movement in real interest rates corresponded to what the conventional deficit hawk view would have suggested to be the case, given the budget deficits of the time. And in only *one* of the five periods did real interest rates end up at a level that reflected changes in the level of *public debt*.

(The reader may want to keep referring back to Figures 2 and 4 throughout this discussion.)

The first period extends from 1947 to 1963. Fiscal restraint ruled the roost: the federal government ran surpluses in seven of those 16 years, and incurred a deficit of more than 1 percent of GDP just four times. Federal debt fell from a post-war peak of 109 percent of GDP to 42 percent of GDP by 1963. Politically, Presidents Truman and Eisenhower placed priority on annual balanced budgets. Eisenhower in particular placed balanced budgets above all else—in his budget address of 1960, he defended the punitively high tax rates of the time by saying that "sound fiscal policy requires a budget surplus ... to increase the supply of savings available for the productive investment so essential for economic growth." He killed tax cuts, kept the top federal tax rate at over 90 percent, and generated three recessions on his watch. Real GDP grew by just 23 percent in the eight years from 1953 to 1961.

Contrary to the expectations set by Rubinomics, real interest rates actually rose slightly during this period of fiscal restraint; the real, inflation-adjusted 10-year government bond yield edged up from 170 bp in 1953 (when the 10-year was first issued) to 280 bp in 1961. Nominal yields rose as well, from under 300 bp in 1953 to just over 400 bp in the early 1960s.

The next period extends from 1963 to 1970. President Kennedy championed across-the-board tax cuts to invigorate economic growth, proclaiming in 1962: "It is a paradoxical truth that tax rates are too high today and tax revenues are too low, and the soundest way to raise the revenues in the long run is to cut the tax rates."

The first stage of Kennedy's tax cuts were enacted in 1963 — few remember this today, but Barry Goldwater's 1964 campaign actually featured attacks on the Kennedy tax cuts — and the top income tax rate fell from 91 percent to 70 percent. Under Kennedy and his successor, President Lyndon Johnson, the economy grew by 47 percent in the eight years from 1961 to 1969, far outpacing the performance in the Eisenhower years.

Despite the tax cuts, growth in federal revenues remained robust, climbing by 87 percent during this period. Federal debt continued to fall as a percentage of GDP, albeit at a slower pace. By 1969, it was down to 29 percent of GDP. During this era of small deficits and declining debt, real bond yields were quiescent, falling back to about 160 bp. This is what the deficit hawks would expect. Note, however, that real long term interest rates in 1969 were about where they had been in 1953, when the federal debt had been over twice as large in relation to the economy.

The third period extends from 1970 to 1982. Both fiscal and monetary policy turned stimulative; the budget deficit frequently ran at about 3 percent of GDP, but a massive inflation held the real value of the debt in check. Federal debt remained very steady near 28-29 percent of GDP, but real long-term interest rates fluctuated dramatically — a complete rejection of the notion that public debt is a key driver of interest rates. Real long term bond yields rose to 360 bp in 1972, dropped to *negative* 350 bp in 1975, and soared to almost 800 bp in 1982. Clearly, whatever relationship might have existed between the debt and interest rates had come unhinged.

This period was characterized by runaway statism, which destroyed the role of interest rates as a market signal. In the 1968 *Republican Papers*, Raymond Saulnier — President Eisenhower's former chief economist — had urged for "a temporary tax increase" to "prevent further escalation of interest rates." President Richard Nixon actually *increased* the capital gains tax in 1969, and when the economy blew up in the early 1970s he turned to easy credit and (when a vicious inflation arose) wage and price controls as solutions. Under President Carter, taxes, spending and the federal deficit all rose sharply, reaching post-WWII highs, and inflation spiraled out of control.

The fourth period extends from 1982 to 1993. The first stage of President Reagan's tax cuts took effect in 1982, and fiscal policy remained stimulative throughout the 1980s. The Federal Reserve ratcheted up interest rates and clamped down on money supply growth to quell the double-digit inflation of the late 1970s and early 1980s. Federal debt jumped rapidly, hitting 40 percent of GDP in 1986 and remaining there for the last three years of Reagan's presidency. Real long-term interest rates declined throughout the 1980s, falling from over 680 bp in 1982 to just over 300 bp in 1990, as the budget outlook gradually improved — this seems to corroborate the view of the deficit hawks. Real interest rates remained higher than they had been historically, which is also consistent with the view that a large accumulated debt and chronic deficits can drive real interest rates higher.

The final period is 1993 to 2001. President Clinton raised taxes in 1993, and a combination of strong economic growth, capital gains-driven tax revenues, and spending restraint after Republicans took Congress in 1995 brought the deficits to heel. Here again, the expectations of the deficit hawks were confounded. In 1993, with federal debt at a post-WWII high in terms of GDP and large expected deficits looming on the horizon, the 10-year bond yield bottomed out at 5.25 percent that year. The real 10-year yield was 290 bp. After President Clinton and Treasury Secretary Rubin raised taxes, the deficit picture improved; however, the 10-year note rose to over 7 percent. Real interest rates remained above 400 bp until 1998, when federal debt stood at 43 percent of GDP. From 1999 to 2001, federal debt fell sharply to 33 percent of GDP, and the real 10-year bond yield fell to about 220 bp as the economy spun into a recession.

In sum, the evidence from these various periods of American history yields a decidedly mixed bag. During two of the five periods—1963 to 1970, and 1982 to 1993—real interest rates behaved in a manner that was consistent with what the deficit hawks would predict. Only in the 1982 to 1993 period did the level of real interest rates seem to correspond even remotely to the level of public debt outstanding—yet even here, the high level of interest rates probably owed as much to the restrained monetary policy of the inflation-quashing Volcker Fed as it did to the chronic deficits and rising public debt.

Throughout all of the five periods, it appears that even large swings in the amount of federal debt outstanding have had no impact on the ultimate, absolute level of real interest rates.

An International Comparison

A review of industrialized economies abroad offers a richer landscape from which we can better draw out relationships between public debt, deficits and interest rates. Table 1 shows the relationship between the general government budget deficit — including federal, state, and local government budget balances — and the 10-year government bond yield. Two separate, recent three-year periods are covered, in order to smooth out annual variations in interest rate or budget cycles.

Table 1
Budget deficits and long term real interest rates abroad
Average 2001-2003

	Budget surplus, as a % of GDP	Real 10-year bond yield
United States	-2.9%	4.5%
Canada	1.1%	5.2%
United Kingdom	-1.2%	4.7%
France	-2.9%	4.6%
Italy	-2.6%	4.8%
Germany	-3.5%	4.6%
Japan	-6.9%	1.2%

Average 1998-2000

	Budget surplus, as a % of GDP	Real 10-year bond yield
United States	1.2%	5.6%
Canada	1.9%	5.7%
United Kingdom	1.2%	5.3%
France	-1.9%	4.9%
Italy	-1.6%	5.1%
Germany	-0.7%	4.8%
Japan	-6.3%	1.6%

Source: OECD Economic Outlook, No. 74 (Dec 2003)

The data shows that there is no relationship between interest rates and budget deficits. In fact, in both periods, the country with the highest interest rates (Canada) had the best fiscal track record; the country with the lowest interest rates (Japan) had the worst. This is exactly opposite from what Rubinomics would predict.

The same story holds for public debt. The country with the highest public debt burden—Japan, with debt in excess of 150 percent of GDP—has the lowest short term and long term interest rates, in both real and nominal terms. The euro area is far more indebted than the U.S., with Italy, Germany and France sporting public debts of around 105 percent, 62 percent and 64 percent of GDP, respectively. Yet, their interest rates have been either in line or lower than those of the U.S. for the last six years, which has a debt burden of around 36 percent.

The Relationship between Fiscal and Monetary Policy, Public and Private Savings

I believe that there are two major reasons why the deficit hawks have consistently overstated the relationship between long term interest rates and the federal debt. First, they fail to account for the interaction between fiscal policy and monetary policy. One of the principal tenets of macroeconomics is that an expanding economy requires increased credit. If the public sector debt contracts, the private sector must take on an expansion in credit in order to compensate.

For instance, between 1996 and 2000, federal public debt fell from 49 percent of GDP to 33 percent of GDP. During this period, the economy was growing at over 4 percent a year, and household and business debt was climbing rapidly in order to facilitate the expansion in national income. Even as the federal government was reducing the federal debt, monetary policy had to accommodate an increase in household debt.

Between 1997 and 2003, total household debt (the sum of mortgages outstanding and consumer credit) expanded from 67 percent of GDP to 86 percent. (For the sake of comparison, in the six-year economic expansion prior to 1997, household debt expanded only modestly, from 64 percent to 66 percent of GDP.)

Today, our household sector is far more indebted than ever before; over the past 35 years, the household debt-to-GDP ratio has averaged 58 percent.

Total business debt also rose from 1997 to 2003, albeit less sharply, from 58 percent of GDP to 68 percent of GDP. In the 1991-1997 period, business debt had actually contracted, from 61 percent of GDP to 58 percent of GDP.

Paradoxically, the Rubinesque effort to reduce federal debt since 1997 has coincided with a 37 percentage point *increase* in total non-federal debt, and a 38 percentage point increase in total non-financial debt, to 204 percent of GDP. The mantra of "paying down the debt" has led the federal government to a course of action that resulted in a rapid monetary easing by the Federal Reserve, which in turn has left the private sector far more indebted than it was at the beginning of the era of fiscal restraint.

Second, the hypothesis that increased taxes result in increased national savings is flawed. Analytically and empirically, the relationship between public and national savings is a tenuous one. Proponents of tax increases routinely ignore the impact of higher taxes on key drivers of savings—personal incomes, corporate profits, returns on investment and economic growth.

Robert Eisner published a survey called "National Savings and Budget Deficits" in 1994, in *The Review of Economics & Statistics*, in which he concluded that deficits had no demonstrable effect on savings. The conclusion of that study has been borne out by at least three subsequent natural case studies of major industrialized economies that intentionally adopted budget policies during the 1990s that deliberately veered from previous fiscal paths.

In the United States, the federal government ran considerable deficits averaging nearly 4 percent of GDP from 1981 to 1989; during this period, gross national savings averaged 18.2 percent of GDP. Between 1990 and 1997, the government's finances improved considerably, but gross national savings actually fell.

From 1998 to 2001, when the federal budget was in surplus, gross national savings was just 17.1 percent of GDP.

In the United Kingdom, the gross national savings rate was 17.8 percent of GDP between 1984 and 1987, when the budget was in deficit, but dropped to 17.2 percent of GDP in 1988 and 1989 when the budget moved to surplus. British deficits averaged almost 5 percent of GDP from 1990 to 1997, and then moved to modest surpluses from 1998 to 2001. During both of these periods, gross national savings averaged just under 16 percent of GDP.

Australia is the third case study. That country ran a series of deficits, averaging about 3 percent of GDP, from 1986 to 1997, and then moved to surpluses from 1998 to 2001. The gross national savings rate during the years of chronic deficits was 19 percent of GDP, almost exactly where it was during the surplus years.

Conclusion

Although there is a schism in the economics community, it appears there is no statistical support for the criticism George W. Bush receives from modern day deficit hawks—that higher budget deficits or accumulated public debt will drive up interest rates and "crowd out" private savings. There is some statistical support for the weak form of the anti-deficit view, that *changes* in deficits can drive *changes* in interest rates, at least in the short term. However, as long as budget deficits are temporary, this argument fails to prove that deficits *per se* either permanently raise interest rates or endanger economic growth.

There is certainly no evidence to support the notion that the absolute level of long term interest rates is affected by the modest increases in public debt envisioned by President George W. Bush. Both time series data from the United States and the international scene give evidence that the current and projected public debt of the United States is well within a range that can support continued low interest rates and robust economic growth.

More worrisome than deficits *per se*, in my view, is the growth of government spending, which tends to crowd out private spending whether it is financed by taxes or by borrowing. Real, non-defense, discretionary federal government spending is up an average of 7.2 percent a year since 2000. A continuation of this trend could indeed cause real economic damage by diverting labor and capital from private capital goods production—that is the real "crowding effect" that economists should worry about.

We live in an era of almost universal budget expansion—since 1960, national defense spending has risen about 5 percent per year, roughly in line with the inflation rate, but almost every other area of government has seen substantial, real increases in spending over the past 10, 20, 30 and 40 years. Health and Social Security expenditures now consume over 40 percent of our federal budget, and those areas have been growing at annualized after-inflation rates of 6 and 3 percent respectively since 1990.

If rising government spending persists, then federal deficits may become permanent fixtures of the economic landscape rather than the transient and harmless interlopers they are projected to be.

Chapter Thirteen

THE SECOND TERM DIET

Grover Norquist

Grover Norquist is the president of Americans for Tax Reform, a coalition of taxpayer groups, individuals and businesses opposed to higher taxes. He is also a former executive director of the National Taxpayers' Union and serves on the boards of the National Rifle Association and the American Conservative Union. The following article appears with the permission of The American Spectator, *which first published it in March 2004, and of the author.*

W hen the Republicans became the majority party in the House and Senate in January 1995, federal spending was 20.7 percent of the gross domestic product (GDP). After six years of a Republican Congress and the Democrat Bill Clinton in the White House, federal spending fell to below 18.5 percent of GDP. Today, after three full years of a (mainly) Republican Congress and Republican President, George W. Bush, federal spending has climbed back to almost 20 percent of GDP. [29] Total federal spend-

---

29.   *Economic Report of the President* (Feb. 2004), Table B-79.

ing increased $300 billion in fiscal years 2002 and 2003 combined[30] and is expected to increase another $136 billion in fiscal year 2004. [31] These increases amount to 4.2 percent in 2001, 7.9 percent in 2002, 7.3 percent in 2003, and a projected 7.5 percent in fiscal year 2004.[32]

What happened? Has the Republican Party turned liberal? Hardly. Bush and a Republican Congress have cut taxes three times in three years, and taken on not only the liberals but much of the world in repudiating the ABM treaty that limited America's ability to develop and deploy strategic defenses, and the Kyoto treaty that would have curtailed America's economic growth. Partial birth abortion was outlawed. Tort reform passed the House and awaits a few more Republicans in the Senate. Conservative judges have been appointed—some confirmed, others also awaiting a few more Republican Senators. In the war on terror, the Taliban government of Afghanistan has been removed for supporting Al Qaeda and Saddam Hussein's regime in Iraq is ended. The anger of Howard Dean and John Kerry supporters is entirely rational—there isn't a liberal bone in this Republican Administration.

Indeed, the President and Republican Congress have been rock solid on almost everything—except federal spending. How could that be? If the professed goal of the Republican Party is to limit the size and scope of government so as to maximize individual liberty, how can it fail to limit federal spending? Something is wrong when everything on the agenda gets attention— except the one big thing.

One reason for the out of control spending is the makeup of the conservative coalition. Taxpayers vote for Bush because they want him to cut taxes. They would also like lower spending. Gun owners vote for Bush because they want their guns left alone.

---

30. Ibid, Table B-78.
31. "The Budget and Economic Outlook: Fiscal Years 2005 to 2014," *Congressional Budget Office*.
32. Budget of the United States, historical tables, http://www.whitehouse.gov/omb/budget/fy2005/hist.html.

THE SECOND TERM DIET

They would also like lower spending. Pro-lifers vote for Bush because they value life. They would also prefer lower spending. Ditto property owners, small businessmen and women, traditional values conservatives.

Everyone wants lower spending. But for all organized parts of the conservative movement it is a second priority. There is no National Rifle Association, National Right to Life Committee, or National Federation of Independent Business organized around the single issue of controlling spending. A second problem is that the pro-spending forces are well organized and well funded. The largest lobbying and law firms in Washington are hired by clients who want more spending. I cannot identify a single client of the top ten lobbying shops whose goal is a reduction in federal spending. A third problem is that unlike fighters for "pro-life," "taxpayer" and "death tax" issues, the forces of limited spending have given away the language. In the 1950s conservative Republicans—a minority within a minority—fought against spending. But because they believed their cause wouldn't gain majority support, they targeted "deficit spending" to win over all the Methodists who hate debt.

Liberals responded by arguing that deficits were meaningless because "we owed the money to ourselves." But by the 1980s the Democrats discovered that deficits were an important weapon in opposing tax cuts and supporting tax increases. They dropped the word "spending" to harp on the evil of "deficits" caused by lower taxes. When Ronald Reagan and Jack Kemp now argued that "deficits" didn't matter, they were defending tax cuts.

Back in 1995, the newly elected GOP Congress slowed federal spending just a tad and put a stop to Bill Clinton's plans to nationalize health care, pensions, and raise taxes. As a result, the economy took off and the federal budget went into surplus. Then came a moment of clarity. Republicans asked Democrats: "You said you opposed tax cuts because of the deficits: Now that we are in surplus, will you support our tax cuts?" "No, no," the Democrats replied. "We were lying. We always oppose tax cuts."

The Democrats asked back: "Hey, Republicans, you said you were against spending on various domestic programs because of the deficit. Now that we have a surplus, will you support new spending programs?" And the Republicans answered, "No, we were lying. We oppose more spending period, surplus or deficit." For a few years in the late 1990s, the focus remained on spending. And spending as a percentage of the economy fell. Actually fell.

But Bush inherited a recession, and with the war on terror and overspending the budget went back into deficit. We are now once again focused not on the important numbers—how much the government spends and how much it takes by force—but on the unimportant difference between those two numbers, i.e., the federal deficit. The Bush Administration's greatest strategic error occurred when Josh Bolten of the Office of Management and Budget announced in the *Wall Street Journal*—and the President reiterated in his recent State of the Union address—that the Administration's goal was to cut the federal deficit by half in five years. The White House obviously doesn't even recognize the problem—spending.

Worse, we know Democrats cannot compete with Republicans if the fight is over who can control federal spending. But the Democrats can compete just fine, thank you, if the problem is defined as the deficit. "End the Bush tax cuts." "Bring back the death tax." Problem solved.

If the problem is spending: Republicans win. If the problem is deficits, Democrats can claim to have one of two equally valid answers—spending or raising taxes. One understands why CBS and Ted Kennedy want the discussion to be about "deficits." But it is wrong, and suicidal, for any Republican to so frame that debate.

Some conservatives now argue that the combination of a Republican Congress and a Democratic President from 1995 to 2000 led to a decline in federal spending as a percentage of the economy. By contrast, having George W. Bush as President alongside a Republican Congress has led to an equally sized increase in federal spending as a percentage of the economy. Perhaps, then, there is a case for wishing ill luck to Bush/Cheney in 2004 and a return to "divided" government. Fortunately for Republicans and conservatives who want a re-elected George W. Bush to continue to nominate judges, cut taxes, and pursue a foreign policy independent of the United Nations, Bush's re-election is also the key to real reductions in government spending. This is not to excuse the inexcusable explosions of spending such as the recrudescence of farm subsidies, expanded foreign aid, and more federal funds to finance the National Education Association's precinct workers.

Six Reforms to Reduce Federal Spending

The good news is that the Bush Administration has begun six serious reforms that—if Bush is re-elected with the mandate he is seeking—will put us on a path to smaller government. The first reform is competitive sourcing. Bush's policy is to take 850,000 federal civilian jobs that could be performed by private contractors and require that they all be put to bid. For example, the fellows who mow the lawn at the Pentagon are government workers. Nice people in the yellow pages offer similar services. Government lawn mowers will now have to bid periodically against outside contractors for that work. When the Defense Department tried competitive sourcing on a limited basis, it found that the same work can be performed at a savings of 30 percent. This experiment will end if a Democrat is elected. Only a Republican Congress plus a Republican President can maintain this reform, at an annual savings of $25 billion. And this is just the tip of the iceberg. Once outsourcing becomes standard operating procedure for the federal government, it's inevitable that the more competent Governors will follow suit. Since there are 15 million state and local government workers, at least one-third or five million of these jobs could be competitively sourced for a savings of more than $125 billion each year. And this savings comes (sadly) without reducing any "government services." The feds and the states would do everything they do today at 30 percent savings. It would change the culture of government work, which would no longer be a sinecure. That's reason enough to get out of bed on Election Day, November 2nd.

The second reform is the base closings legislation. We are in the middle of the fifth round. This brilliant evenhanded Base Closings Commission idea was put forward by then-Texas congressman Dick Armey in 1988. The first commission saved taxpayers an initial $4 billion with an additional $1 billion annually. This was followed in 1991 with an initial $8.4 billion and $2 billion annual savings thereafter. Then 1993's commission saved taxpayers $4.7 billion initially and $2.3 billion annually. The fourth commission was undercut by Bill Clinton's politically motivated exempting of two California bases, resulting in an actual net cost to taxpayers in 1995. Congress didn't pass another base closing bill until the election of a President who wouldn't cheat. Thus under Bush Congress passed another base closing bill in 2003, and the commission will issue its report in 2005. The Secretary of Defense has called for closing one-quarter of domestic bases and one-quarter of foreign bases. The success of this commission and the creation of future commissions will require a re-elected Bush.

The third reform is to move Social Security toward a fully funded, individually controlled, portable pension system. President Bush bravely touched (heck, fondled) the third rail of American politics when he came out for such reform in the 2000 election. His re-election campaign will outline three principles: give every American the opportunity to put roughly half of their FICA taxes into personal savings accounts like an IRA, oppose any cuts in present benefits, and oppose any tax hikes. Should Bush win his mandate, the 70 percent support this idea already commands will ensure passage by a Republican Congress. I believe that any American who chooses to invest some of his

FICA taxes in a personal savings account will eventually demand the right to do so entirely. Should every young American make this choice, according to the Social Security Actuary, over time we will reduce the Social Security tax, the largest tax paid by most Americans, by 83 percent and turn 20 percent of the federal budget into a forced savings plan. The $2 trillion shift to personal accounts will be the largest reduction of federal taxes and spending in American history. This is a large enough reform to forgive periodic falling off the wagon for expensive trips to Mars or the creation of taxpayer-funded electric grids in other people's countries.

The fourth reform is the Doha round of trade negotiations scheduled for completion in 2005. U. S. Trade Representative Robert Zoellick has called for eliminating manufacturing tariffs and lowering tariffs on agricultural products in exchange for the reduction/elimination of American and European agricultural subsidies. The latter would reverse the damage done by the restoration of direct farm subsidies in 2001 and save $170 billion over ten years. It's a particularly important budget cut in that existence of farm subsidies is the only reason the good, honest, and patriotic peoples of North and South Dakota inflict on our nation the four Bolsheviks they send to the U.S. Senate. Without subsidies to fight for, there's no need for Democratic Senators.

The fifth reform is the health savings accounts enacted as part of the Medicare expansion legislation that will increase federal spending by at least $50 billion each year to provide pharmaceutical benefits that most Americans already receive through the private sector. Conservatives have fought for years for health savings accounts. They will allow Americans to put money in HSAs and buy high deductible insurance. Any money not spent will roll over and accumulate tax free. The more Americans pay for their own basic health care directly, the more competition will lower health care costs for all Americans. While health care costs have increased in double digits for five consecutive years (because consumers do not shop directly but simply send the bill to the government or their health insurance provider), the cost of cosmetic surgery—which is not covered by insurance and therefore is competitively priced—has declined in real prices every year for a decade. Laser eye surgery has fallen 35 percent in cost in the last three years for the same reason. Simply put, when people have a stake in the process they shop around.

And with the state and federal governments already spending nearly $600 billion on Medicare and Medicaid, HSAs have the ability to keep government health-care spending in line with GDP growth, which will cut projected government health-care spending from the Medicare trustees in half from nearly 12 percent to 6 percent of GDP. This will save taxpayers hundreds of billions of dollars.

The sixth reform is parental choice in education. Bush and the Republican Senate have just won school choice for 1,700 students in Washington, D.C. That may seem like no more than a small crack in the public school monopoly, but when Hungary allowed a few hundred East Germans to cross its border to the west in 1989 the fate of Communist East Germany was sealed. Government education K-12 costs 4.5 percent of GDP. Private schools spend half as much per student as government schools spend, employing as they do 2.1 million Democratic precinct workers belonging to the National Education Association. Over time, if public schools are required to compete for parents' money with independent schools and home schooling, costs will fall. If government schools become as productive as private schools, total costs could be cut by half or 2.5 percent of GDP. There's a reason why the NEA fights so hard against the smallest "experiment" in school choice. It knows best the shoddy quality of its work.

The above six spending reforms are all underway. They will move forward under a re-elected George W. Bush and a Republican Congress. They will all be delayed for years if not decades if a Democrat wins the Presidency.

CHAPTER FOURTEEN

WELFARE REFORM, PART II

STAR PARKER

Star Parker, a former single Los Angeles welfare mother, is the Founder and President of the Coalition on Urban Renewal and Education (urbancure.org), a non-profit organization facilitating national dialogue on issues of race and poverty in the media, inner city neighborhoods, and public policy. A renowned social policy consultant, she gives frequent testimony before the U.S. Congress, and serves as a regular commentator on CNN, MSNBC and Fox News. Her books include the newly released UNCLE SAM'S PLANTATION: HOW BIG GOVERNMENT ENSLAVES AMERICA'S POOR AND WHAT WE CAN DO ABOUT IT.

"The new culture said if people were poor, the government should feed them. If criminals are not responsible for their acts, then the answers are not in prisons, but in social programs…A culture of dependency was born. Programs that began as a temporary hand-up became a permanent handout, regarded by many as a right."

President George W. Bush, *A Charge to Keep*

Anyone still looking to politics and government to synthetically engineer a better society is just not looking, or doesn't want to look, at what we've learned over the last fifty years. Political experiments, from communism and socialism to the New Deal and the War on Poverty, have blown up in the smoke of their own claims.

The explosive growth of government-sanctioned and mandated public education programs, the increased use of racial quotas to ensure "fair play," and the bloating of the welfare state in the latter half of the last century have handicapped rather than helped the nation's poor, the very people these programs were created to assist. Poverty has become more entrenched, crime and promiscuity more widespread, and hopelessness and bitterness the prevailing mentality in our nation's inner cities. America's war on poverty has clearly failed. By promoting dependency, victimization, materialism and helplessness, the welfare state and entitlement mentality have undermined the very values of faith, fidelity, love, community, and personal responsibility that build character and provide the framework for dealing with adversity.

The 1996 welfare reform act (a key component of the Contract With America), along with current initiatives such as No Child Left Behind and the Faith-based Initiative, move America in the right direction, promoting personal responsibility and private sector approaches. However, the question of the viability of public education and welfare programs still remains. The propensity of any nation to turn to government for its answers to all of life's problems is itself a sign of a fundamental loss of moral direction.

Today we are well beyond intellectual arguments and need only to look at the clear and simple picture the data conveys. Wherever we look in the world, whether in the Middle East or Africa or in America's inner cities, the preponderance of government and the absence of freedom go hand in hand with ignorance, poverty, and human suffering. We have seen, and continue to see, that government interference, in any form which stands in the way of individuals taking responsibility and control over their own lives, produces disaster.

African Americans have paid a dear price for turning their lives over to politicians. The civil rights movement of the 1960s was about pure freedom. Anyone who doubts this should re-read Dr. King's magnificent "I Have a Dream" speech. A defining moment of the civil rights movement, it was an appeal to a nation to live up to its own great vision and standards, and ensure that none of its citizens be denied the freedom guaranteed for all. There was no hint in Dr. King's words suggesting that blacks were not ready or capable of sharing in the American dream or that they needed anything from government other than the same protection afforded to all Americans.

Yet, Dr. King's successors carried a very different message on to their black constituencies. The moral message of Dr. King, echoing the message of our founders, that all men are endowed by our Creator with inalienable rights, and that men create government for the sole purpose of securing those rights, was manipulated by the current black leadership into a political message that rights and justice are meted out by politicians and judges. After the passage of the landmark civil rights legislation in 1964, instead of returning home to provide the moral leadership necessary for strengthening family and community, the new black leadership, weaned in the black church, fell in love with the political process and political answers. They soon joined hands with white liberals and spent the next thirty years passing welfare and social engineering programs that blacks supposedly needed over and beyond constitutional protection.

Black leaders began to depend heavily on the courts and the Congress to atone for the social ills confronting their communities. Court rulings ordered the states to racially integrate their institutions. For example, the U.S. Supreme Court ruled that the public schools in several cities had to be racially balanced. This decision led many states to pass laws to force the busing of black students from urban neighborhoods to those of predominantly white schools. Almost overnight, an exodus of white students from the public schools began to occur.

Government controlled and directed public education has caused particular problems for the African American community. Since the establishment of the U.S. Department of Education in 1979, federally-encouraged and state-mandated requirements have left our public schools, especially those in minority and/or inner-city neighborhoods, in shambles by stripping them of their moral foundations. In the name of so-called neutrality, public schools peddle distinctly left-biased, morally empty curricula that satisfy the politicos who design these programs and destroy the children who are held captive to them.

Education research uniformly shows that the greatest predictor of success for children in school is the values they are taught at home. Black children suffer both on the home front and the school front, and the problems on both fronts can be traced back to government. The welfare state has all but destroyed the black family; seventy percent of black children are reared today in single parent homes. As result, the likelihood remains high that black children will not, in today's environment, show up in school with a background to succeed. The environment in school is therefore particularly important to black children.

Unfortunately, black children, badly in need of truth, values, and authority, are fed morally relative, politically motivated programs in school that lead them further down the path of pointlessness. Hence, the public school system produces dropouts and criminals rather than educated young adults.

The purging of values from education leaves one purpose to education—career training. However, when the point becomes acquisition with no framework for values, children quickly grasp that school is not necessarily the best use of their time. Drugs and crime can pay off far more quickly. Illiteracy and pregnancy rates amongst American teenagers have risen to heights that have left our forefathers weeping in Heaven. Metal detectors and drug-sniffing dogs have become permanent fixtures in many of our urban school districts. Suicides, contraceptive dispensers, and abortions are as commonplace as jump ropes and sack lunches. Unfortunately, this so-called education (the tool by which a culture hopes to transmit its beliefs and values to the next generation) has left millions of Americans, especially African Americans, in an on-going state of poverty.

The Compton Unified School District (CUSD) is a sad example of the state of public schools in inner-city and minority neighborhoods. Located in south central Los Angeles, CUSD has a large percentage of black students. In 2003, CUSD students performed dismally on their California Standards Test. According to the California Department of Education, 58% of sixth-grade students and 63% of seventh-grade students tested below the basic or far below the basic mean scaled score in math. Test results in English Language Arts were not much better with 57% of sixth and seventh graders below basic or far below basic. As students moved into high school in the CUSD, test results fell even lower. Only 34% of eleventh-grade students tested at the basic level or above in English.

At the same time, the city of Compton was identified by the University of California, Berkeley, as one of the eighty-two "hot spots" in California for the highest birth rates for teenage mothers ages 15 to 17. I seriously doubt that any of those young women were married before they conceived their first child. Rather than teaching children to read and write, and to abstain from sex until after marriage, CUSD, along with thousands of other public schools, believes that a so-called values-free education will lead children down the road to success. In reality, depending on government-designed education has only led their students down the drain.

And what a drain it has been. Not being able to read, write, or do basic math calculations by graduation (if they graduate at all) has left thousands of poor Americans competing for the same limited number of minimum-wage jobs. Teenage girls find it particularly difficult to raise a child, continue their education, and work a part-time job—all at the same time.

Poverty abounds in many African-American communities for these very reasons. According to the U.S. Census Bureau, only 8% of black married couples were living in poverty in 2001. Compare that to the staggering 35% of black families led by a single mother during the same year.

Welfare reform legislation in 1996 showed that change is possible; but we must continue down the path that this legislation initiated.

Although many on the Left continue to protest welfare reform, the problems and dynamics of welfare as we used to know it remain clear. Politicians divert large amounts of tax dollars toward subsidizing housing and medical care for the needy, and giving money and food to unemployed women raising children without husbands. Prior to welfare reform, this frequently had the perverse effect of encouraging the very behaviors it was designed to alleviate: inner city teenage girls often found the federal financial incentives to actually get pregnant irresistible. Under the Great Society-era Aid to Families with Dependent Children (AFDC), such girls could, once pregnant, get federal housing assistance (move away from home) as well as direct aid (spending money), provided that they were truly needy (refused support from their parents and didn't marry their child's father) and stayed home with their child (dropped out of school and didn't get a job). To many girls, this seemed almost like a dream come true: until, of course, they were trapped by the perverse moral choices the system had enticed them to make.

The old system hurt blacks more than anyone, especially ironic since it was supposed to help them most. Out of all American families who received welfare benefits in 1992, 37.2% were black. This is a sad state of affairs when one considers the fact that blacks as a whole represent only 13% of the entire population of the United States.

Welfare reform as a whole has been a grand success, not least by removing most of AFDC's incentives for perverse, harmful behavior. Welfare rolls from 1996 to 2001 were cut in half. However, minorities continue to lag in being weaned off this destructive machine. More stringent work requirements and limited life welfare benefits provide strong incentives to get off the system. But what is really needed is inculcation of values that make such behavior shameful and unthinkable. We need to move beyond a society in which race translates into categories and quotas. The *Grutter v. Bollinger* decision justifying race in university selection processes was a step backward and a slap in the face to blacks. Justice O' Connor's remarks implying that blacks are not capable of competing academically was insulting and counterproductive. Blacks can compete. The solution to blacks' educational problems is in reconstructing the homes into which black children are born, not in engineering preferential selection processes at universities. Many will cry out that racial quotas even the playing field in a world where whites have been the ones who have called all the shots. There is no doubt that discrimination has existed throughout our history, and still continues even to this day. But it has always been the individuals who refused to let backward-minded white folk hold them back that ended up being the greatest success stories.

For example, one only needs to look at the success of the late Reginald Francis Lewis, chairman, CEO, and principal shareholder of TLC Beatrice International Holdings Inc., for inspiration in overcoming one's circumstances. He was born on December 7, 1942, in East Baltimore at a time when black people couldn't shop or even try on clothes at many downtown stores, eat in certain restaurants, or go to certain movie theaters; he became a successful corporate lawyer who remade himself into a financier and buyer of corporations. Lewis bought McCall Patter Company for $22.5 million, guided it to record earnings, sold it for $65 million, and then went on to leverage a buyout of Beatrice International Foods, a global giant with sixty-four companies in thirty-one countries, for just under a billion dollars. Where might he have been instead had he waited for a "fair" playing field to "even" his chances of succeeding?

A friend of mine who really enjoys watching college football told me a story about how Tom Osbourne, former head coach of the Nebraska Cornhuskers, viewed bad referees and how they affected his team's success. Apparently Coach Osbourne said that bad refs and bad calls are all a part of the game, and to win (which is, after all, the goal of playing the game) often required rising above the circumstances. Great teams always win in spite of an uneven playing field. Coach Osbourne ended up with three national championships.

Some may think that I'm trivializing the subject by comparing real life events with football, but the lesson is the same for all arenas of life. Winning in spite of the odds and seeing obstacles as challenges to overcome are essential ways we must approach our careers. Can anyone imagine Venus and Serena Williams asking for thirty-point advantage before play begins at Wimbledon, simply because they are black? They win because they put their all into their practice sessions and matches, not because of the color of their skin; and indeed, to be given such an unfair advantage would rob them of the credit they deserve.

We must appreciate that the creeping moral relativism of our country is most damaging to blacks. Children growing up in intact homes, in which age old values are transmitted, are far less likely to be captured by the distorted and destructive sense of the world transmitted by popular culture. However, among blacks, where, thanks to forty years of welfare state politics, family life and values are already in shambles, moral relativism takes a profound toll.

Statistics speak for themselves. The percentage of black babies born to unwed mothers has tripled over the past thirty years, along with the percentage of black children growing up in fatherless homes. In the inner city, the percentage of young black males who have both dropped out of school and are unemployed now approaches fifty percent. Abortion destroys more than 300,000 black babies every year. The overwhelming majority of them are from unwed mothers. Fifty percent of new AIDS cases are in the black community.

This crisis is the direct result of the replacement of values and virtues with political answers, and middle-class blacks are slowly awakening to the fact that liberalism in general, and liberal government programs in particular, are the problem.

As I point out in my book, *Uncle Sam's Plantation*, the pulsating primitive rhythms and rhymes of rap music simply reflect the truths that are transmitted to blacks through the wafer-thin veneer of popular American culture. Sadly, that same culture, which has become the ideological mother's milk of poor black children, is devoid of eternal ideals and altruism. With all the subtlety of a sledgehammer, our youth are bludgeoned with the message that life is all about money, power, and sex. Promiscuity, illiteracy, and youth crime make it abundantly clear that our children are getting the message.

These problems must be fixed, and in addition to creating an environment to rebuild family life in black America, market-based reforms such as school choice vouchers will help to reverse these trends.

Social Security reform, whereby the current system would be transformed into one of privately-owned retirement accounts, is another crucial reform for low and low-middle income workers, and absolutely essential in order to move into the next phase of welfare reform. The President has advocated moving in this direction and he should by all means follow through.

The current Social Security system is perverse in structure and implementation. The highest tax most low income individuals pay is the payroll tax. Workers are captive in this system until they reach an income level of $90,000. At that point, the worker is free and clear. Thus, perversely, the payroll tax is totally regressive and penalizes lower income workers.

Worse yet, the implicit returns of social security are far below market returns and deny ownership of benefits to those paying into the system. Thus, social security systematically limits wealth accumulation for low income workers. And just to add ultimate insult to crippling injury, the system is designed to begin paying benefits just as the average black man dies. Many never see a dime; neither can their children inherit the fruit of their work.

Let's fix our broken social security system and create a regime that is both more equitable and provides a framework for ownership and wealth accumulation for our nation's low and low-middle income workers and families.

Similarly, our health care system is badly in need of reform and President Bush has led the charge to make some necessary changes. Third party payer arrangements drive up costs and put health care out of reach for low income workers. The answer is a flexible system that returns decisions to consumers, embodied in the newly-enacted Health Savings Accounts. Widespread introduction of such accounts will make health care affordable and health security achievable for every American, especially for those in the low end of the income spectrum.

In sum, freedom, personal responsibility and less government is the answer for poverty. Allow individuals the dignity to choose, return the moral grounding of our country and take politics off the table as the means for solving life's problems— and the artificial lines of race will melt away. President Bush has begun to move our nation in this direction. The key is to work with him to continue leading our country down this path.

CHAPTER FIFTEEN

EXPANDING OPPORTUNITY THROUGH FREE TRADE

HEIDI CRUZ

Heidi Cruz is an energy investment banker at Merrill Lynch in Houston, Texas. She served as the economic director for the western hemisphere at the National Security Council at the White House from 2003 to 2004, and as special assistant to Ambassador Robert B. Zoellick from 2001 to 2002.

International trade policy has been one of the most successful undertakings of President Bush's first term in office. Starting with the campaign, the President has put trade at the center of his agenda for America, relating free trade to opportunity, liberty, democracy, and security. At a speech dedicated to his vision of defense policy at the Citadel in South Carolina in September 1999, the President reminded the nation of the important role that trade plays in the post-Cold War world: "We won a victory, not just for a nation, but for a vision. A vision of freedom and individual dignity—defended by democracy, nurtured by free markets, spread by information technology carried to the world by free trade." As Congressman John Tanner has pointed out, military alliances shaped our relations in the Cold War, but trade alliances would shape our relations in the current era.

The Bush Administration's accomplishments on trade are extraordinary. Just a few years after the multilateral talks in Seattle collapsed, and immediately following the tragic attacks of September 11, President Bush launched global negotiations in the Middle East, in Doha, Qatar. After eight years of failed attempts at obtaining the lapsed negotiating authority from the Congress, President Bush passed the Trade Act of 2002, granting the Executive Branch new authority to close deals with foreign nations. Regionally, the President has worked toward new agreements and solving long lasting disputes in Europe, Latin America, Africa, Australia, Asia, and the Middle East. When the President came into office, there were 130 free trade agreements around the world and the United States was party to only 2. At the time of this writing in June 2004, the United States has launched negotiations with 19 nations, and has concluded talks with 9 of those.

During the Bush-Cheney transition in the winter of 2000-2001, the President named Robert B. Zoellick to serve as U.S. Trade Representative. Ambassador Zoellick has turned a difficult challenge into a resounding success with a carefully crafted strategy and no less than surgical implementation. The strategy began on the campaign, and was carried out with adherence to core principles, compensated for inevitable setbacks and transformed the unforeseen into opportunities. The strategy consists of a few key ideas: making trade policy consistent with our values as a nation, selling the benefits of trade while helping people deal with the challenge of change, building coalitions for trade and creating leverage in negotiations to maximize the opening of markets around the globe, enforcing the rules of the global trading system and defending America when others don't play fair, and using trade to improve standards of living around the world.

This article begins with an overview of the trade policy environment the President faced at the beginning of his term in January 2001, and reviews the causes for the challenges that confronted the Administration. The chapter then outlines the strategy the President and his team developed to overcome these challenges and describes how this Administration turned the trade agenda into a major success of the President's first term. Lastly, it reviews the results of the President's approach.

Difficult Times for Trade Policy

The decade of the 1990s proved tumultuous for America's trade agenda. For reasons well defined in public choice theory, the naysayers outpaced supporters of free trade, both domestically and internationally. While the beneficiaries of trade are widely dispersed throughout the economy and many of the gains are taken for granted, the opponents of trade are often concentrated in particular industries and in certain geographical pockets of the country. The acrimonious environment at home and abroad culminated in 1999 at the doomed third World Trade Organization (WTO) ministerial in Seattle, which was a major setback for the cause of freer trade.

The global economic slowdown, starting in early 2001 and then exacerbated by the tragic attacks of September 11, 2001, further imperiled the environment for openness and risked the possibility that America would take a more isolationist turn.

Failure at Seattle

After the completion of the Uruguay Round in 1994, members of the World Trade Organization (WTO) reconvened in 1999 in Seattle, Washington, to discuss the parameters for launching the next global round of trade talks. Seattle failed for a few key reasons. First, the United States and other countries did not come ready to negotiate. Each came with a list of items that it would demand of the others without considering where common objectives might be found, or where seemingly contradictory demands may be mutually reinforcing. In a consensus body of what was at the time 135 nations (today, there are 148 members in the WTO), such an approach was doomed.

Second, the leading industrialized countries underestimated the concerns of the developing world, which accounted for four-fifths of the membership of the WTO at Seattle. These countries felt left behind in the global trading system in the Uruguay Round—it seemed to them that the rules were slanted to advantage rich countries and that the needs of their populations had not been met by their participation.

Lastly, members of the WTO failed to design a workable agenda to deal with the increasingly complex issues with which the global trading system would have to deal. In 1995, participants in the General Agreement on Tariffs and Trade (GATT) formed the WTO to be a pillar of the globalizing world, an institution that succeeded the GATT as a standing body in Geneva, Switzerland, to build a universal trading system charged with managing the increasing global economic interdependence. With such an ambitious charge, as Renato Ruggiero, the Brazilian director general of the WTO from 1995-1999, pointed out in his reflections on Seattle, the WTO cannot operate in isolation from the concerns of the world in which it exists. Deeper global integration means that commercial exchanges intersect with business and social issues such as investment, competition, environment, labor, health, and education policies.[33]

The irony of Seattle is that the ultimate desires of all the countries gathered were the same, from the United States to the poorest country in Africa: the negotiators wanted the benefits

---

33.   Jeffrey Schott, *The WTO After Seattle* (Washington, D.C.: Institute for International Economics, 2000).

that global trade and economic integration can bring to their countries' populations—economic growth and higher standards of living—but all feared the inevitable adjustments that necessarily result from change. Parties to the negotiation inhibited progress because of lack of preparation and understanding.

September 11

A second factor complicated the environment for reinvigorating multilateral trade negotiations: the 9/11 terrorist attacks. Within a few months of assuming his office, Ambassador Zoellick had already worked to restart global trade talks. The next round of global talks were planned to begin in late November, 2001, in Doha, Qatar.

But then terrorists attacked the Twin Towers in New York and the Pentagon in Washington, D.C. This attack struck against everything that the Bush Administration's trade agenda stands for: greater global economic prosperity; deeper economic and political integration bound by more extensive networks of capital, goods, and services; and the spread of values of freedom and entrepreneurship.

Historically, countries, including our own, have tended to look inward during times of national crisis. For example, in 1930 the United States Congress passed the Smoot-Hawley bill, raising tariffs dramatically just after the stock market crash in 1929, which led to Congress granting authority to the executive branch to negotiate agreements, subject to an up or down vote by Congress.

Yet under the leadership of President Bush, September 11 had a surprising effect on the world trading system. While countries had not been able to find common ground in Seattle, September 11 brought our shared interests into broad daylight: a connectedness in our value systems of respect for life, human rights, and opportunity and prosperity for all. The fact that our financial and political systems are already so connected meant that a loss on the mainland of the United States resulted in cascading economic costs for the global system. Whether we liked it or not, our economic and politico-cultural systems were already hitched.

At the time of the attacks, Deputy U.S. Trade Representative Jon Huntsman was in Vietnam at a meeting of ASEAN economic ministers. In a December 2001 speech to the Washington International Trade Association, he recounted his experience from the morning after the attacks. The U.S. delegation emerged from a sleepless night and were greeted by their Asian counterparts not only with expressions of sympathy and support, but with equally sleepless experiences of searching for loved ones in New York. Thailand's trade minister spent the night calling New York to determine the whereabouts of his son; the minister from Singapore tried to identify those lost to his country's private and public sectors; and the Philippine delegation looked for brothers, sisters, and cousins. The bond with our trading partners was stronger than ever.

Making Trade Policy Consistent with our Values

Seattle and September 11 both highlighted the fact that our trading system and openness are intertwined with our values. Two years earlier, President Bush was already espousing that fact, running for the presidency on the principle that trade policy must be consistent with our values as a nation. And indeed, the core of our trade policy has been shaped by our President's articulation of his foreign policy and our values as Americans.

In November 1999, President Bush outlined his foreign policy objectives in a speech given at the Ronald Reagan Presidential Library in Simi Valley, California. In that speech, he detailed the values America lives by: human freedom, democracy, free movement of people, capital and information mobility, optimism, dignity, and opportunity for all. Trade was at the center of how these values would be expressed in his Administration: "I view free trade as an important ally in what Ronald Reagan called 'a forward strategy for freedom.' The case for trade is not just monetary, but moral. Economic freedom creates habits of liberty. And habits of liberty create expectations of democracy." Seattle lacked this connection to an overarching set of principles that would define what was good for the global trading system and what was in America's interests.

The Administration faced the same debates that had paralyzed the trade agenda in the 1990s—the debate on whether trade policy could address reducing the worst forms of child labor, improvement of environmental standards, and access to medicines for people suffering from HIV/AIDS in Africa. The answer was clear for our President—if the system was worthwhile, it had to address these human concerns.

Selling the Benefits of Trade

Although NAFTA was signed by former President Bush in 1992 and passed by Congress during the Clinton Administration in 1993, the benefits of free trade for the United States and the benefits that accrue to developing countries that open their markets had never been fully explained. This allowed the opponents of free trade to go unchecked for eight years. Even so, exports accounted for 27 percent of U.S. growth in the 1990s, and trade has become an increasingly important component of our economy. Since the 1970s, trade as a percentage of our GDP has tripled from about 11 percent in 1971 to close to 30 percent in 2002. Indeed, as former Treasury Secretary Robert Rubin has observed, productivity increases, resulting in large part from increased global competition, are credited for the high levels of economic growth and low unemployment that coexisted without igniting inflation in the 1990s.

C. Fred Bergsten, director of the Institute for International Economics in Washington, D.C., estimates that lower import prices explain virtually all the decline in inflation between 1996 and 2000. Bergsten estimates that expansion of trade has created 1.5 – 2 percentage points of growth and generated at least 1.5 million jobs while reducing the unemployment rate in the late 1990s by 1.2 percentage points.

While important to account for the macroeconomic benefits of trade, building public support requires that workers and families know the impact of free trade on their pocketbooks. As Ambassador Zoellick emphasizes at every possible turn, opening our markets means lower prices for consumers, greater choice of products to purchase, and the creation of more, higher-paying jobs. Indeed, our exports support about 12 million jobs, and these jobs pay wages 13 percent to 18 percent higher than the U.S. average. To cite the benefits from recent agreements, the combined benefits of NAFTA and the Uruguay Round have been quantified to benefit the average American family of four $1,300-$2,000 per year due to higher incomes and lower prices.

Ironically, those who felt left out at Seattle stood to reap the greatest benefits from trade. Developing countries expressed concern that their labor would be exploited, resources exported, and that they would not have a say in the rules of the game. While these fears must be addressed, what about the benefits to these countries? The World Bank has estimated that the elimination of trade barriers would result in a $539 billion income gain for moderate and low income countries—and that three-fourths of that would be gained from lower trade barriers among moderate- and low-income countries themselves. The World Bank also points out that in the 1990s, the income per person for developing countries that were opening their markets grew by more than 5 percent per year. Developing countries that were *not* integrating with global markets saw annual incomes *decline* by more than 1 percent per year. The study also found that as trade grew and economies expanded, people with lower incomes realized a proportionate share of the benefits. Indeed, absolute poverty in the globalizing developing countries has dropped sharply in the last 20 years. Over the last decade, trade helped to lift 140 million people out of poverty.

Building Coalitions for Trade at Home

Since 1994, when the "fast track" bill (the legislation granting authority to the executive branch to negotiate) lapsed, the United States was unable to negotiate additional trade agreements in 1990s. When President Bush came into office, the United States was falling behind other countries in negotiating free trade agreements. As previously noted, as of 2001 the United States was a party to only 2 of the 130 free trade agreements around world. This had a real impact on U.S. industry, costing market share in key destinations for American goods. For example, the European Union and Canada both negotiated free trade agreements with Chile before the United States and as a result, Canadian farmers gained market share from American potato and wheat farmers.

Facing this reality, Ambassador Zoellick has stated many times that his job is to keep the momentum going in a positive direction for free trade and to negotiate for American interests at the table.

Implementing the trade strategy first required obtaining the lapsed authority from the Congress to negotiate. Renaming the fast-track bill "Trade Promotion Authority" (TPA) signaled that this Administration was changing the tenor of the debate. Trade would be seen positively, as an economic and social good to be promoted, not as a negative force jammed through by naysayers. The Administration would promote good trade deals in careful consultation with Congress.

Trade Adjustment Assistance

To create and maintain a forward momentum for trade, the Administration recognized that it would need to form supportive coalitions for trade at home. This would involve combining our push to open markets with a focus on assistance for workers who needed help if their jobs changed as a result of trade. The Administration made adjustment assistance a key part of the trade strategy. The Trade Act of 2002, which granted TPA, also tripled trade adjustment assistance, providing $12 billion in assistance over 10 years to help workers and families adjust to competition by training them for new jobs.

Enforcement of Trade Rules

Generating support for trade domestically also required vigorous enforcement of trade laws to ensure the game was fair for American businesses. The President expressed in the campaign his belief that American businesses and workers can compete if there is a level playing field for competition and America's trading partners play by the rules of the game.

This Administration has indeed stood up for America's interests. To list a few of the most recent cases, the United States pressed China to live up to its commitments as a new member of the WTO, filed a case against Mexico's protectionist high fructose corn syrup taxes, reopened the Mexican market to American beef, reopened the Indian market to American almonds, and settled ongoing intellectual property rights' disputes with the Dominican Republic. "Enforcing existing trade agreements is no less important than producing new ones," Ambassador Zoellick pointed out in his March 2004 statement to the Committee on Appropriations.

The decision to impose temporary safeguards on steel has perhaps attracted the most attention. In June 2001, the President acted decisively to address the longstanding problem of overcapacity in the global steel industry by announcing a three-part multilateral steel initiative. The initiative included launching an investigation regarding injury to domestic markets caused by imports, negotiating with other steel producing nations to obtain near-term elimination of excess capacity, and negotiations to establish additional disciplines on market-distorting practices.

On March 5, 2002, the President announced temporary safeguards on steel under Section 201 of the Trade Act of 1974. The U.S. International Trade Commission—an independent federal agency responsible for such investigations—found that increased steel imports were a substantial cause of serious injury to our domestic industry. In cases where increased imports are found to be a substantial cause of serious injury, Section 201 can give U.S. industries a limited time to adjust. Section 201 complies with World Trade Organization rules—the WTO recognizes that sometimes temporary restraints are warranted to allow for an industry to adjust and restructure to address change. (Other countries, including Japan, Korea, India, Brazil, and European Union member states have also used safeguards.)

Reciprocity in opening markets is key to maintaining support for trade and further market openings at home. When other countries want us to move quickly to lower barriers but are not willing to lower their own, the United States has an obligation to give its industries a fair chance to compete by enforcing the rules of the game.

For over 50 years, the international steel industry had been heavily subsidized, cartelized, and protected overseas by various means. This situation has created a global problem of overcapacity and low prices, not due to competition but due to governments impeding markets. All the while, the United States has had a higher import penetration and a lower tariff on steel than our competitors. A 1999 OECD report stated that the United States had an import penetration of 30 percent, compared with 16 percent for the EU and only seven percent for Japan. Whereas Brazil's average steel tariff is 14 percent, the U.S.'s average tariff is only one percent.

The United States imposed the safeguard only temporarily, and excluded imports from free trade partners and almost all steel from developing countries.

Improving Standards of Living Around the Globe

Keeping a forward momentum for trade requires facing the debate over labor and environmental standards. Both at home and in the developing world, labor and environmental groups tend to be against free trade. In the United States, unions argue that conducting commerce with countries with lower standards exploits workers in those countries and threatens jobs in our own. Environmental groups of all kinds argue that increased commerce risks eroding the environment particularly in countries where standards are lower than the U.S. standards. These groups span many causes, from preservation of forests, wildlife and endangered species, to the adequacy of environmental reviews of individual projects.

On the other hand, our trading partners, particularly in the developing world where standards lag those in the United States, were adamantly against the inclusion of labor or environmental standards in trade agreements, fearing that we would use these standards against them as protectionist measures to keep their goods and services out.

The Bush Administration, however, saw an opportunity to improve standards through trade. At the Summit of the Americas in Quebec in 2001, the President established that our trade policy would seek to improve conditions around the world.:"Our commitment to open trade must be matched by a strong commitment to protecting our environment and improving labor standards."

Indeed, no country has done more to help the developing world strengthen standards than the United States. The strategy was that "one size does not fit all," that each country would have different needs and should be dealt with accordingly. In general, however, the United States employed a three-part approach. First, the issue with our trading partners is often not the law on the books, but enforcement of those laws. Our FTAs require that countries effectively enforce their own labor and environmental laws. Second, understanding why laws are not enforced is key—often it is a resource question. To address this, the United States has pursued a cooperative approach with other U.S. government agencies, the international development banks, and the private sector to offer assistance and training where needed. Third, where there are gaps in laws, we can help countries improve their laws. For example, during negotiations for the Chile FTA, Chile repealed its Pinochet-era labor laws. Sidelining the issue of standards, or refusing to negotiate with countries that have lower standards than ours, does not improve the lives of people in the developing world. It is through engagement and targeted assistance that we can, and have begun, to make a difference.

Perhaps the Bush Administration's greatest trade-related accomplishment was its use of the WTO agreement on trade-related intellectual property rights (TRIPS) to provide access to affordable medicines for the vast populations in Africa suffering from HIV/AIDS. The difficulty of the problem lies in determining how the developed world could provide access to affordable medicines for those who need them most without undercutting the incentives for profit-driven companies to continue to produce these R&D-intensive innovations.

In August 2003, through the multilateral trading system of the WTO, countries and their private sectors came to a consensus on how to use the flexibilities under the TRIPS agreement to allow countries in a health crisis to access needed medicines. The agreement was carefully considered to focus on countries that could not produce the medicines themselves and could not afford the market price. This monumental step brought developed and developing interests together to solve world problems. Thanks to President Bush's trade agenda, the developing world has begun to feel the benefits of being part of the global system.

Competition for Liberalization

Not only did President Bush change the tenor of the debate at home, he changed the debate abroad from developed versus developing countries at odds with each other, to what Ambassador Zoellick rightly termed the "can-do" countries and the "won't-do" countries.

President Bush did this by turning trade into an economic good sought after by countries that wanted to open their doors to improvement of their societies and gain access to one of the largest markets in the world for their goods and services. Ambassador Zoellick calls this a "competition for liberalization" in which the United States would pursue market openings globally, regionally, and bilaterally. By simultaneously conducting negotiations on multiple fronts, the United States is able to leverage results, thus maximizing progress and quality of agreements. In his first year as the President's Chief Trade Negotiator, Ambassador Zoellick outlined U.S. ambitions on these levels. Globally, the United States planned to launch a new round of world trade negotiations in the WTO. Regionally, the United States wanted to realize the goal of hemispheric free trade through the Free Trade Area of the Americas (FTAA), an idea brewing in various forms since 1820. There were regional opportunities in Asia, Africa, and the Middle East. Bilaterally, the first priorities were to complete deals with Chile and Singapore. Much would be added to this initial list.

The United States coupled the opportunity of opening markets with a strong program of trade capacity building. Capacity building consists of assistance to help countries adjust, training to establish the necessary laws and standards, and education to allay fears that emanate from change. The United States also offers poorer countries advantages in trade access to the U.S. markets such as expanded preferential openings for over 140 developing economies worldwide.

Results

The President's trade strategy implemented globally, regionally, and bilaterally has yielded much.

Globally, the United States was instrumental in defining and launching a new round of global trade talks at the WTO in Doha, Qatar, in late 2001. This was the first global trade round focused on development and developing countries. That same year China and Taiwan completed accessions into the WTO, ending 15- and 9-year negotiations, respectively. The United States was not only central in successfully launching the global negotiations, but it has been the key leader in keeping the negotiations energized. This summer looks promising for making additional progress at the multilateral level, largely thanks to the extraordinary efforts of Ambassador Zoellick, traveling to 40 countries to encourage progress. The World Bank has estimated that a successful round of removing significant barriers to trade could lift 300 million people from poverty.

Regionally, the Administration has made progress in the FTAA and completed a trade agreement with Central America, and is negotiating with the Southern African Customs Union countries. Last year, the President announced a multi-stage initiative to help draw the countries of the Middle East further into the global economy through trade and investment opportunities, with the goal of creating a U.S.-Middle East Free Trade Agreement (MEFTA) by 2013. In the year since this announcement, significant progress has been made toward this goal. The President also recognized America's mutual interests with the Association of Southeast Asian Nations (ASEAN) by announcing the Enterprise for ASEAN Initiative (EAI) in October 2002. The ultimate goal of the EAI is a network of FTAs in the ASEAN region.

Bilaterally, the United States has brought into force agreements with Jordan, Chile, and Singapore. The Administration has launched negotiations with 19 nations,[34] concluding talks with 9 of them.[35] Taken together, U.S. goods exports to these countries—with which the U.S. has concluded negotiations or is in the process of negotiating an agreement—exceeded $66 billion in 2003, which would make these combined markets our third largest export market behind Canada and Japan. In our hemisphere, the FTAs undertaken in this Administration represent over two-thirds of the non-U.S. GDP of the entire hemisphere. These agreements serve as models of openness, and have expanded U.S. access to top goods, manufacturing, and services markets on continents around the globe.

Conclusion

President Bush has enacted an aggressive and extremely successful trade agenda. With the odds stacked against success just four years ago, this Administration has taken decisive action to reverse the tide. This is not to say that the agenda is finished or has been without difficulty. This Administration's trade policy redefined the debate by basing trade on values, forming our agreements as partnerships that improve societies, and using trade as an instrument to reduce poverty around the world. The Bush Administration has sought to find common ground with opposing domestic and international interests, and to meet obstacles with solutions rather than retreat. The Administration has carefully addressed the concerns of those fearing globalization and proven that their concerns are best met by opening markets. In speeches and negotiations, Ambassador Zoellick has consistently demonstrated that there are real benefits to real people, both at home and abroad to free and fair trade.

---

34. Panama, Bahrain, Southern African Customs Union, Colombia, Ecuador, Peru and Thailand.
35. CAFTA-5 (Nicaragua, Honduras, Guatemala, El Salvador, Costa Rica), Dominican Republic, Australia, Morocco, and Bahrain.

Indeed, the question is no longer whether or not we as a nation will be for or against free trade; rather the question lies in how we will continue to work through the increasingly complex agenda that results when nations trade in freedom with one another, when we form partnerships for prosperity and peace.

SOCIAL

POLICY

CHAPTER SIXTEEN

COMPASSIONATE CONSERVATISM: THE STATE OF THE FAITH-BASED INITIATIVE

MARVIN OLASKY

Dr. Marvin Olasky is editor in chief of WORLD MAGAZINE, *the nation's fourth largest weekly news magazine by circulation. He is also a professor of journalism at the University of Texas at Austin. Widely credited as the father of "compassionate conservatism," Dr. Olasky was candidate George W. Bush's chief domestic policy advisor in 2000, and is the author of several noted books, including* THE TRAGEDY OF AMERICAN COMPASSION.

Light streamed into the high-ceilinged offices on a surprisingly bright late February afternoon in 2001. One month into a new Administration, President Bush's Office of Faith-Based and Community Initiatives opened for business next door to the White House, and its staffers were padding around on clean carpets with new badges on chains around their necks.

The badge photos captured the deer-in-the-headlight look of driver's license art. That was appropriate since office head John DiIulio—who would be gone before the end of the year—and his fellow bucks sensed that vehicles from many directions were intent on running them down. Pundits on the Left were pressing Uncle Sam-I-am: Will you fund green eggs and ham? Is all this faith-based stuff a sham? Will some church get a new computer? Will that be OK with David Souter?

The Left's play-it-both-ways argument was clever: Churches are so strong that they'll take over government and so weak that government will take over them. Many liberals portrayed the initiative as a conspiracy to move big bucks from secular to Christian groups. Then *The New York Times* front-paged a new dimension with a scare story about Scientologists possibly tapping federal funds. Pat Robertson jumped at that bait: What if cultists want a grant? Should my taxes fund their rant?

Little of this argument was basic to the simple-enough purpose of President Bush's faith-based initiative: the attempt to end governmental bias against religious groups that provide social services and are not willing to become government look-alikes in the process. As Governor and during the 2000 campaign, George W. Bush had advocated creation of "a level playing field" for all groups. He proposed that organizations be evaluated not by their doctrines but by their effectiveness in helping the poor to move from welfare to work or to leave behind alcoholism, drug addiction, or revolving-door prison experience. The initiative was a key and crucial component of compassionate conservatism and certainly long overdue.

The initiative's initial goal was to audit federal agencies to find out which rules and practices hinder faith-based groups. Tax code changes were also part of the plan President Bush had promoted: He wanted expanded deductions for charitable contributions and incentives to create state income tax charity tax credits as well. This approach could have been expanded to include federal income tax credits for poverty-fighting. That way, theists would not be compelled to support Scientology and non-Christians would not be compelled to support Christian efforts, while all Americans would be better enabled to unleash their own creative energies in the charitable poverty-fighting manner for which their private talents were best suited.

Some tensions were inevitable, not only because of the disparate groups involved in social service provision but because the hoped-for outcomes of any Christian anti-poverty program are likely to be broader than governmental goals. For the government, success is the single mother getting off welfare or the ex-convict not committing more crimes, no matter how miserable the newly freed remain. By comparison, the Christian goal is holistic: Socioeconomic advance, yes, but that is likely to last only when the ex-con is convicted by Christ and the mother develops a relationship with the Heavenly Father.

But early in 2001 the task became even harder when John DiIulio, an academic Democrat appointed head of the Office of Faith-Based and Community Initiatives in an attempt to gain media and bipartisan support for President Bush's initiative, attacked the initiative's evangelical base of support. Mr. DiIulio even promised to refuse funding to groups engaging in religious teaching, a move that would have rendered the program moot. Mr. DiIulio, voicing a strong faith in social science, heavily emphasized a governmental grants program, overriding conservative complaints that it is as difficult to get a government grant-making program right as it is for a camel to fit through the eye of a needle.

His approach lost the initiative conservative support without gaining liberal backing, and Mr. DiIulio resigned after seven months on the job (and later attacked the Bush Administration as a haven for "Mayberry Machiavellis"). At the time it appeared that Mr. DiIulio had merely wasted a window of opportunity and that new opportunities would arise. Then came the events of September 11, 2001, and the attention of the Administration and the nation necessarily turned from domestic concerns to the international battle against terrorism.

2002

President Bush's legislative package to promote the faith-based initiative foundered in Congress, where the Senate had passed to Democratic hands. On December 12 he signed executive orders that changed regulations in a way that accomplished big chunks of what could have been achieved legislatively. The speech he gave that day promoting the faith-based initiative also showed where his heart is.

For example, President Bush presented an Iowa example of the "pattern of discrimination" against faith-based groups: "The Victory Center Rescue Mission was told to return grant money to the government because the mission's board of directors was not secular enough." The President argued that "government can and should support social services provided by religious people … faith-based programs should not be forced to change their character or compromise their mission."

The story behind Victory Center is significant. The homeless shelter in Clinton, Iowa, had applied for a Housing and Urban Development (HUD) grant to build transitional housing. Victory Center had noted on its application form that it was a religious organization designed "to provide both spiritual and professional help and counseling to the needy." But several months after the grant was received, a HUD inspector complained about the shelter's chapel service and Bible studies. HUD cancelled the grant and demanded that Victory Center secularize its board of directors and program or pay back $100,000 already spent.

President Bush, by going to bat for the shelter, was saying that a program which includes religious teaching is still eligible for overall support. A second statement from his speech bulwarks that point: "FEMA [the Federal Emergency Management Agency] will revise its policy on emergency relief so that religious non-profit groups can qualify for assistance after disasters like hurricanes and earthquakes." The White House offered up Seattle Hebrew Academy, a school that integrates religious teaching with all aspects of life, as the type of group that now will be treated just like other social service organizations that suffer damage.

2003

In late September 2003 the Bush Administration accelerated the regulatory revamping that will allow more religious groups to compete for government grants. The amount of money involved is potentially huge. The Department of Health and Human Services finalized regulations giving faith-based organizations access to nearly $20 billion in HHS grants related to welfare, substance abuse, mental health, and community services. New regulations within the Department of Housing and Urban Development will make faith-based groups eligible to compete for $8 billion in HUD grants.

The danger that faith-based applicants will have to leave their faith behind is still present, but Team Bush has taken into account many of the concerns voiced by evangelical organizations. The Administration specified that rescue missions "will be able to apply for HUD funds while maintaining their religious identity." A group will no longer have to form a secular non-profit arm to receive HUD money to build or repair a building for social service.

The Department of Labor stated that those who receive job-training vouchers will be able to use them not only at barber schools and truck-driving academies but at institutions that prepare them for employment at church or other religious organizations. The Department of Justice said that its programs for giving forfeited assets to community organizations will not discriminate against religious groups.

It remains to be seen whether organizations will be able not only to retain their religious identity but to express that religious identity in every aspect of their programs. At universities, dogmatic deans don't mind Christian professors who go to church on Sunday but minimize the importance of the Bible during the rest of the week. Similarly, social service secularists can live with Christian organizations that maintain a religious identity but marginalize it.

Still, it was good to see DiIulio successor Jim Towey sticking close to the compassionate conservatism script: Create a level playing field, treat all equally, do not discriminate against or in favor of those with religious faith. He defended the rights of Jewish groups to hire Jews or Christian groups to hire Christians by noting that the World Wildlife Fund hires people who share its beliefs: Otherwise-qualified religious groups should not be denied government grants if they "hire people that share their vision and mission."

The danger in all this, of course, is that the federal grants system still centralizes power in Washington. Tax credits and vouchers that decentralize funding by empowering direct givers and receivers of aid would be an enormous improvement, but Republicans are not immune to the pleasures of speaking softly while carrying a big pork barrel. Much remains to be done.

2004: Does George W. Bush Deserve Our Support?

"Join the club." That's what President-elect Bush said in December 2000, when I told him I was journalist first, Bush supporter second, and would probably be criticizing some of his decisions early and often. That's the way it has worked out, and it's easy to enumerate complaints. No vetoes of pork-barrel spending. No nationwide vouchers or tax credits to begin creating parental choice in education. Missed opportunities during the first year of the faith-based initiative. And so on.

Nevertheless, my plea to conservatives is this: Remember that we're better off now than we were four years ago (when Bill Clinton was in office), or than we will be a year from now if millions of us stay home in November and John Kerry takes over.

Much could be said about our war against terrorism, but I'll concentrate here on President Bush's continued commitment to compassionate conservatism. He keeps asking Congress to act "so people of faith can know that the law will never discriminate against them again." The faith-based initiative's emphasis on grants has been frustrating—tax credits and vouchers would work better both practically and politically—but as long as we have big government, the President is right to fight against red-lining religion.

I wish the naysayers could have heard President Bush's remarks at Union Bethel AME Church in New Orleans on January 15, 2004. There he laid out a bottom-up political philosophy that is the opposite of the top-down approach demanded by Democrats and relished by liberal Republicans. Sometimes reaching for words, he spoke of problems beyond the ability of government: "Intractable problems, problems that seem impossible to solve can be solved. … Miracles are possible in our society, one person at a time. But it requires a willingness to understand the origin of miracles. Miracles happen as a result of the love of the Almighty."

He stated well the problem for religious groups: "Government policy says, on the one hand, perhaps you can help; on the other hand, you can't practice your faith. Faith-based programs are only effective because they do practice faith. It's important for our government to understand that. Government oftentimes will say, yes, you can participate, but you've got to ... conform to our rules. The problem is, faith-based programs only conform to one set of rules, and it's bigger than government rules."

Why does President Bush persist in talking this way? Maybe because he's the first President since Grover Cleveland to have turned around his life as an adult in conjunction with a coming to biblical faith. He still speaks about this haltingly: "Addiction is the problem of a heart—of the heart. I know—I told this story before. I was a drinker. I quit drinking because I changed my heart. I guess I was a one-man faith-based program. I'm comfortable in pushing the change, because I know the nature of the work that is taking place."

The President can say, as he did in New Orleans, "Many of the problems that are facing our society are problems of the heart," because he knows his own heart and knows that he needed and needs God. That realization leaves him attuned to the goals of life-changing groups in a way unlikely for someone who knows only theoretically the importance of transformation. Despite the frustrations of the faith-based initiative in Washington, the President has continued to praise and spotlight the work of local faith-based volunteers wherever he goes.

Liberal journalists don't worry that President Bush is a hypocrite: They see that he's not one, and that makes some frantic. Yes, conservatives should not minimize the cost of veto-less government spending. (Billions.) We should not minimize the cost of not pushing for school vouchers. (Many miseducated kids.) Those costs are high, and we need to keep pushing for change—but does anyone see Democrats as the party of frugality?

And, what is it worth to have not only an adult in the Oval Office, but an adult who knows deep down that he was dying and was born again, an adult who hopes to help millions of others change their lives as well? Priceless.

CHAPTER SEVENTEEN

MUTED BUT MONUMENTAL: ACHIEVEMENTS OF BUSH'S FAITH-BASED INITIATIVE

DON WILLETT & SUSANNA DOKUPIL[36]

Don Willett currently serves as Deputy Texas Attorney General for Legal Counsel. He previously served in the presidential and gubernatorial administrations of George W. Bush, most recently as Deputy Assistant Attorney General for Legal Policy at the U.S. Department of Justice and Special Assistant to the President for Domestic Policy at the White House. The views expressed are his own, and not necessarily those of the Texas Attorney General.

Susanna Dokupil is an attorney and writer in Houston, Texas. She has a J.D. from Harvard Law School, where she was editor in chief of the JOURNAL OF LAW & PUBLIC POLICY, *and holds a M.A. in Church-State Studies from Baylor University. After law school, she clerked for The Honorable Jerry E. Smith, U.S. Court of Appeals for the Fifth Circuit,*

---

36.   The authors are deeply indebted to Stanley W. Carlson-Thies of the Center for Public Justice for his gracious and excellent input.

before joining a Texas law firm. Her work has appeared in THE WASH-INGTON TIMES, NATIONAL REVIEW ONLINE, THE AMERICAN ENTERPRISE, THE LOS ANGELES DAILY JOURNAL, *and* THE HOUSTON CHRONICLE.

A few years ago, the U.S. Department of Housing and Urban Development asked the archbishop of Los Angeles if it would be possible to rename the local St. Vincent de Paul Shelter, which received federal aid from HUD, the *Mr.* Vincent de Paul Shelter. As humor columnist Dave Barry says, I am not making this up. Reality has surpassed parody.

It is a great art, says the fable, to do the right thing at the right time. On July 22, 1999, then-Governor George W. Bush combined this lesson from Aesop with another one—do boldly what you do at all—and delivered his first major policy speech as a presidential candidate. The topic was deliberate, and also illuminating. This was no rote recitation of rhetorical retreads—low taxes, a strong military, results-driven education reforms, and so on—but the audacious pronouncement of compassionate conservatism and the unveiling of a signature, uniquely Bush priority: rallying America's armies of compassion to lift the lives of the least, the last and the lost.

Half a decade later, President Bush's vision for a federal government that is hospitable to the everyday heroics of faith-based charities is quietly but steadily packing on muscle. True, no sun-splashed, bill-signing ceremony has graced the verdant Rose Garden lawn, but the heart of the President's faith-based initiative has *never* been legislative. From day one, the major media have suffered acute tone-deafness when covering this agenda—viewing its success or failure as inextricably linked to legislation blocked in the Senate—but the muscle and sinew of the agenda has always been the heavy lifting of regulatory reinvention. And on this urgent front, when it comes to overhauling America's bureaucratic machinery to make it more benevolent and faith-friendly, President Bush can boast colossal success.

A Historical Snapshot of Good Samaritans Receiving Public Support

Cooperation between government and private charities is not a uniquely Republican invention, born of a crass desire to woo evangelical voters. Two months *before* Bush's July 1999 speech, Vice President Al Gore also expressed support (albeit qualified support) for increasing collaborations between government and faith-based service groups.[37] Indeed, church-state social service partnerships predate the modern political parties altogether and hearken all the way back to colonial times, when taxpayers subsidized clergy to care for the needy. President Bush today is simply directing his Administration to ratify a very old precept of American civic life: that fruitful collaboration between church and state need not lead to corruption.

Fast-forward to 2004 when governments at all levels routinely partner with community-serving religious groups. In fact, faith-based charities, especially in urban communities, form the backbone of the nongovernmental charitable sector. Some are religious-affiliated service providers who, while perhaps motivated by their faith, provide purely secular services in a purely secular fashion. But others are, as Stephen Monsma pointed out in his 1996 study, *When Sacred and Secular Mix*, downright faith-drenched—groups like church-run daycare centers that are not merely inspired by their faith to do good works but who infuse those government-funded works with heavy religious content (i.e., offering Bible-based instruction and worship, displaying religious icons and symbols, hiring only like-minded believers, praying before meals).

So it's true that many faith-based charities don't flinch from receiving public funds, but innumerable other faith-based

---

37. This modest flirtation was short-lived, though. The Democratic base went apoplectic over the speech—Gore's first and only major speech on religion during his eight years as vice president—and he never mentioned the idea again.

organizations (FBOs) "wouldn't touch the money with the proverbial ten-foot pole," as one religious leader said. The governing legal and regulatory landscape is too fraught with peril, they say, and that's indeed how many faith-based groups view it: no government shekels, no government shackles. Or, as some believe, "Once you get in bed with government, you'll never get a good night's sleep."

President Bush, though, knows firsthand the transforming power of religious devotion, and he is revolutionizing the tired script of sacred-secular skirmishes. He is cheering and harnessing the life-changing power of religious charities—the army ants of civil society—and integrating them into our social safety net, but without forcing them to conceal or compromise the distinctive qualities that explain their uncommon success.

Done Right, Funding the Civic Purposes of Sacred Places Is Entirely Constitutional

The principle animating the Bush philosophy is a simple one: neutrality, pluralism, evenhandedness, and nondiscrimination. If government contracts with non-profits to deliver social services, it should do so fairly, giving all groups an equal opportunity to participate. Historically, though, government officials have stiff-armed fairness and routinely tilted the playing field against religious groups. Why? Because they stubbornly misperceive the requirements of the First Amendment and have failed to bring their stale policies in line with recent U.S. Supreme Court rulings that have cooled church-state hostility by supplanting rigid separationism with what the Court has called the "guarantee of neutrality." The American people, for their part, want religion in the public square. A 2001 Public Agenda survey, *For Goodness' Sake: Why So Many Want Religion to Play a Greater Role in American Life*, revealed that about 70 percent of Americans believe the country would be better off if religion—any religion—had a greater influence on society.

In case after case, the modern Supreme Court has said that merely permitting religious groups equal access to public fora and resources on the same basis as secular organizations does not unconstitutionally advance religion. In response, Congress has repeatedly enacted programs that embrace this concept of equal treatment and honor the unique character and practices of religious charities.

The four iterations of the revolutionary Charitable Choice Law that Congress enacted four times during the Clinton presidency, beginning with the omnibus 1996 welfare reform overhaul, embody the clearest and most high-profile legislative embodiment of this neutrality theory.[38] Charitable Choice, which Governor Bush implemented aggressively in Texas, today applies to four federally funded programs—welfare, welfare-to-work, certain activities of community action programs, and drug-treatment programs—and advances four fundamental principles:

- Faith-based providers cannot be disqualified for being religious or "too religious;"
- Government cannot force participating FBOs to conceal or compromise their distinctive religious character;
- Clients' religious liberty must be honored; and
- No direct public money may support inherently religious activities like sectarian worship, religious instruction, or proselytizing.

Charitable Choice says religious groups can deliver federally funded social services and still control the "definition, development, practice, and expression" of their religious mission. It enshrines religious autonomy and assures FBOs, "You can

---

38.   Notably, President Clinton, when he signed these various Charitable Choice provisions into law, contemporaneously signed interpretive comments designed to subvert Charitable Choice and to retain barriers that obstruct faith-based groups who refuse to check their faith at the door.

partner with government to deliver valid public services without being forced to secularize, bleach, or surrender your unique religious character in the bargain."

Perhaps a bigger hurdle than constitutionality, though, is convincing some religious service groups to cooperate with government at all. Experience teaches that FBOs can negotiate government support and maintain their spiritual vitality, but many charities say, "Thanks, but no thanks." Public scrutiny follows public dollars, and sometimes Good Samaritans do grow dangerously dependent on public support. Each organization must decide for itself whether government strings create too tight a noose or sap groups of their spiritual energy, and some groups will rightly decide that government collaboration is not for them.

President Bush wants to end the secularizing drift of federal programs and has implemented a can-do regime in ten agencies to meet his goals within the parameters of the Constitution. Since he took office in January 2001, his team has worked quietly, and ingeniously, to bulldoze barriers that thwart successful partnerships with groups that tackle—and conquer—our most intractable social problems. In addition, the U.S. Department of Justice has established a special counsel for religious discrimination within the Civil Rights Division to enforce aggressive federal laws against religious discrimination. Together, this double-barreled approach has fostered an atmosphere of pluralism—a welcome mat extended to "Methodists or Muslims or Mormons, or good people of no faith at all," as the President puts it—and ushered in a new era of nondiscrimination that is scraping the residue of unabashed discrimination from America's legal and regulatory scene.

The White House Office of Faith-Based and Community Initiatives and the Ten Related Cabinet Centers

On January 29, 2001, in his first presidential executive order, President Bush created the White House Office of Faith-Based and Community Initiatives (OFBCI). This move swiftly fulfilled his campaign promise to launch a specific White House office to push the agenda aggressively. President Bush has dubbed the office "the engine that drives the Administration's goal of reorienting federal social policy across the board."

Executive Order 13199 created the OFBCI and explained the overall goal:

> Section 1. Policy. Faith-based and other community organizations are indispensable in meeting the needs of poor Americans and distressed neighborhoods. Government cannot be replaced by such organizations, but it can and should welcome them as partners. The paramount goal is compassionate results, and private and charitable community groups, including religious ones, should have the fullest opportunity permitted by law to compete on a level playing field, so long as they achieve valid public purposes, such as curbing crime, conquering addiction, strengthening families and neighborhoods, and overcoming poverty. This delivery of social services must be results oriented and should value the bedrock principles of pluralism, non-discrimination, evenhandedness, and neutrality.

The OFBCI facilitates the participation of FBOs in government programs; coordinates with the agencies to implement policy; and educates state and local governments and the public about opportunities to involve faith-based and grassroots initiatives in the provision of social services through successful programs.

President Bush also signed Executive Order 13198 that day, establishing Centers for Faith-Based and Community Initiatives in the five key cabinet departments most involved in domestic social policy and humanitarian aid: the Departments of Justice, Education, Labor, Health and Human Services, and Housing and Urban Development. The President believed that it was vital to have a high-ranking and hard-charging presence within key cabinet agencies that could drive a dynamic intradepartmental reform agenda. He has since added centers in the Department of Agriculture, the United States Agency for International Development, the Department of Commerce, the Small Business Administration, and the Department of Veterans Affairs.

EO 13198 placed a heavy emphasis on action and required each center to conduct:

> A department-wide audit to identify all existing barriers to the participation of faith-based and other community organizations in the delivery of social services by the department, including but not limited to regulations, rules, orders, procurement, and other internal policies and practices, and outreach activities that either facially discriminate against or otherwise discourage or disadvantage the participation of faith-based and other community organizations in Federal programs.

Identifying Obstacles that Impede Good Works

On August 19, 2001, a blockbuster OFBCI report, titled *Unlevel Playing Field: Barriers to Faith-Based and Community Organizations' Participation in Federal Social Service Programs*, revealed that government often discriminated against religious charities, in ways big and small, overt and hidden, and intentional and inadvertent. Additionally, it highlighted the shortcomings of specific federal programs, particularly the abject failure of HHS to implement the 1996 Charitable Choice Law and promote compliance with the new requirements.

Unlevel Playing Field also unearthed a large disparity between the organizations supported by federal programs and the organizations that actually provide the bulk of everyday services to everyday Americans in need, particularly the lean, shoestring budget organizations that supply the lion's share of good works in distressed inner cities. In other words, faith-based organizations help thousands of people every day—often with spectacular results—but receive only a small fraction of federal funding.

Why the asymmetry? Because the federal government is decidedly "inhospitable to their involvement" and succumbs to "an
overriding perception by Federal officials that close collaboration
with religious organizations is legally suspect." Still other FBOs
opt against participating in government programs because they
don't want to become too dependent on government and fear
that the creep of secularization might accompany public money
or because their theological beliefs caution them to remain
independent. Others simply don't know how to get involved.
According to one leading researcher, more than 50 percent of
clergymen and 60 percent of black and Latino clergymen want to
participate in government partnerships once they become
informed about it. Yet, less than one in ten have even heard of it.
So, although in some cases, groups fear the strings attached to
government dollars, in others, the lack of information poses the
only obstacle.

   Unlevel Playing Field described numerous barriers to the participation of grassroots faith-based charities in government
programs in four key categories: unequal treatment, hiring
restrictions, noncompliance with current law, and administrative
burdens. All of these barriers produced measurably bad consequences for neighborhoods where FBOs are the primary social
service providers.

Unequal Treatment

   Most importantly, the report discovered a widespread and
hard-wired government suspicion of working with faith-based
groups, likely due to erroneous assumptions that the Establishment Clause mandates all-out secularism and disqualifies
religious providers. In New York, for example, a government
official told the Metropolitan Council on Jewish Poverty—a
council of secular organizations—that it could not apply for a
grant because of the word "Jewish" in its name.

This hostility in turn fuels the skittishness of faith-based charities, which opt for pre-emptive capitulation over proactive collaboration. Moreover, this anti-faith-based bias prompts federal administrators to view applicants on a secularization continuum—those that are "too religious" cannot get funding, but those that are "sufficiently secular" can. The Supreme Court plurality said in Mitchell v. Helms, however, that the religious character of an organization does not matter—all that matters is its ability to further the state's legitimate purpose.

Furthermore, federal programs imposed undue restrictions on the FBOs that did participate. Some program administrators, though not required to do so, compelled providers to cover all religious signs and symbols. The city of Chicago, for instance, erroneously told childcare providers in the Head Start program that they could not participate without removing religious symbols from their facilities. These regulations came solely from the bureaucrats; they furthered no specific legal mandate.

Hiring Restrictions

Many faith-based groups want to hire employees with a strong faith commitment. Naturally, personnel play a vital role in a program's success or failure, and many FBOs insist on the freedom to hire those who share their deepest beliefs and ideals. Several federal laws prohibit service providers from discriminating against beneficiaries, but employment is fundamentally different. Generally speaking, religious groups can use religious criteria in hiring. Title VII of the Civil Rights Act of 1964, which protects citizens from various types of employment discrimination, also safeguards the hiring rights of religious entities, making it clear that they can require staff to live out the organization's beliefs and mission. The Supreme Court—understanding the difference between the Salvation Army and 7-Eleven—unanimously upheld that protection in 1987. Yet, even though none of the agencies surveyed in the 2001 audit had across-the-board limitations on hiring in their enabling statutes passed by Congress, some implemented such restrictions anyway.

Noncompliance with Current Law

The federal government had done little or nothing to help state and local agencies comply with the four Charitable Choice Laws already passed by Congress. So, failure to implement laws already on the books to help FBOs compete on an equal basis with secular groups was itself a major obstacle.

HHS, for example, provided almost no guidance to the states about the applicability of Charitable Choice Law to its programs. For Temporary Assistance to Needy Families Funds, it did not oversee states to ensure that they were complying with the law and leveling the playing field for faith-based providers. For the Community Service Block Grants, the guidance provided omitted key provisions, like the right of religious organizations to hire people of their own faith and the prohibition on using federal support for inherently religious activities.

This demonstrated failure to urge compliance with governing law explains the urgency of a key Bush Administration priority: to educate and press state governments that receive the bulk of funding under Charitable Choice-covered programs to honor its myriad religious liberty protections for FBOs and clients. It is not enough to pass statutes that gather dust on a shelf; we are a nation of laws, and we must strictly follow those laws. In addition, given the rather limited programmatic scope of Charitable Choice—covering only four federal programs—President Bush also favors expanding these faith-friendly reforms across the board to govern virtually all domestic social service spending.

Administrative Burdens

Applying for federal funding involves an incalculable amount of paperwork. Grant applications, then, are difficult for those unfamiliar with the Byzantine process. Even experienced organizations with larger budgets may still feel obligated to hire a professional grant consultant. Plus, proving compliance with program regulations and fiscal accountability is such an enormous burden that it deters many smaller groups from trying.

Unlevel Playing Field concluded that the federal government had (1) discriminated against faith-based groups and (2) discouraged groups offering successful community programs from even applying for government funds. If community-serving groups have a successful track record in rescuing people from addiction, conquering poverty, combating crime, and so on, then government must take note and cheer and welcome these civic entrepreneurs as partners. In light of the barriers identified in the audits, the Bush Administration has taken bold steps to tear down these walls so that faith-based charities wishing to cooperate with government may compete for grants on an even footing with secular groups. These changes have made a measurable impact on FBOs across the country and on the communities they serve.

Enacting Faith-Friendly Reforms to Level the Playing Field

By definition, fostering equal treatment is essential to fair play among faith-based and secular organizations. To that end, President Bush, fed up with partisan opposition in Congress to the legislative component of his faith-based initiative, issued in December 2002 Executive Order 13279, which extended Charitable Choice-like protections for religious groups to all other federally funded social service programs.

Executive Order Mandating Evenhandedness and Nondiscrimination

Executive Order 13279 requires equal treatment of faith-based and community organizations that compete for federal financial assistance to provide social services. This landmark executive order ended discrimination against FBOs in federal social welfare programs. Moreover, it increased protections for the FBOs such that they would not have to secularize their identity and religious mission to partner with government.

EO 13279 addresses several of the core concerns that impede FBOs' participation in the federal grants process. It protects FBOs from having to abandon their religious character, allowing them to engage in inherently religious activity, so long as they don't underwrite those activities with government money. They may still share their faith with participants by inviting them to voluntarily attend religious services at another place or time. For example, a church receiving direct government aid for a homeless shelter may invite those who come to the shelter to attend a Bible study at a different time, but the church must clarify that attendance is purely optional.

Furthermore, to avoid "impairing [the] independence, autonomy, expression, or religious character" of the organizations, EO 13279 allows them to leave religious symbols, art, or icons in the space where they provide federally funded services. A faith-based organization receiving federal funds may also "retain religious terms in the organization's name, select its board members on a religious basis, and include religious references in its organization's mission statements."[39]

Moreover, this executive order goes well beyond Charitable Choice, which applied only to a few programs. EO 13279 applies to every social-service program using federal funds, including programs that state or local governments administer. However,

---

39. Some grant programs, however, have specific requirements for board composition that depart from this general rule.

because the EO articulates principles for implementing existing law rather than creating new law, its reach, though far broader than Charitable Choice, is not as deep. Congress itself must act to remove the impediments that are statutorily embedded in some federal laws.

Responses in the Cabinet Departments

Usually, hell hath no fury like a bureaucrat unturfed, but cabinet agencies have achieved extraordinary success in overhauling the rules that govern their social service programs. The Departments of Education and Justice have drafted robust equal treatment regulations applicable to all of their programs. HUD has eliminated regulations that completely excluded religious organizations from eight programs.

The move toward equal treatment has helped immeasurably. The Seattle Hebrew Academy in Seattle, Washington, was able to get a disaster relief grant from the Federal Emergency Management Agency to repair earthquake damage. Touro Synagogue in Newport, Rhode Island, and the Old North Church in Boston, Massachusetts (noted for its role in Paul Revere's famous ride), were able to receive "Save America's Treasures" grants as a result of the new nondiscriminatory policies. The Jewish Renaissance Medical Center in Perth Amboy, New Jersey, is using a $1.7 million grant from HHS to quadruple the number of patients it serves, from 5,000 to 20,000.

Safeguarding FBOs' Fundamental Civil Right to Hire Staff Who Share Their Beliefs

For a generation, Title VII of the Civil Rights Act of 1964 has protected the right of religious groups to hire people who share their faith. And the U.S. Supreme Court upheld that fundamental right 9-0 in a 1987 ruling. Although federally funded FBOs cannot discriminate among whom they serve, President Bush firmly believes that religious charities must maintain their established right to hire like-minded and like-hearted believers.

While numerous FBOs hire people of other beliefs, many other ministry leaders believe their staff should share a common religious mission and vision. At the Bowery Mission, a successful city-funded program in Manhattan for homeless addicts, virtually all staffers are deeply religious. The mission's president, Ed Morgan, notes that "The clients can sense our staff really cares, because they don't report just to me. They report to a higher power." For groups like this, Title VII carves out an exception from the general prohibition on religious discrimination and says religious groups can staff using religious criteria. While religious staffing freedom is the rule, criticism erupts when a FBO receives government support. Unfortunately, too many inside and outside of Congress think that this cornerstone religious freedom—the right of religious groups to staff on a religious basis—suddenly becomes immoral and intolerable bigotry once those Good Samaritans partner with government to serve the needy.

The President believes that FBOs must be able to take faith into account in staffing just as secular non-profits can consider ideology. He wants to safeguard that fundamental protection—a core civil right for religious groups—when FBOs receive federal support. As the White House statement on religious hiring rights explains: "President Bush believes that—regardless of whether government funds are involved—faith-based groups should retain their fundamental civil rights, including their ability, protected under Title VII, to take their faith into account when they make employment decisions." Many people helped by church-based programs need the influence of religiously rooted values, and some non-profit leaders argue that if the group's staff doesn't embody those ideals, the program's efficacy is compromised. Just as Planned Parenthood may consider applicants' views on abortion and decline to staff its clinics with pro-life Catholics, a faith-based non-profit should be able to consider whether an applicant lives out the group's values. Quoting again from the White House statement, "That is why President Bush believes the right of all organizations—including faith-based groups—to keep their identity when they receive federal funds should be a straightforward proposition." The President's policy advances equal treatment for all and discrimination against none.

Some laws governing federally funded social service programs protect a FBO's right to consider religion in hiring, but others do not. Charitable Choice, for example, explicitly protects the religious hiring rights of FBOs. But other programs, like the Department of Labor's Workforce Investment Act, have statutory language that specifically mentions nondiscrimination in employment. For programs with these sorts of provisions, FBOs could forfeit their well-established hiring rights. Plus, some state and local governments have additional laws that prohibit discrimination on the basis of religion without providing exceptions for religious organizations receiving state funds. Because state and local entities often administer the federal funding programs, they often impose these non-federal laws on entities with which they contract, even if the underlying federal law retains the hiring protection for FBOs.

Executive Order 13279 from December 2002 removes one monumental barrier to hiring freedom. Section 4 of EO 13279 amends a previous executive order requiring all government contractors to sign nondiscrimination provisions and agree to hire on the basis of affirmative action. The President's directive preserves FBOs' longstanding Title VII right to consider religious beliefs when making staffing decisions, even when they are delivering federally funded social services. The Department of Labor passed its own regulation honoring this exemption last September.[40]

---

40.   This executive order is significant, but its reach is limited only to those programs whose underlying statutes do not affirmatively prevent FBOs from hiring on a religious basis. To eradicate any statutorily embedded restrictions, Congress must act separately.

The Department of Veterans' Affairs has also proposed a rule creating such a hiring exemption for FBOs. As more agencies adopt such exemptions, faith-based charities will have more freedom to participate in partnerships with government without having to hire staff who reject their religious mission, which in the FBOs' view, expunges an element of faith from their caregiving.

Honoring the constitutionally protected right of FBOs to safeguard their religious identity through staffing merely sets them on an equal footing with any ideologically motivated secular employer. And it represents another way that the President is eliminating special burdens against FBOs that do not hamper secular organizations.

Ensuring Compliance with Existing Charitable Choice Laws

Because state and local governments have often failed to follow existing law, HHS has promulgated strong Charitable Choice regulations. Now, when these governments receive formula grants, they understand they cannot exclude a group because they suspect it is "too religious." A better understanding of the conditions under which the federal government provides funds (and which apply to state funding commingled with federal funding) will help alleviate unnecessary and illegal discrimination against faith-based applicants.

HHS has taken impressive steps to bring its practices in line with Charitable Choice. Last September, it implemented three rules on the same day. One rule ensured that FBOs could participate in the Community Services Block Grant program on an equal footing with secular organizations, including protections for the religious character of faith-based groups approved by Congress in 1998. Another clarified the rights of beneficiaries under Temporary Assistance to Needy Families, the rights and obligations of organizations providing the services, and the role of state and local governments. The third applied Charitable

Choice directives to grants available through the Substance Abuse and Mental Health Administration. Putting the landmark Charitable Choice reforms into practice will further facilitate fruitful partnerships with FBOs and improve the lives of countless Americans in need.

Helping Prospective Applicants Navigate the Grant-Making Maze

To help with the complex grant application process, individual agencies have set up workshops, posted information on their Web sites, and offered informational assistance so that smaller groups can traverse the paperwork labyrinth.

Moreover, the White House OFBCI has produced several informational booklets to help faith-based and community organizations tap into the federal dollars for which they might be eligible. It has released a grants catalogue and has created two guidance booklets: *Guidance to Faith-Based and Community Organizations on Partnering with the Federal Government and Protecting the Civil Rights* and *Religious Liberty of Faith-Based Organizations: Why Religious Hiring Rights Must Be Preserved.*

In addition, OFBCI has sponsored a number of day-long regional conferences and training sessions around the country to educate interested organizations about the grants process. Conferences in twelve cities over the past two years—including the first-ever White House National Conference on Faith-Based and Community Initiatives on June 1, 2004—have attracted about 15,000 attendees.

These efforts offer valuable information that helps formerly crowded-out FBOs decipher how to apply for government funding and evaluate the pros and cons of getting involved. Application assistance further levels the playing field by reducing the natural advantage that larger, experienced organizations have in the grants process. Making the procedures more layperson-friendly and accessible helps ensure that the groups with the best programs, not just those with the best grant-writers, get the opportunity to help.

Leadership from the OMB

Early in the Bush Administration, the Office of Management and Budget (OMB) released The President's Management Agenda, announcing the President's "strategy for improving the management and performance of the federal government." The Agenda outlines six broad reform initiatives, including notably a "faith-based and community initiative," a specific reform effort targeting the ten cabinet departments that have Centers for Faith-Based and Community Initiatives.

OMB—the 800-pound gorilla in terms of enacting the President's key management priorities—ensures that the agencies encourage faith-based participation by incorporating faith-based and community initiatives into its performance management system. OMB aims to improve overall efficiency in the Administration by using management scorecards with green, orange, and red traffic lights to rate performance improvement among government departments and programs. By incorporating faith-based and community initiatives into the traffic lights scheme, departments that do not improve accessibility of grant information or maintain rules that unnecessarily secularize programs will receive OMB scorecards awash in red or orange lights rather than green ones. OMB's incentive structure helps the various agencies make faith-based and community initiatives an omnipresent part of their daily concerns.

The General Results

Since the first Charitable Choice legislation in 1996, but particularly since the Bush-led administrative reforms began taking hold, FBOs have increasingly chosen to contract with the government. Amy Sherman and John Green studied faith-based organizations involved in programs governed by Charitable Choice in their 2002 study, *Fruitful Collaborations: A Study of Government-Funded Faith-Based Collaborations in 15 States*. This study surveyed FBOs with government contracts governed by Charitable Choice rules. They found that 70 percent of organizations surveyed highly valued laws that allowed retention of religious character. And clients have liked the services faith-based organizations provide—only 9 percent reported anyone leaving the program for an alternative.

According to Sherman and Green, the most likely collaborators are African-American evangelical protestant non-profits (not congregations) operating with a $1 million to $5 million budget and a membership of 100 to 500. Many are relatively new to the contracting process: over 56 percent of contractors surveyed began participating after the passage of the first Charitable Choice legislation in 1996. About 20 percent of the FBOs and over half of the congregations had received their first contract ever.

Faith-based providers have used government funds both to expand existing programs and to develop new ones. Sherman and Green report that 87 percent of faith-based organizations surveyed said that government funds enabled them to serve new clients. Seventy-six percent reported expanding an existing program, and 65 percent added a new service to an existing program.

Significantly, Sherman and Green found, 90 percent of organizations surveyed disagreed with statements suggesting that partnership with government had undermined their religious mission, decreased their ability to raise funds from private sources, or threatened their ability to criticize the government. Of the contractors surveyed, most fully express their faith within the parameters of the law by inviting clients to participate in religious activities outside of the program.

Another remarkable finding: 93 percent of faith-based organizations surveyed were happy with their partnership with government, and 92 percent would do it again. On the whole, they found that faith-based organizations diligently observed the laws while maintaining their religious character. This is precisely what President Bush has tried to support—the simultaneous expression of service through religious community-serving organizations without forcing clients to participate in religious exercise.

Sherman and Green's findings mark the slow change that began before President Bush's executive order mandating equal treatment for faith-based providers. Their data still show, however, that when government protects the unique character of FBOs, such groups are ready, willing, and able to enter successful partnerships with government. More importantly, the study's findings demonstrate that, over time, President Bush's muscular reforms will markedly increase the number of these fruitful collaborations.

HHS and HUD exemplify the trend of increased faith-based participation. From fiscal year 2002 to 2003, the number of awards from HHS to faith-based groups grew from 483 to 680, and the amount increased from $477 million to $568 million. At HUD, grants increased from 659 to 765. During this period the awards to first-time faith-based grantees soared; the number of HHS grants increased from 86 to 129, and HUD hiked the amount of first-time funding from $56 million to $113 million.

Eliminating the barriers to participation has augmented the role of faith-based providers in local communities, welcoming them as indispensable allies in our efforts to lift people's lives and have an equal opportunity to cooperate with the government to serve those in need. President Bush's efforts have made tremendous strides toward eliminating unnecessary barriers. As a result, the hungry, the homeless, the elderly, the addicted, the ex-offender, and countless others now have the hope of a richer array of providers to boost their life chances.

Complementary Faith-Friendly Activities

In 2002, President Bush pushed Congress to appropriate money for the Compassion Capital Fund (CCF), a $30 million appropriation to HHS. The Compassion Capital Fund targets grassroots organizations that serve families in poverty, prisoners reentering the community, the homeless, and at-risk youth.

The CCF supports four activities: (1) technical assistance to intermediary organizations; (2) the Compassion Capital National Resource Center; (3) research regarding best practices and services of community organizations; and (4) field-initiated research grants. The technical assistance sponsors intermediary organizations that can help smaller organizations operate efficiently, access funding, and replicate successful programs. The National Resource Center is designed to work directly both with intermediary organizations and with faith-based and community groups to provide information about best practices and to offer technical assistance. CCF will further sponsor research into best practices and the most effective provision of services. The field grants support short-term research into promising approaches to homelessness; hunger; helping prisoners, addicts, and at-risk children; and transitioning from welfare to work. During its first year, the CCF awarded $24 million to 21 intermediaries, and last year it awarded over $30 million to 81 intermediaries.

One of these intermediaries, Father Joe's Villages, enabled Food Finders Inc. of Long Beach, California, to get $40,000 to purchase a refrigerated truck. With that truck, Food Finders expects to deliver an addition 2 million pounds of food, which is enough to provide three meals per day for nearly 4,000 people. Lending a hand to smaller organizations even at miniscule dollar amounts (at least on the government-spending scale) can make a huge difference in the lives of those the organization serves.

In the 2003 State of the Union Address the President proposed two additional initiatives: Access to Recovery, a voucher program for drug treatment, and the Mentoring Children of

Prisoners Initiative. For Access to Recovery, Congress has appropriated $100 million to HHS for a program in 15 states, and, for the first time, recipients can use the funding at the program of their choice, including a faith-saturated program if they wish. Under the mentoring initiative, $50 million will be available through HHS this year to serve the almost 2 million innocent victims of crime whom the President believes have a special claim on our conscience and on our resources.

In his 2005 budget, President Bush proposed a four-year, $300 million Prisoner Reentry Initiative. The program is designed to curb recidivism and to reduce the societal costs of incarceration.

The President has also advanced his faith-based initiative at the state and local level, a critical priority given the front-and-center role of nonfederal actors in implementing modern federal social service programs. New laws and regulations at the federal level are little more than ink blots if the frontline officials who implement the program flout the reforms and stick with the tired old ways of doing business. A bipartisan group of 21 governors have liaisons or offices focused on faith-based and community initiatives. The United States Conference of Mayors has opened a faith-based office, and over 100 mayors now have offices or liaisons for FBOs and other community-serving grassroots groups.

The Justice Department's Special Counsel for Religious Discrimination

President Bush's commitment to eliminating discrimination against religious groups extends beyond the government contract arena. The Civil Rights Division in the Department of Justice has established a special counsel for religious discrimination. Before President Bush took office, no one at the Justice Department had religious liberty as their sole focus. The special counsel's office coordinates DOJ's efforts to enforce federal laws against discrimination on the basis of religion in employment, education, housing, public accommodations, and access to public facilities. It also pursues suits under the Religious Land Use and Institutionalized Persons Act of 2000 (RLUIPA), which outlaws unduly burdensome zoning restrictions and gives prisoners certain rights to religious exercise.

Since the creation of the special counsel's office, its efforts have protected Muslims' rights to wear the hijab or kuffi as a government employee, a public school student, or a prisoner. It has defended the rights of seniors to use the city's senior center for religious activities they initiated and organized. It has also contended that religious-oriented student activities should have equal rights to disseminate information. It has argued that the city of San Diego wrongfully invalidated the Boy Scouts' lease of a city aquatic center (in whose construction the Boy Scouts had invested) on the grounds that the Boy Scouts is a religious organization.

The office has investigated at least 15 claims of unfair zoning regulations under RLUIPA. Most significantly, the Civil Rights Division recently won a case in the Eleventh Circuit that upheld the constitutionality of RLUIPA. At issue was two Orthodox Jewish congregations' right to use commercial space they had rented for worship services. The Eleventh Circuit held that RLUIPA mandates equal treatment for religious and nonreligious assemblies.

The religious liberties work at DOJ complements President Bush's faith-based initiative. Both seek to eradicate discrimination against religious organizations and individuals. Both promote the prevailing constitutional understanding that government should be neutral towards matters of religion. And both foster a superior environment for people of faith to put their beliefs into practice (within constitutional parameters).

Conclusion

The Washington press corps suffers from a fatal blind spot when covering the progress of the President's faith-based initiative. To the D.C.–centric, those who revel in full-contact, political blood sport and fixate on which way one's arrow points from week to week, legislation is she who must be obeyed and the President's agenda is all about enacting legislation to send money to church-related charities. The media and opponents of the initiative embrace a flawed syllogism: The initiative is legislative; the legislation has stalled; the initiative has stalled.

Wrong. From day one, the heart of the Bush faith-based initiative has been a government-wide administrative reform agenda—a determination to flex political muscle to uproot deeply entrenched biases. True, zero-sum partisan politics have tragically prevented President Bush from passing key legislative changes, even changes that enjoy wide, bipartisan support— like tax reforms that, as studies confirm, will spur an outpouring of private charitable giving to America's neighborhood helpers and healers. But, even though Capitol Hill squabbles consume the media oxygen, the real meat and potatoes of President Bush's initiative is the unglamorous but essential work of conforming day-to-day administrative policies and practices to equal treatment principles. And on that front, the Bush vision of inventive, compassionate government is taking shape, from South Central Los Angeles to North Central Philadelphia.

President Bush has done much to elevate the civic importance of America's Good Samaritans. As a direct result of President Bush's executive orders, ten executive agencies are revising their policies—policies that govern the disbursement of billions of dollars—to eliminate disparate treatment for neighborhood-based religious charities. And now that the federal underbrush is mostly cleared, the White House is turning attention to an even stiffer challenge: winning similar reforms from state and local governments that administer federal social service funds.

The real beneficiaries of President Bush's policies, though, are not the FBOs, but those whose lives are being transformed by good will and good works. People like Veronica, a refugee from Liberia who, thanks to the Catholic Social Agency in Allentown, Pennsylvania, has just completed her training to be a nursing assistant. People like Elijah Anyieth, who fled his war-torn village in rural Sudan, then was rescued by the Commonwealth Catholic Charities. With the program's help, Elijah graduated from high school with honors last year. People like Brad Lassiter, a prisoner and drug addict who turned his life around with the help of Gospel Rescue Mission.

Every day and in every corner of America, community-serving ministries are conquering every single problem afflicting our nation. And President Bush, by ending government discrimination against religious charities, has extended their reach and amplified their potency. Taking the side of America's quiet heroes who are helping their needy neighbors—this is the centerpiece of compassionate conservatism. And those fortunate enough to hear the President speak about this agenda and his belief that we must seek, not shun, divine help when tackling America's social ills are witnessing Bush unvarnished and impassioned, barely able to stay in his boots. He unflinchingly believes faith is a civic virtue, not a civic virus.

President Bush merits much acclaim for his Reaganesque grit and tenacity in championing this hopeful, optimistic vision to unleash the best of America and to fortify our country's promise as a "shining city on a hill."

CHAPTER EIGHTEEN

THE FEMINISM OF
GEORGE W. BUSH

CANDICE E. JACKSON

Candice Jackson is an attorney living in the Los Angeles area. She is the former litigation counsel for Judicial Watch, Inc., a non-profit legal organization. Her articles have appeared in THE INDEPENDENT REVIEW, REASON magazine, and THE FREEMAN. She is currently working on a book on President Clinton's abuse of power with respect to his treatment of women.

Despite President Bush's best efforts in the 2000 campaign to style himself as a pro-woman candidate, feminist groups systematically decried him as the worst thing to happen to women since the defeat of the ERA during the Reagan years. With the now-familiar gender gap looming yet again in the 2004 election season, the Bush team is no doubt worried about positioning Bush as a female-friendly President.

Bush garnered praise from the mainstream media, and even grudging kudos from liberal feminists, by appointing four women to his Cabinet: Condoleezza Rice, as National Security Adviser; Elaine Chao, as Secretary of Labor; Gale Norton, as Secretary of the Interior; and Ann Veneman, as Secretary of Agriculture. Chao was the first ever Asian American woman to serve in the Cabinet. Bush also tapped Karen Hughes to be White House Counsel, making her the first woman ever to hold that post, and asked Christine Todd Whitman to head up the EPA.

Yet supposed women's rights organizations quickly wrote off Bush's appointments of women to powerful Administration positions. Radio talk show host Laura Flanders recently authored a book entitled *Bushwomen*, profiling six of Bush's female appointees. According to Ms. Flanders, "The Bushwomen are the media-friendly face of an extremist Administration, one that's lawyered by anti-civil rights, anti-government fanatics, and fuelled by the theocratic Right."[41] The women active in the Bush Administration "act as a cover for both a presidency that seeks to dominate the world, and religious autocrats who would like to rewrite the nation's laws according to their interpretation of the will of some god." [42] In other words, any women who balk at modern notions of "civil rights" that amount to burdensome regulations, think of government as a backdrop rather than as a savior for society, and believe in a power greater than ourselves, are really pawns in some sort of World Domination game set up by aging white males. Paranormal belief in the vast Right-Wing Conspiracy lives on.

It cannot be denied that a gender gap has plagued the GOP for the past quarter of a century, ranging from 4 to 11 percent in Presidential elections since 1980.[43] And it's not worth trying to argue that President Bush promotes any of the policies deemed

41.   Laura Flanders, *Bushwomen: Tales of a Cynical Species* (New York: Verso, 2004), 28.
42.   Ibid.
43.   For example, Darlisa Crawford, "Women Voters in the 2004 Election," *Election Focus 2004*, Iss. 1, No. 8, (U.S. Department of State, April 14, 2004) , http://usinfo.state.gov/dhr/democracy/ elections/elections_newsletter.html.

by the National Organization for Women (NOW) to be "women's issues" in need of federal government attention. But can it still be argued that more than Bill Clinton, more than John Kerry, and more than any President in recent history, George W. Bush deserves the women's vote? I believe such a case can and should be made—not because I personally support all of President Bush's policy initiatives, nor because I think leftist feminists can be convinced to support Bush, but because I believe that George W. Bush exemplifies, through substance rather than symbolism, a viable, respectable, meaningful view of women's rights.

Feminism as a Call for Freedom

The entire debate over so-called women's issues needs to be redefined so that women on the Right (and libertarian women like me who hover "above" the Left-Right dichotomy) can advocate policy positions consonant with their political philosophy without being denigrated as traitors to their gender. Similarly, the debate needs redefinition so that whether a leader is regarded as "women friendly" no longer turns on support for abortion services, affirmative action in employment and education, and federal intervention in routine criminal violence policy. In short, the 1970s-era myth must be exploded: leftist political positions do not represent the only path to genuine feminism.

I am no stalwart defender of the Republican Party; nor am I a member of the Christian Right. However, the point of this essay is that to a libertarian like myself, President Bush is a "woman's candidate" because he honors women as individuals, praising and supporting them for their involvement in activities deemed venerable by his own ideological standards. For example, Bush touts the benefits and importance of small business to the national economy, and doles out recognition to women who succeed in that arena. In every speech where Bush thanks our military forces for their sacrifices he unfailingly praises our "men and women" in uniform.

Rather than singling out women as a group defined by mere biology or physiology to be politically exploited, Bush appreciates women on par with any men who take actions which Bush believes warrant praise. George W. Bush truly views women as equal to men in every respect, and that view should be at the core of any valuable version of women's rights. He even congratulated the Detroit Shock at the Rose Garden on winning the 2003 WNBA championship as heartily as if he had been slapping Pistons players on the back, speaking highly of the "talent and the flare and the charisma of the [Shock] players."[44] If anyone is intent on not re-electing Bush, it should be for honest disagreement with the President's policies, but it most certainly should not be for his view on women's rights.

In its fundamental form and at its origins, the modern movement for women's liberation was a decidedly laissez-faire call for freedom. Expressed most eloquently in the Declaration of Sentiments and Resolutions penned by Elizabeth Cady Stanton in 1848, the early women's movement called for legal and social recognition of moral, political, and civic status equal to that enjoyed by men—that is, to be left alone rather than dominated. Legally this included a demand to marry without losing basic rights and an end to *de jure* and *de facto* laws that permitted men (especially husbands) to control a woman's actions by force. Politically, this meant suffrage; socially, this meant opportunity for women to participate intellectually in matters of church and state, education and professions.

Modeled after the Declaration of Independence, Ms. Stanton's document set forth the injustices against women for which she demanded redress. Conspicuously absent is any demand for government-funded abortions, paid family leave, or

44. George W. Bush, "Remarks by the President in Photo Opportunity with the Detroit Shock" (May 24, 2004), http://www.whitehouse.gov/news/releases/2004/05/20040524-1.html.

anti-sexual harassment laws in the workplace. Instead, the Declaration of Sentiments highlighted abuses of men toward women such as "He has made her morally, an irresponsible being, as she can commit many crimes with impunity, provided they be done in the presence of her husband," and "He has denied her the facilities for obtaining a thorough education, all colleges being closed against her," and further decries the exclusion from women in any significant "public participation in the affairs of the church." The Resolutions of the document call for repeal of all laws "which prevent women from occupying such a station in society as her conscience shall dictate," and for men to encourage women to speak and teach in all religious assemblies. Socially and legally, "the same transgressions should be visited with equal severity on both man and woman"— patently, these feminists saw no need for a federal Violence Against Women Act. The Resolutions exhort men and women to work untiringly to secure to women "an equal participation with men in the various trades, professions, and commerce." In its final paragraph, the Declaration of Sentiments proclaims that it is a "self-evident truth growing out of the divinely implanted principles of human nature" that "it is demonstrably the right and duty of woman, equally with man, to promote every righteous cause by every righteous means; and especially in regard to the great subjects of morals and religion ..."

For these true proponents of women's rights, women's thoughts and opinions on political and spiritual issues should be encouraged and embraced, and the laws in place should treat men and women *equally* with respect to taxation, punishment, marriage and divorce, and access to education.

Deliberately, the women's rights movement did not demand government action (much less *federal* action) to remedy every kind of injustice. For example, they called for laws granting them the elective franchise, and for changes in divorce laws to take into consideration the well-being of women and their children, but spotted no role for the law in forcing the complete social acceptance of women in religious and professional life. That level of social acceptance was pleaded for not with demands for legal action but with a natural rights appeal to the consciences of men.

The pioneers of the women's movement in this country had sufficient faith and confidence in the greatness of this country and in the strength of individual women to believe that the removal of actual obstacles burdening the female gender was all that was needed to permit women the opportunity to live full and meaningful lives. Their vision of women as equal participants in our country is embraced by President Bush. The President's policy positions are no more about punishing women than legal drinking age requirements are about punishing teenagers.

The President's policies can and should be debated, but let's at least approach them with enough honesty and civility to admit that being pro-life and pro-business does not equal an attempt to return women to second-class status. In his most recent proclamation on Women's Equality Day, President Bush praised Elizabeth Cady Stanton and others who "advanced the fight for equal rights," and lauded the women across America whose "accomplishments in education, business, science, art, medicine, athletics, and every other field have made America better and stronger."[45] This is a President, and a man, who honors and appreciates women who work, learn, and fight alongside men in every aspect of our society.

I'm not arguing that Bush is creating a gynocentric government or social order; he no doubt cringed at presidential candidate Dennis Kucinich's vision of goddess worship in the United States.[46] However, the fact that Bush's view of women encompasses genuine respect for women as individuals and unblinking

---

45.   George W. Bush, "Woman's Equality Day 2003, By the President of the United States of America, A Proclamation" (August 26, 2003), http://www.whitehouse.gov/news/releases/2003/08/20030826-1.html.

46.   Dennis John Kucinich, "Formal Announcement Speech" (October 13, 2003), http://kucinich.us/announce-news.htm. The speech states in part: "I am running for President of the United States to enable the goddess of peace to encircle within her reach all the children of this country and all the children of the world."

acceptance of their equality with men should be quite sufficient to rebut charges of misogyny hurled at him by modern feminists.

A Feminism Beyond Abortion Rights

A brief look at the top reasons cited by today's feminists for labeling George W. Bush such a danger to women is enough to demonstrate that President Bush has strong, principled convictions on issues that remain controversial in our society, but also shows that the President's stance on these issues does not qualify him as anti-woman. First and foremost on the feminist agenda is attacking Bush for lack of support for abortions and other euphemistically-named "family planning" devices, domestically and internationally.[47] Feminists' next biggest complaint is Bush's other pro-life stances, such as signing the Partial Birth Abortion Ban, supporting legal protection for human embryos on par with protections for other human research subjects, and signing a law providing a separate criminal offense for killing or harming an unborn fetus during commission of another crime. The third tier of charges consists of a collection of items that strikes me as really reaching for proof of Bush's alleged hatred of women—for example, charges that the Bush Administration deleted information about women's programs from government websites, that Bush strong-armed the Food and Drug Administration (FDA) into refusing to approve over-the-counter emergency contraception (the "morning-after" pill), that Bush improperly ordered non-profit organizations that refuse to endorse Bush's "abstinence only" philosophy to be audited by the government, and that Bush's Attorney General, John Ashcroft, failed to prepare a required report under the Violence Against Women Act.

---

47. For example, consider the March for Women's Lives, held in Washington, D.C. on April 25, 2004. This event featured organizers intent on demonizing Bush for being the leading enemy of abortion rights, which seemed to be the biggest—if not the sole—source of their characterization of Bush as waging a "war on women."

These categories of charges supposedly prove President Bush's secret agenda to force women and girls to live in a country "where the judiciary system looks like Iran, the air looks like Tokyo, and their rights look like Saudi Arabia."[48] The most vitriolic attacks concern Bush's lack of support for abortion and other "family planning" devices, although NOW and other women's rights groups also level bitter condemnations of all conservative policies, no matter how tenuously connected to "women's rights" those may be.[49] Modern feminists' inability to support any person—male or female—who subscribes to conservative principles clearly indicates that their self-described campaigns on behalf of "women" are really a front for advocating leftist ideology. It is modern feminists themselves, not George W. Bush, who have abandoned Elizabeth Cady Stanton's call for embracing and appreciating women's intelligence, opinions, and perspectives on social and political issues, evidenced by feminists' dismissals of the contributions of any woman who refuses to endorse far-left liberalism.[50] If any crowd has betrayed the female gender, it is modern feminists, not the Bush Administration. President Bush speaks his conscience and accepts or rejects the views of people as individuals, regardless of gender, while expressing respect for people who hold beliefs different from his own.

If support for abortion rights is the litmus test for being pro-woman, then George W. Bush clearly fails. As someone who believes that the government ought to leave women free (and informed) to choose how to handle unwanted pregnancies, I respect the principled stance of Bush and other pro-lifers who

---

48.   Kim Gandy, *National NOW Times* (Summer 2002), http://www.now.org/nnt/summer-2002/viewpoint.html.

49.   Ibid. Gandy indicates that Bush's judicial appointments are "focused on using the courts to return us to a pre-Civil War era of unquestioned state's rights, to roll back legislation that has advanced civil rights, women's rights, reproductive rights, environmental protection, health and safety standards ..."

50.   In fairness, not all feminists have railed against President Bush; for example, see Phyllis Chesler, "A Radical Feminist Comes Out for Bush," *FrontPageMagazine.com* (January 9, 2004), http://www.frontpagemag.com/Articles/Printable.asp?ID=11669.

genuinely believe that funding, encouraging (or even allowing) abortions weakens society's respect for life and leaves the unborn child's rights out of the equation. But I also believe that the vast majority of pro-lifers hold their positions with absolutely no animus toward women whatsoever, and even view themselves as trying to prevent women from suffering potential pain and regret over a choice to abort.

President Bush's decision to strengthen the "gag rule" preventing U.S. dollars from going overseas to groups that help women obtain abortions, his decision to sign the Partial Birth Abortion Law, his insistence that domestic funds go to groups that advocate "abstinence only" methods of "family planning," and his numerous other pro-life policies in no way represent a betrayal of *women* as such. Rather, they represent his ardent belief in the sanctity of all human life, and his desire to use his position as Leader of the Free World to encourage people of all nations to *value* children, women, families, and marriage as inherent "goods" and as means to better societies. Painting Bush as anti-woman on the basis of his pro-life convictions makes as much sense as accusing anti-war activists of being pro-terrorism. Just as a fervent belief that war is never the answer doesn't mean an activist *desires* foreign aggression, neither does being pro-life mean the advocate desires that women suffer undue burdens.

Equating women's rights with abortion rights has been a powerful weapon for the Left in the liberal-conservative cultural war in America over the past thirty years. Conservative and libertarian women (and men) have fought back by demonizing "feminism" as a dirty word and dismissing feminism as "wacky" left-wing extremism.[51] Unfortunately, this tactic has left conser-

---

51. This tactic appears to have been quite successful—in a recent poll, three out of four women perceived the word "feminist" as an insult. See Dr. Janice Shaw Crouse, "Feminism and the Family," *Remarks at the World Congress of Families III* (March 29, 2004), http://www.cwfa.org/articledisplay.asp?id=5435&department=BLI&categoryid=commentary. See also, "Feminists meet to discuss future of the movement," *CNN* (April 2, 2000), http://www.cnn.com/2000/US/04/01/feminist.majority/. This article reported that only 20 percent of women self-identified as feminists,

vatives and libertarians vulnerable to being perceived as unsupportive of women's rights, when we can and should claim for ourselves a powerful, inspiring version of feminism. Touting Bush's appointments of women to powerful positions is all well and good, though it will always lead to an ideologically unpleasant numbers battle—for example, the feminists quickly counted heads and declared that only 26 percent of Bush's initial Administration appointments were women, compared to Clinton's 37 percent.[52]

Trying to portray President Bush as female friendly while silently accepting the premise that women's rights are equivalent to reproductive rights will do little to help President Bush narrow the gender gap in November 2004. The Bush team, and anyone who balks at the idea of a President Kerry, should instead highlight the way President Bush unflinchingly accepts women in every facet of our society, including government, education, professions, business, the military, and sports; the President simply *assumes* that women are every bit as capable as men in all these arenas. They should focus on Bush's efforts to alleviate abuses of women worldwide,[53] and should explain to America that principled reasons for refusing to extend government's sphere of influence have nothing to do with hating women and everything to do with promoting freedom and prosperity.

John Kerry's campaign website[54] lists "Women's Issues" as a separate tab and insists that "President Bush's actions have made

down from 31 percent in 1991.

52. For example, Marie Tessier, "Women's Appointments Plummet Under Bush," *Women's Enews* (July 5, 2001), http://www.now.org/eNews/july2001/070501appointments.html. This NOW publication commented, "Though the Bush White House appeared purposeful in its initial, highly visible appointments, three-quarters of its later nominees have been men, and four of every five appointees are white."

53. See e.g., "Fact Sheet: U.S. Commitment to Advancing Women's Rights," *U.S. Department of State, International Information Programs* (April 15, 2002), http://usinfo.state.gov/usa/women/rights/fs041502.htm. See also George Bush and Laura Bush, "Remarks by the First Lady and the President on Efforts to Globally Promote Women's Human Rights" (March 12, 2004), http://www.whitehouse.gov/news/releases/2004/03/20040312-5.html.

54. See http://www.johnkerry.com.

American women less safe and less secure—on the job and on the streets." Kerry promises to help women by defending affirmative action, expanding the Family and Medical Leave Act to help women "balance the needs between work and family," appointing only pro-choice justices to the Supreme Court, promoting family planning, assuring women contraceptive insurance coverage, increasing regulations to narrow the pay gap, supporting the Violence Against Women Act, defending Title IX against Bush Administration efforts to change its proportionality requirements, and increasing funding for breast cancer research.

President Bush's official re-election website,[55] by contrast, has no banner specifying "women's issues" and lacks any evidence of outreach to women. Small wonder. Conservative and libertarian principles prevent a candidate like Bush from pandering for the women's vote by supporting *any* of the so-called "women's issues" flaunted by Kerry, because they all require inappropriate government intrusion into business and the economy and/or conflict with pro-life principles.

That is no reason, however, to shy away from championing President Bush as a true advocate of women's rights. While the far Left will never be persuaded, many women would appreciate hearing an alternative version of feminism that comports with the President's conservative agenda. In his personal life and as a public leader, President Bush puts into action the legal and social aims of Elizabeth Cady Stanton's Declaration: respect for women as individuals; appreciation for their efforts in business, government, church, and society; and confidence in women's abilities to succeed in America. Rather than playing politics with women as John Kerry does, or actually abusing them as Clinton did, George W. Bush views women as equal, vital members of society whose human rights are unquestionable.

---

55. See http://www.georgewbush.com.

If "women's rights" is your pet issue, your candidate is President Bush.

CHAPTER NINETEEN

EDUCATION AND HEALTH CARE POLICY

MICHAEL NEW

Dr. Michael New is an adjunct scholar at the Cato Institute. He received his Ph.D. in Political Science from Stanford University and is currently a post-doctoral fellow at the Harvard-MIT data center. His research interests include limitations on government, tax revolts, welfare reform and campaign finance reform. He is currently writing a book on the history of the tax revolt movement.

Education and health care are two issues where many conservatives and libertarians have raised their most strident objections to the policies of President Bush. Specifically, many have been disappointed with both the federal mandates and the spending increases in the No Child Left Behind Act, which was enacted in 2001. Furthermore, many oppose the prescription drug entitlement which President Bush signed into law in 2003.

These criticisms have some merit. However, to his credit, President Bush has also succeeded in enacting education and health care reforms that are worthy of praise. Specifically, President Bush has signed into law legislation authorizing school vouchers for Washington, D.C., schoolchildren. Furthermore, the Medicare Modernization Act which was enacted in 2003 significantly expanded Medical Savings Accounts (MSAs). MSAs and vouchers will introduce market forces and competition into two sectors of the economy where the government plays an especially large role. As such, both are important policy objectives for conservatives and libertarians.

Now, it is true that both of these reforms are somewhat incremental in nature. However, history indicates that incremental policy successes often lead the way to larger reforms. Indeed, these school vouchers and Medical Savings Account programs may well pave the way to more ambitious market based reforms that will lower costs, provide more choices, and improve the quality of health care and education for all Americans.

Vouchers for D.C. Children

One of President Bush's most noteworthy achievements was his signing of an appropriations bill on January 22, 2004 that authorized a school voucher program for Washington, D.C., students. These vouchers will give 1,700 school children the opportunity to escape the District's troubled school system. Indeed, vouchers in the District are long overdue, because students in Washington public schools have consistently lagged behind their counterparts elsewhere. For instance, in the late 1970s at the University of the District of Columbia, it took one year of remedial training to bring D.C. public high school students up to speed. In 2002 the average was two years. Furthermore, 85 percent of D.C. public high school graduates who enter the University of the District of Columbia need remedial educa-

274

tion.[56] According to the U.S. Department of Education's National Center of Education Statistics, an estimated 40 percent of students who start the 8th grade in Washington, D.C., public schools leave or drop out before graduating.

Based on objective measures of performance, public school students from the District mightily underachieve their national peers. The College Board reports that, in 2001, Washington public school students scored 222 points below the national average on the SAT. On the Stanford 9 achievement test in 2001, 25 percent of D.C. students read and 36 percent performed math at the "Below Basic" level demonstrating little or no mastery of fundamental knowledge and skills at their grade level.[57]

The evidence clearly indicates that public schools in the District of Columbia have failed to provide students with an adequate education. Meanwhile, all of this has occurred at a time when spending for Washington, D.C., public schools has been steadily increasing. In 2001, expenditures per pupil in D.C. public schools were $12,046. This is one of the highest figures in the nation.

Now the District of Columbia is certainly not the only city with a troubled public school system. However, D.C. schools present Congress with a unique opportunity. This is because with regard to schools in the District, the Constitution grants Congress authority to "exercise exclusive legislation in all cases whatsoever."

Voucher Success Stories

For years, conservative and libertarians have recommended school vouchers as a means to improve education. Most proposed voucher plans would grant students from low income

---

56. Valerie Strauss and Sari Horowitz, "Students Caught in a Cycle of Classroom Failures," *The Washington Post* (February 20, 1997), A01.

57. Paul L. Vance, *A Five Year Statistical Glance at D.C. Public Schools: School Years 1996-1997 through 2000-2001* (Washington, D.C.: Washington D.C. Division of Educational Accountability, Student Accounting Branch, February 2002), 43-44.

families a voucher or tax credit that could be used to defray the cost of attending a private, parochial, or even another public school. These vouchers would give students from low income families the opportunity to escape failing public schools. Furthermore, the increased competition from private and religious schools would push public schools to improve.

Vouchers have been gaining steam politically in other cities. In the early-1990s, through the dogged efforts of Wisconsin state legislator Polly Williams, Milwaukee became the first city in recent times to have a school voucher program. However, this program was fairly limited as students could only use their vouchers to attend private schools that were not religious in nature. Some other cities followed suit. Most notably, Cleveland enacted a more comprehensive school voucher program in the mid-1990s which included both private and parochial schools. In 2002 the Supreme Court found the Cleveland school voucher program constitutional in *Zelman vs. Simmons-Harris*.

Academic researchers who have examined these programs have found that vouchers benefit both students and the public school system as a whole. Caroline Hoxby of Harvard University found that public schools in Milwaukee pushed to increase achievement because of the competition from vouchers. [58] Other studies have also verified the effectiveness of vouchers in test improving results. Harvard Political Scientists Paul Peterson and William Howell concluded that black students who received vouchers in lotteries had higher standardized test scores than black students who entered lotteries but did not receive vouchers. [59] Finally, Princeton economist Cecilia Rouse found that Milwaukee students who received vouchers showed significant improvement on standardized tests. [60]

58. Caroline M. Hoxby, "How School Choice Affects the Achievement of Public School Students," *Choice with Equity*, ed. Paul T. Hill (Stanford, California: Hoover Institution Press, 2002), 150.

59. William G. Howell and Paul E. Peterson, *The Education Gap: Vouchers and Urban Schools* (Washington: Brookings Institution, 2002), 145-147.

60. Cecilia Rouse, "Private School Vouchers and Student Achievement: An Evaluation of

Previous Attempts at Reform

There have been previous attempts to reform the Washington, D.C., public schools, but most have not met with success. In 1981 an initiative placed on the ballot by the D.C. Committee for Improved Education would have allowed families earning less than $20,000 a year to receive a $1,200 local income tax credit to be used for private school fees or to pay for supplemental programs at public schools. However, supporters of this measure were vastly outspent by opponents who included the League of Women Voters, the American Federation of Teachers, the entire city council, the entire D.C. school board, the Washington teachers union, the local chapter of the NAACP, Mayor Marion Barry, and every candidate running for Mayor. In the end, this measure lost by a 9 to 1 margin.

More recently, in 1998 Congress passed a school voucher plan for the District. The District of Columbia Student Opportunity Scholarship Act (HR 1797) cosponsored by House Majority Leader Dick Armey (R-TX) and Representative William Lipinski (D-IL). It would have offered up to $3,200 in tuition subsidies to 2,000 low income students for use at the public, private, or parochial school of their choice. However, this bill was vetoed by President Clinton.

Prospects for educational choice seemed quite dim until the election of George W. Bush in 2000. President Bush did not make vouchers for Washington, D.C., schoolchildren a major part of his campaign in 2000. However, candidate Bush emphasized education and seemed interested in giving parents options beyond public schools. In fact, a school voucher plan was included in the original version of President Bush's No Child Left Behind Act, but Congressional Democrats were strongly opposed to vouchers and the plan was removed during negotiations.

---

the Milwaukee Parental Choice Program," *The Quarterly Journal of Economics* 113 no. 2, (May 1998): 593.

Fortunately three subsequent events should give voucher supporters some hope. First, on June 27, 2002, the Supreme Court found the Cleveland school voucher program—a program which included both religious and non-religious schools—constitutional in *Zelman vs. Simmons-Harris*.

Second, Anthony Williams, the mayor of Washington, D.C. came out in support of a voucher program. Other Washington, D.C. officials, who had previously opposed vouchers including D.C. Council member Kevin P. Chavous and school board President Peggy Cooper Cafritz would later join Mayor Williams. The fact that Mayor Williams and others were supportive would make vouchers easier to implement.

Third, Republicans retook control of the U.S. Senate in the 2002 elections. This increased the number of Senators who were sympathetic toward vouchers and would make it easier to schedule a vote on a bill that authorized vouchers. After the election, Congress went back to work and in December 2003 the House of Representatives passed an omnibus spending bill that included $14 million for Washington, D.C. school vouchers.

Voucher proponents faced more opposition in the Senate. However, President Bush remained a strong ally of vouchers. Speaking to a group of Catholic educators in the East Room of the White House on January 9, 2004, Bush said the District voucher program would expand on the spirit of the No Child Left Behind Act, making public schools more accountable by expanding parents' choices.

"For the sake of educational excellence and for the sake of trusting parents to make the right decision for their children; for the sake, really, of helping to begin a change of education around the country ... the Senate needs to pass this bill and make school choice in Washington, D.C., a reality," Bush told 250 members of the National Catholic Education Association.

In the end, a voucher bill passed the U.S. Senate and on January 22, 2004, President Bush succeeded where President Clinton and others failed and promptly signed the bill into law. For the first time, many Washington, D.C. parents will have the means to send their children to private and parochial schools.

The legislation permits Secretary of Education Rod Paige to launch a five-year pilot program designed in consultation with Mayor Williams to provide annual, taxpayer-funded grants of up to $7,500 a year for at least 1,700 District schoolchildren to attend private and parochial schools beginning in the fall of 2004.

These "Opportunity Scholarships" would be limited to children in families earning up to 185 percent of the poverty level—about $36,000 for a family of four—with priority going to children attending low-performing public schools. Already these opportunity scholarships have gotten a great deal of attention. During the spring and summer, hundreds of eager parents have attended the informational meetings about these vouchers.

Better yet, President Bush is committed to expanding educational choice across the country. After signing the voucher bill for D.C. students, President Bush said he would renew a request from Congress in next year's budget for $50 million for a "national choice incentive fund" to send federal tax dollars to seed future school voucher programs across the country. Indeed, President Bush's commitment to educational choice will provide families with more choices, spur competition, and extend better educational opportunities to all Americans.

Health Savings Accounts

Rising health care costs are a problem that has attracted interest from many across the political spectrum. One driving factor that makes health care so expensive is the fact that most health care costs are paid for by third parties, such as insurers, employers, or the government. As such, consumers typically have little incentive to economize or bargain for better prices.

One way to bring market forces back into health care transactions is through Health Savings Accounts (HSAs). Health Savings Accounts have two components. First, they are an insurance plan with a high deductible. These less costly insurance plans would provide protection from catastrophic health care expenses, but would require consumers to pay for routine health care expenses, such as checkups, out of pocket.

These high deductible insurance plans would be coupled with tax free savings accounts. These savings accounts would allow individuals to make deposits for health care expenditures without a tax penalty. The money saved by purchasing a plan with a higher deductible would be placed into the savings account. This pool of money could then be used for routine health care expenses.

These tax free savings accounts are an important component to these health savings accounts. Health insurance that is purchased or provided through an employer is not considered taxable income. However, the money that an employee would save through the purchase of a high deductible plan would be taxed, making these plans considerably more costly. Tax free savings accounts would eliminate this bias, and make health savings accounts a better option for health care consumers.

History of Medical Savings Accounts

Congress first launched limited opportunities to open tax-advantaged Medical Savings Accounts as part of the 1996 Health Insurance Portability and Accountability Act (HIPAA). Eligible individuals who purchased qualified catastrophic health insurance coverage also could direct tax-deductible contributions to accompanying savings accounts set up to handle other health care expenses.

However, regulations, design problems, and unnecessary complexity made it difficult for many to acquire these Medical Savings Accounts. First, these accounts were temporary, set to expire in December 2000. Furthermore, they were only available to businesses with fewer than 50 employees. Finally, the total number available was limited to 750,000. These restrictions and others confined the access and market opportunities for these medical savings accounts. At the end only 100,000 individuals set up MSA health care coverage.

After the passage of HIPAA, there was little subsequent discussion about Medical Savings Accounts. Indeed, during the presidential election in 2000, the health policy issue that received the most attention was the expansion of Medicare coverage to include prescription drugs, which George W. Bush supported. In 2003 President Bush delivered on this promise when he signed the Medicare Modernization Act in 2003.

However, the Medicare Modernization Act also featured provisions to include a larger more ambitious program of Health Savings Accounts for the general population. These Health Savings Accounts keep the basic framework of the traditional Medical Savings Accounts that were enacted in 1996, yet they possess considerably fewer regulatory and design obstacles.

In particular, these Medical Savings Accounts are not restricted to those who work for small businesses and the overall number is not capped. Furthermore, the minimum deductible for an insurance plan that can qualify for an HSA has been lowered which makes eligibility easier for many individuals.

In particular, to qualify for an HSA, a high-deductible plan must have a minimum deductible of $1,000 for an individual policy and $2,000 for a family policy. Maximum annual out-of-pocket spending, including deductibles and co-pays, can be no more than $5,000 for an individual or $10,000 for a family.

Furthermore, the Medicare Modernization Act establishes several basic rules for contributions to MSAs. The maximum that can be contributed is the lesser of the amount of the high deductible or $2,600 for an individual and $5,150 for a family. Besides the individual owner of the account, an employer and others can also make contributions on behalf of the individual.

Now, there still exist some obstacles that need to be overcome for HSAs to be properly implemented. In some states, regulations make it very difficult, if not impossible, to purchase health insurance coverage with a high enough deductible to qualify for an HSA. Furthermore, even though money placed into an HSA is exempt from federal taxes, in some states, individuals would have to pay state taxes on this money. Still, President Bush deserves credit for signing legislation that will result in more options and greater freedom for many health care consumers.

Thoughts about Public Policy

Many conservative and libertarian activists express frustration with their seeming inability to enact major policy changes. This disappointment is understandable. However, history indicates that larger changes in federal policy are often preceded by either smaller changes or policy reforms at the state level.

For instance, the tax revolts of the late 1970s paved the way for President Reagan's substantial tax reductions in 1981. In particular, California's Proposition 13—which dramatically cut and then limited property taxes—indicated that taxes could be reduced without truly draconian cutbacks in vital state services. Furthermore, the economic expansion that followed Proposition 13 demonstrated that tax cuts were economically beneficial. All of this made President Reagan's 1981 tax cuts much easier.

A more current example involves welfare reform. Before President Clinton signed the welfare reform bill in 1996, most serious attempts to reform welfare took place at the state level. For instance, in 1971, Governor Ronald Reagan of California signed a welfare reform bill that tightened eligibility requirements and implemented stringent antifraud measures. Within three years, California's AFDC caseloads declined by 17 percent, saving taxpayers $2 billion.[61] Furthermore, because benefits were maintained for those unable to work, Reagan's plan earned plaudits from many across the political spectrum.

---

61.   Lou Cannon, *Governor Reagan and his Rise to Power* (New York: Public Affairs, 2003), 360.

State level welfare reform efforts intensified during the 1990s. The most notable of these reforms was signed into law by former Wisconsin Governor Tommy Thompson who is currently serving as President Bush's Secretary of Health and Human Services. Thompson eliminated Aid to Families with Dependent Children (AFDC) for many welfare recipients, replacing it with a jobs program. This earned him the nickname "Governor Get a Job."

Governors in other states also authorized ambitious welfare reform proposals. The fact that many of these state efforts enjoyed success in moving people from welfare to work gave the general public more confidence in welfare reform. This paved the way for President Clinton to sign the Personal Responsibility and Work Opportunity Reconciliation Act (PRWORA) in 1996 which ended the entitlement status of AFDC and gave states more freedom to implement welfare policy. Eight years later, welfare rolls have fallen dramatically[62] and many more former welfare recipients are self-sufficient as a result.

Similarly, school vouchers for Washington, D.C. schoolchildren and Health Savings Accounts may not have dramatic short term effects. However, both of these programs should provide visible, concrete examples of how market forces can improve the quality and lower the cost of both health care and education. These reforms will hopefully increase the demand for further market based reforms that can only result in better health care and education for all Americans.

---

62.   Data on caseloads obtained from Administration for Children and Families at http://www.acf.dhhs.gov/news/stats/aug-dec.htm.

CHAPTER TWENTY

DEFENDING AMERICA'S FAMILIES

JAMES DOBSON

Dr. James Dobson is founder and chairman of Focus on the Family, as well as of Focus on the Family Action, a cultural organization dedicated to addressing the moral, social and political issues that threaten the family today.

To many, the crowning achievement of George W. Bush's first term in office will be his bold and decisive response to the terrorist attacks of September 11, 2001, and his principled leadership in the subsequent War on Terror. To be certain, these are amazing accomplishments that will ensure him a place among America's most revered and respected national leaders.

I shudder at the thought of what our country might look like today if a less principled individual had held the office of President in the weeks following 9/11. Americans everywhere—and freedom-loving people around the globe—owe President Bush a deep debt of gratitude for his willingness to make tough decisions during a time of overwhelming uncertainty and turmoil.

For me, however, the most significant contribution that President Bush has made—and continues to make—to the fabric of American life is his staunch support for the institution of the traditional family. His own words, as recorded in the National Family Week Proclamation of November 2001, demonstrate the extent of his deep commitment to this essential building block of society:

> My Administration is committed to strengthening the American family. Many one-parent families are also a source of comfort and reassurance; yet a family with a mom and dad who are committed to marriage and devote themselves to their children helps provide their children a sound foundation for success. Government can support families by promoting policies that help strengthen the institution of marriage and help parents rear their children in positive and healthy environments.

That simple yet profound statement is music to the ears of someone who, for the past 30 years, has fought tooth and nail to protect and defend the precious institution of the family! Unfortunately, some of the most difficult battles during that time have been fought against Presidents and other national leaders who, through dangerous policies and utter disregard for the will of the people, have seemed determined to either undermine the family or dismantle it altogether. By stark contrast, President Bush's support for this fundamental institution remains bold and unwavering. It is reflected in his consistent defense of pre-born babies, his strong support for traditional marriage, and in myriad other ways.

Indeed, on countless occasions, President Bush has taken a principled stand in defense of what is right, even in the face of serious opposition from his liberal opponents and, at times, some members of his own political party. When he makes a statement in support of something, such as the aforementioned proclamation, he is not merely giving a political sales pitch. You can be sure that he will back up such statements with appropriate policies and legislation. I am profoundly thankful for his commitment to promoting the family in both *word* and *deed*.

Nowhere has the President "walked the talk" more clearly than in his unwavering support of the sanctity of human life. Even during the campaign leading up to the 2000 election, it was clear that Mr. Bush had an unshakable commitment to the pro-life cause. Throughout the campaign, he stated unequivocally that his desire was to create a culture in which every child is welcomed in life and protected in law, and that he would appoint judges who are strict constructionists when it comes to interpreting laws not only related to abortion, but a host of other critical issues as well.

During his first few days in office, President Bush re-instated the "Mexico City Policy," a Reagan-era provision that prohibits federal funding of abortions overseas. (Not surprisingly, that important policy had been rescinded during the Clinton years.) In addition, Mr. Bush signed into law the Born Alive Infant Protection Act, which states that if, at delivery, a baby—no matter what stage of gestation—is attempting to move or breathe or has a heartbeat, that child is legally a "person" protected by the 14th Amendment. With important policies such as these, which are designed to protect the tiniest and most helpless members of society, the President breathed new life into the concept of "compassionate conservatism."

One of the most significant moments in the President's first term came on August 9, 2001, when Mr. Bush appeared before the nation in a televised address and declared that his Administration would stand against any move to use federal funding for destructive stem cell research involving human embryos. In the same speech, he pledged $250 million toward more ethical forms of stem cell research, including cells from adults, umbilical cords, placentas, and animals, and created a presidential commission to monitor progress on stem cell research. Mr. Bush's brave decision came amidst howls of protest from the liberal media, the entertainment industry, and others who supported the creation and subsequent destruction of life for research purposes. Columnist Robert Novak rightly observed that "the pro-life rhetoric of [President Bush's] 11-minute speech surpassed anything Ronald Reagan or Bush's father ever said," while Chuck Colson noted that, "For the first time, in my memory at least, a sitting President has grappled publicly with a critical moral issue and, unapologetically, drawn a line in the sand... Human life is sacred."

As encouraging as Mr. Bush's handling of the stem cell issue was, even better news was coming. In 2003, after more than a decade and a pair of vetoes from the pen of former President Clinton, the Partial Birth Abortion Ban Act was passed by Congress and signed into law by the President. This landmark legislation was the first federal restriction on abortion since *Roe v. Wade,* paving the way for an end to a procedure so horrendous that it could have been a favorite tactic in the torture chambers of Nazi Germany. Even though the ban was immediately challenged in the courts by pro-abortion forces, the President had sent a clear and decisive message to the American people that *no* argument about a "woman's right to choose" can ever justify, even in the most liberal mind, the brains being sucked from a baby's head in the eighth and ninth months of development. It is not an exaggeration to suggest that Mr. Bush's bold endorsement of the Partial Birth Abortion Ban Act of 2003 marked a significant step toward dismantling our nation's culture of infanticide.

Of course, the protection of life in the womb is but one of *many* family-related issues upon which President Bush has taken a pivotal stand. He has consistently demonstrated support for the institution of traditional marriage, particularly as it relates to amending the Constitution to define marriage exclusively as the union of one man and one woman. His commitment has been resolute, even in the face of rabid attacks from the homosexual activist community and other opponents at the opposite end of the ideological spectrum. With rogue judges and local officials in several states embracing same-sex "marriage" in utter disregard for both the law and the will of the people, our President called on Congress "to promptly pass, and send to the states for ratification, an amendment to our Constitution defining and protecting marriage as a union of one man and one woman."

We face an uphill battle in endeavoring to get the Federal Marriage Amendment passed. But I believe that, with George W. Bush in office, there is hope. If the past four years have shown us anything, it is that President Bush is a man who will stick to his guns and follow through on his promises. That is why I am able to retain a certain sense of optimism in the face of our culture's continued attacks on traditional marriage. If, by God's grace, the Federal Marriage Amendment *does* become a reality, it will be because George W. Bush had the courage and fortitude to guide our country in that direction. I know that millions of Americans are praying that God would grant him the strength and fortitude to do just that.

Space does not permit me to write at length about the numerous other reasons why I would like to say a heartfelt "thank you" to President Bush. However, a few additional points do immediately come to mind. He has fought hard for tax cuts that benefit struggling families. He has championed the idea of allowing faith-based organizations to partner with government entities to help fight poverty. He has consistently nominated principled, conservative individuals to key federal court positions, even though his Democratic opponents have done everything within their power to hijack the judicial nomination process. And on a more personal note, he has been a gracious host to my wife, Shirley, and her staff each year as they oversee the National Day of Prayer events in Washington, D.C. In fact, Mr. Bush has made room in his incredibly hectic schedule for the National Day of Prayer every year that he has been in office. Shirley and I are both extremely grateful for his participation, and I know that Americans from coast to coast appreciate his willingness to publicly express his faith and his leadership while encouraging others to do the same.

For these and many other reasons, I am thankful that the Lord, in His providence, has allowed George W. Bush to serve as President of the United States during this pivotal time in the history of our nation. He is a man of conviction, a man of principle, and, most importantly, a man of faith. May divine grace and protection surround him, Laura, and their children in the days ahead. And while I write in my capacity as a private citizen and not as a representative of any organization, I know I am joined by millions of God-fearing Americans in praying that, God willing, he may lead our nation for another four years as it embraces the challenges of the new millennium.

THE ROLE

OF THE LAW

CHAPTER TWENTY-ONE

A LEGACY ON THE COURTS

TARA ROSS

Tara Ross is an attorney and a professional writer. She graduated from the University of Texas at Austin's Law School, where she served as editor in chief of the TEXAS REVIEW OF LAW & POLITICS. *She is currently working on a book about the Electoral College.*

While campaigning for the presidency, then-Governor George W. Bush promised that, he would nominate federal judges who will "strictly interpret the Constitution and not use the bench for writing social policy."[63] His words reflected an appropriate understanding of a judge's proper role. Judges act constitutionally when they remain faithful to the original meaning of laws and the Constitution, interpreting them as they were

---

63. George W. Bush, "The First Gore-Bush Presidential Debate at the University of Massachusetts in Boston," *Commission on Presidential Debates* (October 3, 2000), http://www.debates.org/pages/trans2000a.html.

first written. The restraint exercised by these judges leaves Americans free to govern themselves, and their actions are consistent with democratic government.

Once elected, Bush reaffirmed his desire to identify and nominate judges who will abide by this philosophy of judicial restraint. He has maintained this position despite the unprecedented obstructionism that his nominees have faced. His actions are important. The nominations that a President makes (or fails to make) to the courts can impact the nation for years, even decades, after his term of office comes to a close.

The Importance of Judicial Nominations

The judiciary is the only branch of the federal government that is not elected. Federal judges are nominated by the President, confirmed by the Senate, and (once confirmed) may hold their positions "during good behavior." [64] Moreover, the President and the Congress may not remove federal judges from office or slash their salary if particular judicial decisions do not meet their political needs. The Constitution protects the independence of the judiciary, leaving judges free to apply the law neutrally.

The Constitution frees federal judges from *outside* political pressure, but it is equally critical that they avoid succumbing to pressures from *within*. The personal philosophies and wishes of a judge ought not to matter. His job is to pronounce what the law *is*, not what he thinks it *should be*. Although state judges are often elected rather than appointed as federal judges are, they should abide by a similar judicial philosophy as well.

A judge's judicial philosophy is his theory regarding the proper role of a judge in society. Judge Jerry Smith (Fifth Circuit) has compared a judge's role to that of an umpire in a baseball

---

64.   U.S. Const, Art II, § 2; id. Art III, § 1.

game.[65] Umpires may not create or alter the rules of baseball based on their personal preferences or the mood of the fans. Instead, umpires neutrally apply the rules of the game to the situation before them. While honest disagreements may arise about whether a particular pitch was within the strike zone, all umpires recognize the existence of the strike zone and their duty to call balls and strikes accordingly. They cannot suddenly change the strike zone because they like the batter at the plate.

Judges with a judicial philosophy of *restraint* see themselves as the umpires of the legal arena. They may have honest disagreements on how to read a particular legal provision, but they strive to interpret the law as it was first written. They recognize that the Constitution has one meaning that does not change over time and that shifting political considerations should be reflected in the legislature, not in judicial opinions. After all, legislators who misread the political tea leaves can be voted out of office. Judges cannot.

Other judges, by contrast, maintain a more *activist* judicial philosophy. These judges tend to speak of the Constitution as a "living" document with a meaning that changes over time. Such a statement is as ridiculous as believing that an umpire can unilaterally change the strike zone over the course of several games, months, or years. A formal rule change is needed before an umpire can start calling balls thrown at ankle height a "strike." In the same way, if and when an amendment to the Constitution or laws is needed, it is the job of lawmakers, not judges, to begin this process.

A judge's judicial philosophy stands in direct contrast to his political ideology. The former is a legitimate matter for consideration by the Senate; the latter is not. Indeed, Senators who take political ideology into account essentially say to judges: "You are

---

65.   Howard Bashman, "Interview with Judge Jerry E. Smith of the U.S. Court of Appeals for the Fifth Circuit," *How Appealing* (January 24, 2003), http://appellateblog.blogspot.com/2003_01 _01_ appellateblog_archive.html#90229950.

expected to make political, rather than legal, decisions." Such expectations are wrong.

It is admittedly difficult to identify those individuals who are truly willing and able to act solely as legal umpires. However, identifying these nominees should always be the goal. Bush's public statements and actions reflect a commitment to identifying and nominating these candidates. The public statements[66] and obstructionist efforts of many liberals in the Senate indicate that they, instead, increasingly evaluate candidates based on political ideology.

Obstructionism of Judicial Nominees

On November 12, 2003, Republican Senators initiated a 39-hour "talkathon" on the Senate floor. Majority Leader Bill Frist (R-TN) opened the session, charging that Senate Democrats have engaged in "unprecedented" new tactics, blocking the President's judicial nominees and "erod[ing] two centuries of Senate tradition."[67] Democrats denied the charges. "[W]e have supported and confirmed 168 judges," Senator Charles Schumer (D-NY) stated, "We have blocked 4."[68] His words contradicted earlier statements by the Democratic minority leader. In 2001, Senator Tom Daschle (D-SD) warned: "[W]e'll cooperate when [judicial nominees are] from the center, but we are going to be very concerned if they're from the far right *and we'll use whatever means necessary.*"[69] After Daschle's 2001 warning, how, then, could liberal Democratic Senators in 2003 simultaneously denounce Bush's nominees as being "on the far, far right of the political and philosophical spectrum,"[70] yet claim unusual levels of cooperation by Senate Democrats?

---

66.   For example, see Charles E. Schumer, "Judging by Ideology," *New York Times* (June 26, 2001), A19.

67.   *Cong. Rec.,* 108th Cong., 1st sess., 2003, 149, S14, 528.

68.   Ibid, S14, 533.

69.   Tom Daschle, Minority Leader, United States Senate, press briefing, Washington, D.C., (February 1, 2001). Emphasis added.

70.   *Fox News Sunday with Tony Snow,* Fox television broadcast (November 16, 2003).

The misleading nature of liberal Senators' claims can be seen most easily by deconstructing the numbers that they throw around as supposed proof of their cooperative attitude in the face of Republican intransigence.

168 to 4

Many Democrats repeatedly argued during the 2003 talk-athon that they had allowed the confirmation of 168 of Bush's nominees and blocked "only" 4 nominees. On May 22, 2004, after a handful of additional confirmations, the website of Senator Patrick Leahy (D-VT) claimed that this number was 176 to 3.[71] William Pryor (Eleventh Circuit), Janice Rogers Brown (D.C. Circuit), and Carolyn Kuhl (Ninth Circuit) were named as the three blocked nominees.

Leahy's claim ignores the existence of many other nominees who would, in the absence of obstruction by liberals in the Senate, be sitting on the bench today. Consider the following partial list of blocked nominations, not included in Leahy's May 2004 tally:[72]

- Three nominees who were filibustered before the 2003 talkathon commenced: Priscilla Owen (Fifth Circuit), Charles Pickering (Fifth Circuit), and Miguel Estrada (D.C. Circuit).
- William Myers (Ninth Circuit) and William Haynes (Fourth Circuit), first nominated in 2003. Their

---

71.   Senator Patrick Leahy of Vermont, "Judicial Nominations Worksheet: The Truth About President Bush's Judicial: Nominations," *United States Senate* (May 22, 2004), http://leahy.senate. gov/issues/nominations/index.html.

72.   All nomination, confirmation, hearing, and vacancy dates relied on in this chapter were obtained from the United States Courts (http://www.uscourts.gov), the Federal Judiciary Center (http://www.fjc.gov), the Library of Congress (http://thomas.loc.gov/home/nomis.html), the Office of Legal Policy (http://www.usdoj.gov/olp/ judicialnominations.htm), or the Senate Judiciary Committee (http://judiciary.senate.gov/). Any calculations from those dates are the author's own. This chapter addresses judicial nominations to the Article III courts only.

nominations are expected to remain pending on the Senate floor indefinitely.

- Seven nominees, first nominated in 2001 to 2002, whose nominations remain pending in committee due to opposition from their home-state Senators: Senators Carl Levin (D-MI), Debbie Stabenow (D-MI), or John Edwards (D-NC). The three Senators have stated no particular objection to any of the nominees. Efforts to discharge the nominations from committee have failed, despite majority support, due to a threatened filibuster.

When tallying the number of blocked Bush nominees, liberal Senators construe the numbers too strictly, selectively including only a portion of nominees who are victims of their filibusters and excluding many others who have, by any reasonable definition, been blocked. They do not grant Republicans the same privilege when tallying the number of supposedly blocked Clinton nominees.

63 to 4

Several Democrats have consistently claimed that Republicans blocked 63 of Clinton's nominations, compared to the "only 4" Bush nominees that they have blocked.[73] This number appears to include anyone and everyone who was ultimately not confirmed, regardless of the reason that the nomination failed and appears to inappropriately include the following nominees:

- Eleven nominations that were withdrawn by Clinton, including nominees such as Charles Stack. Stack admitted at his hearing that he had limited

---

73.   *E.g., Cong. Rec.,* 108th Cong., 1st sess., 2003, 149, S14,539 (statement of Senator Richard Durbin [D-IL]).

experience in criminal law and "would rely heavily" on other judges to "educate me in those areas in which I feel limited."[74] He subsequently asked Clinton to withdraw his nomination. Other nominees have similar stories.

- Eleven nominations that were submitted approximately three months (or less) before the 2000 presidential election. The Senate lacked time to send these nominees through the confirmation process.

- Thirteen nominations that were allowed to expire and were not resubmitted for further consideration, including nominees such as Barbara Durham. Durham withdrew herself from consideration, citing her husband's poor health. In many of these cases, Clinton nominated a second nominee to the same position and this nominee was quickly confirmed.

- Some argue that several of Clinton's failed nominations, opposed by home-state Senators, should not be attributed to Republicans. Reasonable arguments can be made either for keeping or eliminating these Senate procedures that allow home-state opposition to stall a nominee. Regardless, Republican Senators during the Clinton years, by and large, followed these procedures as they have historically been understood. Levin, Stabenow, and Edwards have not done the same. Bush consulted with these Senators, as is customary, but did not let them choose his nominees for him. They have retaliated by blocking nominees who have majority support on the Senate floor, even though they have no particular objection to these nominees.

---

74. U.S. Senate Committee on the Judiciary. *Confirmation Hearings on Federal Appointments,* 104th Cong., 2d sess.,1996, S. Hrg. 104-512, S521-28.

In short, when liberals claim that 63 nominees were blocked during the Clinton years, at least half and as many as two-thirds of these nominations are illegitimately included. They dishonestly manipulate the numbers to exaggerate their claims. Liberal Senators are not comparing apples to apples. They have chosen the most damaging manner of tallying numbers and use these statistics as a sword against Republicans.

Apples to Apples

It is admittedly difficult to compare apples to apples in this area, as the dynamics between the President and the Senate in any given year may change. However, one method of comparing Bush and Clinton's presidencies is simply to do a straight analysis on all nominees for each President's first term. Each President governed for two years with his party in control of the Senate and then two years with the opposing party in control. Bush made his judicial nominations more quickly than did many of his predecessors. He put an early priority on judicial nominations, making 66 nominations during his first year in office, compared to Clinton's 47 nominations (see Table 1).

Table 1
Number of Nominations for Article III Courts, By Year
Clinton and Bush: First Two Years in Office

	TOTAL		Courts of Appeal		District courts	
	Clinton	Bush	Clinton	Bush	Clinton	Bush
Nominations in first year	47	66	5	29	42	37
Nominations in second year	93	65	17	3	76	62
Total nominations	140	131	22	32	118	99
Total confirmed	126	100	19	17	107	83
% confirmed	90%	76%	86%	53%	91%	84%

Note: The charts in this chapter do not include two nominations made and confirmed to the Supreme Court during Clinton's first term. All District Court numbers include nominations made to the U.S. Court of International Trade.

Bush's early nominations should have given the Senate more time to conduct hearings and make decisions on his nominees. Instead, the Senate took longer on average to process nominations during Bush's first term than it did during Clinton's first term. Perhaps most egregiously, 40 percent of Bush's Courts of Appeals nominees were pending for one year or more, compared

Table 2
Time Before the Full Senate Acted on Nominations

	TOTAL		Courts of Appeal		District courts	
	Clinton	Bush	Clinton	Bush	Clinton	Bush
Less than 1 year	96%	86%	92%	60%	97%	94%
More than 1 year	4%	14%	8%	40%	3%	6%

to 8 percent for Clinton (see Table 2). Although Bush's nominations took longer to process, it appears that he will close his term with a higher percentage of his district court nominees confirmed than Clinton. However, a much smaller percentage of his nominees to the U.S. courts of appeals will be confirmed (see Table 3).

Generally speaking, nominations to the courts of appeal are considered more important than nominations to the district courts. The courts of appeal can reverse the decisions of district courts, and district courts must follow their precedents when considering future cases. Only the Supreme Court can overrule the courts of appeal. Republicans argue that district court nominees are being confirmed in greater numbers to hide the low confirmation rates for Bush's nominations to the more influential courts of appeal.

Table 3
**Confirmation Rate for Article III Judicial Appointments
Clinton and Bush: First Two Years in Office**

	TOTAL		Courts of Appeal		District courts	
	Clinton	Bush[75]	Clinton	Bush	Clinton	Bush
Nominations	238	224	39	52[76]	199	172
Confirmations	201	198	30	35	171	163
% confirmed	84%	88%	77%	67%	86%	95%

Obstructionism of Judicial Nominees

In 1998, Leahy observed, "I have stated over and over again ... that I would object and fight against any filibuster on a judge, whether it is somebody I opposed or supported; that I felt the Senate should do its duty."[77] His words were echoed the following year by Daschle, who stated: "I find it simply baffling that a Senator would vote against even voting on a judicial nomination."[78] Despite these statements, these two men have helped to lead their fellow Senate Democrats into multiple filibusters of Bush's judicial nominees. As of May 22, 2004, liberals in the Senate had filibustered six nominees, each discussed above: Estrada, Brown, Owen, Pickering, Kuhl, and Pryor. Other nominees have not been voted on due to the threat of additional filibusters.

"Filibuster" refers to a particular use of Senate rules to prevent a vote on a matter. A question cannot be put to a vote as long as one Senator holds the floor or seeks to speak on that

---

75. The number for Bush is expected, not actual. It includes the actual confirmations as of May 22, 2004, plus the additional confirmations that are anticipated as a result of a deal cut by Democrats and Republicans in May 2004. More confirmations are certainly possible, but they seem unlikely.

76. Fifty-two nominations were made to fill 50 positions during the 107th and 108th Congresses.

77. *Cong. Rec.*, 105th Cong., 2d Sess., 1998, 144, pt. 9:12727.

78. *Cong. Rec.*, 106th Cong., 1st sess., 1999, 145, S11,919.

issue. This debate may be ended in one of two ways: First, the Senate can agree to end debate by unanimous consent. Second, debate can be ended through a successful motion for cloture. This cloture vote is won and debate is ended if at least three-fifths of Senators (60, if no vacancies) vote for the cloture motion. Cloture votes indicate the existence of a filibuster when 41 or more Senators refuse to vote for cloture regardless of how much debate is had on an issue. They are not voting to continue the debate because they feel more discussion is helpful or necessary; instead, they are voting to extend debate simply to prevent a final vote from ever being taken.

Historically, filibusters have not been used to block judicial appointments. Cloture votes have occasionally been used to extend debate on a particular nominee, but until George W. Bush's first term, no more than two cloture votes were ever needed for any nominee. With one exception (discussed below), these nominations have always gone forward to a full Senate vote. In fact, Bush's nomination of Estrada to the D.C. Circuit Court was the first nomination ever to fail because a minority of Senators used cloture votes to permanently filibuster a nomination that would otherwise have been approved.

Many Democrats reject this characterization of past nomination battles. They argue that Republicans routinely use the filibuster and are only objecting now because the filibuster is being used against their nominees. As proof of this statement, Leahy lists on his website several judicial nominations that were "Republican filibusters." Among these examples, he includes Marsha Berzon (Ninth Circuit, 2000), Richard Paez (Ninth Circuit, 2000), H. Lee Sarokin (Third Circuit, 1994), Rosemary Barkett (Eleventh Circuit, 1994), Stephen Breyer (First Circuit, 1980), and Abe Fortas (Supreme Court, 1968).[79]

---

79.   Senator Patrick Leahy of Vermont, "Republican Filibusters Of Nominees Reported To The Floor," *United States Senate* (May 22, 2004), http://www.leahy.senate.gov/issues/nominations/pastfilibusters.html.

In fact, none of these examples constitute a precedent for the actions that liberal Democrats are taking against Bush's nominees. To the contrary, each nominee but Fortas (discussed below) eventually received a vote and was confirmed by the Senate.

Berzon was a controversial nominee nominated by Clinton. Although many Republicans opposed her nomination, they also opposed use of the filibuster to prevent her confirmation. In November 1999, Republican Majority Leader Trent Lott (R-MS) promised an up or down vote on her nomination before March 15, 2000. [80] He later personally filed the motion for cloture on her nomination himself. The cloture motion passed, 86 to 13, and Berzon was confirmed by a vote of 64 to 34. Several Republicans voted to end debate on Berzon's nomination, but then voted against confirmation. Similar situations existed for two other Clinton nominees, Paez and Sarokin. A motion for cloture was presented on the fourth Clinton nominee, Barkett, but it was withdrawn by unanimous consent shortly before she was confirmed. Arguably, Breyer's nomination to the First Circuit was a temporary filibuster, but those opposing the move to a full Senate vote did not seek to permanently delay the vote. Instead, they wanted improper committee procedures remedied. Eventually, a second cloture motion passed 68 to 28, and Breyer was confirmed 80 to 10. Breyer sits on the Supreme Court today.

The Fortas nomination came closest to setting a precedent for filibusters of judicial nominations, but even that example fails to qualify. In 1968, Fortas was nominated to be Chief Justice of the Supreme Court. Opposition to his nomination was bipartisan, in large part due to serious ethical problems that had been alleged against him. One cloture vote was taken and failed, 45 to 43. President Lyndon B. Johnson withdrew the nomination before further debate and voting could go forward, most likely because he could see that Fortas lacked the 51 votes needed for confirmation. Fortas later resigned from the Supreme Court as a result of

---

80.   *Cong. Rec.*, 106th Cong., 1st sess., 1999, 145, S14,503.

the allegations of ethical impropriety that had been made against him.

A filibuster of Fortas's nomination, if in fact it existed, was bipartisan. Opposition to Fortas was caused by ethical concerns, and he did not have majority support in the Senate. From the historical record, it seems likely that the Fortas nomination (had it not been withdrawn) would have gone to a full vote before the Senate, and it would have been defeated. Johnson withdrew the nomination to prevent this political embarrassment; he was not forced into withdrawing the nomination by the existence of a filibuster.

Bush's filibustered nominations, by contrast, have majority support in the Senate. In each case, a minority of Senators are consistently voting to prevent the remaining majority from approving the nomination. They have shown that their intent is not to fully debate a nominee, but to prevent votes (that they are sure to lose) from ever occurring. When asked how much time Democrats needed to debate the Owen nomination, Senator Harry Reid (D-NV) responded that "there is not a number in the universe that would be sufficient." [81]

During Bush's first term, liberals in the Senate have chosen to use the filibuster abusively. Their actions have no historical precedent and have upset the balance of power between the President and the Senate with regard to judicial nominations.

Steadfast Under Pressure

Liberal Senators have shamelessly undermined Bush's efforts to fill vacancies on the courts. The President, to his credit, has refused to modify the nature of his judicial nominees, even in the face of the blatantly partisan attacks on his nominees. He is standing his ground in three main ways.

---

81.   *Cong. Rec.*, 108th Cong., 1st sess., 2003, 149, S4,949.

Removing the ABA's Special Privileges from the Nomination Process

Prior to Bush's Administration, the American Bar Association (ABA) served as a semiofficial screening panel for candidates to the federal bench. The ABA received names of candidates and rated them before they were nominated. The ABA's special status in the nomination process gave it great power. Indeed, *The Washington Post* stated in an August 1988 editorial that the "ABA has come to have a virtual veto power before a nomination is made." Initially, the ABA was fairly neutral and its reviews were helpful. Over the years, however, the ABA has become increasingly partisan, taking liberal positions on many public policy issues. As it has become more partisan, its reviews of politically conservative candidates have become less and less objective.

When Bush entered office, he changed the practice of submitting candidates' names to the ABA prior to their nomination. The ABA still rates nominees, but it does so after they have been nominated, rather than before. The procedural adjustment puts the ABA on a level playing field with its fellow political organizations.

Making Recess Appointments

Presidents are granted constitutional power to make temporary "recess appointments" of federal judges without Senate approval in certain circumstances. The temporary appointment can be made permanent if the Senate approves the nomination through the regular confirmation process. These judicial recess appointments have a long history of use. [82] Bush has made two recess appointments, each consistent with this historical usage: Charles Pickering (Fifth Circuit) and William Pryor (Eleventh Circuit).

---

82. More information can be found in Stuart Buck et. al, The Federalist Society for Law & Public Policy Studies, *Judicial Recess Appointments: A Survey of the Arguments* (2003) http://www. fed-soc.org/pdf/recapp.pdf.

Liberal Senate Democrats have not supported Bush's legitimate use of recess appointments. Instead, Bush's actions prompted Daschle to declare that Democrats "will continue to cooperate in the confirmation of Federal judges, but only if the White House gives us assurances that it will no longer [make recess appointments]." [83] Democrats and Republicans cut a deal in May 2004. Bush agreed not to use his recess appointments power to appoint judges until the end of his term, and Senate Republicans agreed not to hold additional cloture votes on already-filibustered nominees. Senate Democrats agreed to allow 25 additional judges through the confirmation process.

In the view of this author, the deal was a mistake. It is understandable that Republicans don't want to leave 25 qualified judges pending through 2004 and into 2005 while many courts face workload difficulties without them. However, it is unlikely that liberal Senators could have maintained a filibuster of more than 30 people simultaneously. Had they done so, they would simply have highlighted the egregious nature of their own actions. Republicans granted legitimacy to the obstructionism of liberal Democrats when they negotiated with them. They should not have done so.

Obviously, the recess appointments power should be used prudently, but Bush has met this criteria. Both of his recess appointees were held up by filibusters, despite their majority support among Senators. Both were appointed to vacancies that had been designated judicial emergencies. Both men have exhibited a willingness to exercise judicial restraint.

Maintaining Separation of Powers

Liberals in the Senate have consistently applied pressure on Bush to consult and compromise with them on his selection of judicial nominees. In 2003, Schumer even sent a list of suggested

83.   *Cong. Rec.*, 108th Cong., 2d sess., 2004, 150, S3,2000-01.

Supreme Court candidates to the President. Obviously, Presidents do sometimes consult with Senators, especially home-state Senators, before making nominations to the lower courts. Ultimately, however, it is a President's job to accept or reject the advice that has been given to him.

Historically, the Senate's role in the confirmation process has been understood as a limited one. The delegates to the Constitutional Convention determined that accountability for judicial nominations would be too diluted if they were left in the hands of all or a group of Senators. Members of the Senate, one delegate observed, were "too numerous and too little personally responsible to ensure a good choice." [84] Instead, the Constitution makes one person directly accountable to voters for nominations. The President, Alexander Hamilton later stated, was to be the "principal agent" in the matter of appointments. [85] By contrast, the Senate's role would be secondary, created as an extra form of security.

The public statements of liberal Democrats in the Senate, combined with their obstructionism of many nominees chosen contrary to their advice, indicate that they are dissatisfied with this scenario. Bush has correctly rejected these attempts by many Democrats to encroach on his constitutional power. His actions uphold the separation of powers between the legislative and executive branches.

Conclusion

If re-elected to office, Bush can solidify his legacy in several ways. First, if given the opportunity, it is crucial that he nominate a Supreme Court justice who will exercise restraint on the bench. The ramifications of a poor or mediocre Supreme Court nomina-

---

84.   James Madison, *Notes of Debates in the Federal Convention of 1787* (1787; reprint, Athens, Ohio: Ohio University Press, 1976). Citation is of the statement of Nathaniel Ghorum, delegate from Massachusetts, made on July 18, 1787.

85.   *The Federalist*, ed. Paul L. Ford (Woodbury, Conn.: Research Publications, 1987), microfiche, 433.

tion will reverberate for years, if not decades, to come. Second, if liberal Democrats continue to abuse Senate rules by filibustering nominees, then Bush should encourage a change in those rules. Continued partisan obstruction must be stopped before permanent harm is done to the health and independence of the judiciary. Last, Bush should continue to use his recess appointments power, albeit with discernment, to ensure that the nation's courts are adequately staffed. Many elder statesmen would be willing to assist their country one last time by serving as a judge for a year or two while judicial nominations work their way through the confirmation process.

During his first four years in office, Bush kept his promise to nominate judicial nominees of high caliber who will uphold the law, rather than illegitimately legislate from the bench. He has done so despite pressure from liberal Democrats to compromise and select more "moderate" candidates of their own choosing. His steadfastness in nominating judges with a restrained judicial temperament has already left an important legacy on the nation's courts. Voters should give him four more years in which to solidify this legacy.

CHAPTER TWENTY-TWO

THE USA PATRIOT ACT

JOHN ASHCROFT

John Ashcroft has served as Attorney General of the United States since January, 2001. Prior to that, he represented Missouri in the United States Senate from 1994 to 2001, and served as Governor of Missouri from 1984 to 1993.

The following comments were given at the Federalist Society National Convention on November 15, 2003. They are republished by permission of the author.

Thank you for the invitation to join you here this morning, I would like to know when the Federalist Society began keeping farmers' hours. I mean, a speech at 8:00 AM on a Saturday?

When your friends at the American Constitution Society for Law and Policy held their inaugural event, they let Janet Reno speak at a far more civilized hour. How do you expect me to do this and be fresh for tonight's John Ashcroft Dance Party?

I do appreciate your invitation to speak to you this morning. The Federalist Society and its membership have been resolute defenders of our nation's founding ideals: liberty, the rule of law, limited government. It is in this capacity that the Federalist Society is so necessary today.

For the past two years, you have been part of the debate about how best to preserve and protect our liberty in the face of a very real terrorist threat. America has an honored tradition of debate and dissent under the First Amendment. It is an essential piece of our constitutional and cultural fabric. As a former politician, I have heard a few dissents in my time, and even expressed a couple of my own.

The founders believed debate should enlighten, not just enliven. It should reveal truth, not obscure it. The future of freedom demands that our discourse be based on a solid foundation of facts and a sincere desire for truth. As we consider the direction and destiny of our nation, the friends of freedom must practice for themselves—and demand from others—a debate informed by fact and directed toward truth.

Take away all the bells and whistles—the rhetorical flourishes and occasional vitriol—and the current debate about liberty is about the rule of law and the role of law. The notion that the law can enhance, not diminish, freedom is an old one. John Locke said the end of law is "not to abolish or restrain but to preserve and enlarge freedom." George Washington called this "ordered liberty."

There are some voices in this discussion of how best to preserve freedom that reject the idea that law can enhance freedom. They think that passage and enforcement of any law is necessarily an infringement of liberty. Ordered liberty is the reason that we are the most open and the most secure society in the world. Ordered liberty is a guiding principle, not a stumbling block, to security. When the first societies passed and enforced the first laws against murder, theft, and rape, the men and women of those societies unquestionably were made more free. A test of a law, then, is this: Does it honor or degrade liberty? Does it enhance or diminish freedom?

The founders provided the mechanism to protect our liberties and preserve the safety and security of the republic: the Constitution. It is a document that safeguards security, but not at the expense of freedom. It celebrates freedom, but not at the expense of security. It protects us *and* our way of life.

Since September 11, 2001, the Department of Justice has fought for, Congress has created, and the judiciary has upheld legal tools that honor the Constitution—legal tools that are making America safer while enhancing American freedom. It is a compliment to all who worked on the Patriot Act to say that it is not constitutionally innovative. The act uses court-tested safeguards and time-honored ideas to aid the war against terrorism, while protecting the rights and lives of citizens.

Madison noted in 1792 that the greatest threat to our liberty was centralized power. Such focused power, he wrote, is liable to abuse. That is why he concluded a distribution of power into separate departments is a first principle of free governments. The Patriot Act honors Madison's "first principles," giving each branch of government a role in ensuring both the lives and liberties of our citizens are protected. The Patriot Act grants the executive branch critical tools in the war on terrorism. It provides the legislative branch extensive oversight. It honors the judicial branch with court supervision over the act's most important powers.

The Role of the Executive Branch

First, the executive branch.

At the Department of Justice, we are dedicated to detecting, disrupting, and dismantling the networks of terror before they can strike at our nation. In the past two years, no major terrorist attack has been perpetrated on our soil.

Consider the bloodshed by terrorism elsewhere in that time: women and children slaughtered in Jerusalem; innocent, young lives snuffed out in Indonesia; Saudi citizens savaged in Riyadh; churchgoers in Pakistan murdered by the hands of hate.

We are using the tough tools provided in the USA Patriot Act to defend American lives and liberty from those who have shed blood and decimated lives in other parts of the world.

The Patriot Act does three things:

First, it closes the gaping holes in law enforcement's ability to collect vital intelligence information on terrorist enterprises. It allows law enforcement to use proven tactics long used in the fight against organized crime and drug dealers. Second, the Patriot Act updates our antiterrorism laws to meet the challenges of new technology and new threats. Third, with these critical new investigative tools provided by the Patriot Act, law enforcement can share information and cooperate better with each other. From prosecutors to intelligence agents, the act allows law enforcement to "connect the dots" and uncover terrorist plots before they are launched.

Here is an example of how we use the act. Some of you are familiar with the Lyman Faris case. He is a naturalized American citizen who worked as a truck driver out of Columbus, Ohio.

Using information sharing allowed under the Patriot Act, law enforcement pieced together Faris's activities:

- How Faris met senior Al Qaeda operatives in a training camp in Afghanistan.

- How he was asked to procure equipment that might cause train derailments and sever suspension systems of bridges.

- How he traveled to New York to scout a potential terrorist target.

Faris pleaded guilty on May 1, 2003, and on October 28, he was sentenced under the Patriot Act's tough sentences. He will serve 20 years in prison for providing material support to Al Qaeda and conspiracy for providing the terrorist organization with information about possible U.S. targets for attack.

The Faris case illustrates what the Patriot Act does. One thing the Patriot Act does not do is allow the investigation of individuals "solely upon the basis of activities protected by the First Amendment to the Constitution of the United States."

Even if the law did not prohibit it, the Justice Department has neither the time nor the inclination to delve into the reading habits or other First Amendment activities of our citizens.

Despite all the hoopla to the contrary, for example, the Patriot Act—which allows for court-approved requests for business records, including library records—has never been used to obtain records from a library. Not once.

Senator Dianne Feinstein recently said, "I have never had a single abuse of the Patriot Act reported to me. My staff e-mailed the ACLU and asked them for instances of actual abuses. They e-mailed back and said they had none."

The Patriot Act has enabled us to make quiet, steady progress in the war on terror.

Since September 11, we have dismantled terrorist cells in Detroit, Seattle, Portland, Tampa, Northern Virginia, and Buffalo. We have disrupted weapons procurement plots in Miami, San Diego, Newark, and Houston. We have shut down terrorist-affiliated charities in Chicago, Dallas, and Syracuse. We have brought criminal charges against 286 individuals. We have secured convictions or guilty pleas from 155 people. Terrorists who are incarcerated, deported, or otherwise neutralized threaten fewer American lives. For two years, our citizens have been safe. There have been no major terrorist attacks on our soil. American freedom has been enhanced, not diminished. The Constitution has been honored, not degraded.

The Role of Congress

Second, the role Congress plays.

In six weeks of debate in September and October of 2001, both the House of Representatives and the Senate examined studiously and debated vigorously the merits of the Patriot Act. In the end, both houses supported overwhelmingly its passage.

Congress built into the Patriot Act strict and structured oversight of the executive branch. Every six months, the Justice Department provides Congress with reports of its activities under the Patriot Act.

Since September 24, 2001, Justice Department officials, myself included, have testified on the Patriot Act and other homeland security issues more than 115 times. We have responded to hundreds of written and oral questions and provided reams of written responses.

To date, no congressional committee has found any evidence that law enforcement has abused the powers provided by the Patriot Act. Legislative oversight of the executive branch is critical to "ordered liberty." It ensures that laws and those who administer them respect the rights and liberties of the citizens.

There has not been a major terrorist attack within our borders in the past two years. Time and again, Congress has found the Patriot Act to be effective against terrorist threats and respectful and protective of citizens' liberties. The Constitution has been honored, not degraded.

The Role of the Judiciary

Finally, the judiciary.

The Patriot Act provides for close judicial supervision of the executive branch's use of Patriot Act authorities.

The act allows the government to utilize many long-standing, well-accepted law enforcement tools in the fight against terror. These tools include delayed notification, judicially supervised searches, and so-called roving wiretaps, which have long been used in combating organized crime and in the war on drugs.

In using these tactics to fight terrorism, the Patriot Act includes an additional layer of protection for individual liberty. A federal judge supervises the use of each of these tactics. Were we to seek an order to request business records, that order would need the approval of a federal judge. Grand jury subpoenas issued for similar requests by police in standard criminal investigations are issued without judicial oversight.

Throughout the Patriot Act, tools provided to fight terrorism require that the same predication be established before a federal judge as with similar tools provided to fight other crime.

In addition, the Patriot Act includes yet another layer of judicial scrutiny by providing a civil remedy in the event of abuse. Section 223 of the Patriot Act allows citizens to seek monetary damages for willful violations of the Patriot Act. This civil remedy serves as a further deterrent against infringement upon individual liberties.

Given our overly litigious society, you are probably wondering how many such civil cases have been filed to date. It is a figure as astronomical as the library searches. Zero.

There is a simple reason for this: The Patriot Act has not been used to infringe upon individual liberty.

Many of you have heard the hue and cry from critics of the Patriot Act who allege that liberty has been eroded. But more telling is what you have not heard. You have not heard of one single case in which a judge has found an abuse of the Patriot Act because, again, there have been no abuses.

It is also important to consider what we have not seen: no major terrorist attacks on our soil over the past two years. The Patriot Act's record demonstrates that we are protecting the American people while honoring the Constitution and preserving the liberties we hold dear.

While we are discussing the judiciary, allow me to add one more point. To be at its best, the judiciary requires a full bench.

This is not like football or basketball, where the bench consists of reserves who might not see action. The judicial bench, to operate best for the people, must be at full strength.

Let me say this: President Bush has performed his duties admirably in selecting and nominating highly qualified jurists to serve. The language in a judge's commission reads, "George W. Bush, President of the United States of America ... to all who shall see this, presents greeting: Know ye that reposing special confidence and trust in the wisdom, uprightness and learning, I have nominated ..." You can fill in the blank, with the name Janice Rogers Brown, or Bill Pryor, or Priscilla Owen, or Carolyn Kuhl.

The commission's language may seem anachronistic. The ideals the men and women of the bench must uphold are not: Wisdom. Uprightness. Learning.

The President's nominees personify those noble ideals. They are proven defenders of the rule of law. They should be treated fairly. They deserve to be treated with the dignity that befits the position to which they seek to serve our country and its citizens. You may think that some of the best of the President's nominees are being treated unfairly. In that case, *you* may want to exercise *your* right to dissent. The future of freedom and the rule of law depend on citizens informed by fact and directed toward truth.

To be sure, the law depends on the integrity of those who make it, enforce it, and apply it. It depends on the moral courage of lawyers like you—and our citizens—to insist on being heard, whether in town hall meetings, county council meetings, or the Senate. There is nothing more noble than fighting to preserve our God-given rights. Our proven tactics against the terrorist threat are helping to do just that.

For more than two years, we have protected the lives of our citizens here at home. Again and again, Congress has determined and the courts have determined that our citizens' rights have been respected.

Twenty-six months ago, terrorists attacked our nation thinking our liberties were our weakness. They were wrong. The American people have fulfilled the destiny shaped by our forefathers and founders and revealed the power of freedom. Time and again, the spirit of our nation has been renewed and our greatness as a people has been strengthened by our dedication to the cause of liberty, the rule of law, and the primacy and dignity of the individual. I know we will keep alive these noble aspirations that lie in the hearts of all our fellow citizens and for which our young men and women are at this moment fighting and making the ultimate sacrifice.

What we are defending is what generations before us fought for and defended: a nation that is a standard, a beacon, to all who desire a land that promises to uphold the best hopes of all mankind. A land of justice. A land of liberty.

Thank you. God bless you. And God bless America.

CHAPTER TWENTY-THREE

PROTECTING CIVIL LIBERTIES AND THE PATRIOT ACT

WILLIAM BENNETT

William Bennett served as President Ronald Reagan's chairman of the National Endowment for the Humanities and Secretary of Education, and President George H. W. Bush's director of the Office of National Drug Control Policy. He is currently chairman of the education company K12, Inc., co-director of Empower America, and the chairman of Americans for Victory over Terrorism, a project dedicated to strengthening public support for the war on terrorism.

The following comments were given at a conference hosted by the Heritage Foundation on May 4, 2004. They appear here by permission of the authors.

Introduction by Edwin Meese III

Good morning, ladies and gentlemen, and welcome to the Heritage Foundation.

It's a pleasure to see all of you this morning to talk about a very important topic. After the events of the 11th of September, 2001, a number of things happened. A military action was commenced against the terrorists. We established a Department of Homeland Security, and we passed legislation to provide better means in order to provide investigators and intelligence agents with the legislative authority and instruments to carry on the global war against terrorism and particularly to defend homeland security.

For the most part, what has happened is that various investigative and surveillance techniques that have been applicable to other types of criminal activity such as drug trafficking, organized crime, and the like, have been applied to terrorism. But despite the fact that a great many safeguards were built into the legislation which has become known as the U.S.A. Patriot Act, there still is a great deal of misinformation which has been spread throughout the country, which has caused some people to fear that civil liberties are in danger.

Today we have brought a panel of experts to talk about the Patriot Act, and to talk about civil liberties and Homeland Security, and to set the record straight, and to correct many of the myths that have been carried through the country on this particular subject. I will introduce each of the speakers as they rise to talk to you.

Bill Bennett is well-known, I'm sure, to most of you here. He has a distinguished record of public service. He served as Secretary of Education and chairman of National Endowment for the Humanities under Ronald Reagan and as director of the Office of National Drug Control Policy under the first President Bush. I consider him one of the leading commentators on society and culture, and he has some 14 books that he's either authored or has edited. In addition, he serves as a co-chairman of Empower America.

But as though that wasn't enough, Bill has recently taken on some new responsibilities. He is the chairman of an organization called Americans for Victory over Terrorism, which is a project of the Claremont Institute. He's also the Washington, D.C., fellow of the Claremont Institute and has recently begun a new, nationally syndicated radio show that can be heard in some 76 cities—maybe more. And that was yesterday!

He can be seen on www.bennettmornings.com, which is the Internet version of the radio show.

So, Bill, it's good to have you with us. Please welcome Bill Bennett.

Comments by William Bennett

Good morning ladies and gentlemen. Thank you, Ed, very much.

First, let me address the recent news about the abuse of Iraqi prisoners by American soldiers. Some will no doubt say that a government that cannot be trusted with prisoners cannot be trusted with suspects. That's not true. That's not the government of the United States we are talking about.

I think that John Stuart Mill is appropriate here. He says: "Any standard will work ill if we suppose universal idiocy or barbarism to be conjoined with it." And that's true. As Justice Holmes said once, "The main remedy for most of what ails us is to grow more civilized."

And that I think is an appropriate word to use given the current circumstance, because it is a battle between civilization and barbarism, civilization and nihilism. It makes not a little difference, not some difference, but as Aristotle would say, "all the difference," whether the barbarism is an exception to your standard (as is Abu Ghraib now), or if barbarism is your policy (as was Abu Ghraib under Saddam Hussein).

What's happened over there with some of our military police and others is condemned by a civilized society, and it will be remedied by a civilized society. It is not the policy of a civilized society as it is the policy of some of those who relish in showing these videos over and over again.

I think our first task in talking about civil liberties in the context of this war requires us to remember a few things that some people have forgotten, and to put the whole debate in a general and historical context. Our enemy attacked us in disguise, not in uniform, not in marked war planes from an enemy country. Rather, unlike Pearl Harbor, our enemies trained abroad, moved here, lived here under the guise of legality, trained some more here, and used civilian aircraft, civilian tactics, and other civilians to kill as many innocent people as possible. Also, unlike Pearl Harbor, their targets were not military, but civilian; and unlike Pearl Harbor it appears that much of the money used to finance our enemies came from money raised in the United States and from money raised in countries that are purported allies of the United States.

So, how do we wage war against such an enemy, while at the same time staying true to our own founding ethics—ethics such as freedom and equality and privacy and human dignity? Ethics that seem to be one of the main reasons for our enemies' wrath?

These are not new questions. In Federalist No. 3, John Jay writes the following: "Among the many objects to which wise and free people find it necessary to direct their attention, that of providing for their safety seems to be the first."

Being a country that values such things as freedom, we have, several times, faced the question of how to reconcile that freedom with the first object of government—security, especially in war time. One-hundred and forty years ago Lincoln asked: "Must a government of necessity be too strong for the liberties of its own people or too weak to maintain its own existence?" The answer to Lincoln's question is now as it was then, a resounding "No."

But now, let us look to what's happened since 9/11—again, keeping in mind all the distinctions between that attack and the previous attack on us in 1941. We have not, as Franklin Delano Roosevelt and the great liberal Earl Warren did, established internment camps for over 100,000 U.S. citizens whose only crime was looking like the people we were at war with in another country. Nonetheless, the rhetoric is in some instances more heated about our response to 9/11 than it ever was in the 1940s. So called "conservative libertarians" and liberal libertarians from the spectrum of the American Conservative Union and Bob Barr to the ACLU and John Kerry have at times made this response sound like we live under Mitchell Palmer's Red Scare, or J. Edgar Hoover—or, one might say, Franklin Delano Roosevelt and Earl Warren.

But we don't. We don't live like that and we don't profile like that. We have given trials to those who claim abuses of our post-9/11 system and as Brad Berensen told me and our radio audience, we have even released prisoners from Guantanamo to our detriment, as we now learn that four of those that we released have re-joined Al Qaeda in Afghanistan.

But let's be specific to the Patriot Act. The Patriot Act may be great fund raising fodder for the ACLU. I'm happy to note, however, that the public is not buying into this media and inside-the-Beltway generated crisis. For all of the 2003 Democratic primary attacks on John Ashcroft and the Patriot Act, it is worth noting—as George Will recently did—that such attacks have subsided in the wake of the finding that over 60 percent of the public supports the Patriot Act without even knowing all of its details. Not a surprising statistic, given that 99 Senators voted for it. Who, listening to the Democratic primaries, remembers that fact?

Perhaps nothing concentrated the mind on this so much as Bill Clinton's Attorney General, Janet Reno, telling the 9/11 Commission, just a couple of weeks ago, that "Everything that's been done in the Patriot Act has been helpful." And just last

THANK YOU, PRESIDENT BUSH

October, Senator Joseph Biden called the criticism of the Patriot Act "ill-informed and overblown." Not only Joe Biden, but Senator Dianne Feinstein said, "I have never had a single abuse of the Patriot Act reported to me." And when she asked the ACLU for examples of violations of civil liberties under the Patriot Act, Senator Feinstein came back and said, "They had none."

So, let me part with some of my fellow conservatives who oppose this act, and stand with Democrats such as Joe Biden, Dianne Feinstein, Janet Reno and most conservatives, and re-endorse the Patriot Act. We are not a Jordan, that engages in torture as a matter of policy; we court martial those who torture on our behalf and we revile the practice. In light of the reports coming out of Abu Ghraib, we are rightfully ashamed and angered.

Daniel Moynihan once said that he was not ashamed to speak on behalf of the United States, a less than perfect country. Senator Moynihan said, "Find me a better one. Do I suppose there are societies which are free of sin? No I don't. Do I think ours is, on balance, and comparably the most hopeful set of human relations the world has ever seen? Yes, I do. Have we done obscene things? Yes, we have. How did our people learn about them? They learned about them on television and in the newspapers."

We use the law, we use the courts, we use the press. They are all sources of protection. And in doing so, we use the Patriot Act as well. The Patriot Act is not only commonsensical, but long overdue given the warnings we had for years before 9/11. We need to reauthorize the Patriot Act next year so we can continue fighting our war on terrorism, both at home and abroad, so that we can disrupt terrorist cells both at home and abroad. And so that we don't, in the words of another great Democrat, Justice Robert Jackson, "let our Bill of Rights become a suicide pact."

Thank you very much.

CHAPTER TWENTY-FOUR

THE SAFE ACT WILL NOT MAKE US SAFER

EDWIN MEESE III AND
PAUL ROSENZWEIG

Edwin Meese III served as the Attorney General of the United States, from February 1985 to August 1988. He is now the Ronald Reagan Distinguished Fellow in Public Policy at the Heritage Foundation, and chairman of the Center for Legal and Judicial Studies.

Paul Rosenzweig is a senior legal research fellow at the Heritage Foundation. The following article was previously written for publication on April 30, 2004 by the Heritage Foundation. It is republished here by permission of the authors.

The USA Patriot Act, a law passed with overwhelming support in Congress immediately following the September 11 terrorist attacks, has been the subject of many recent attacks and criticisms. Opponents argue that various provisions of the

Patriot Act, and related laws and practices, have greatly in-fringed upon American liberties while failing to deal effectively with the threat of terrorism.[86]

Criticism of the anti-terrorist campaign is not limited to the Patriot Act; many other aspects of the Bush Administration's domestic response to terrorism have come under fire. To some degree, the Patriot Act as conceived by the public is broader than its actual provisions. Its very name has come to serve as a symbol for all of the domestic anti-terrorist law enforcement actions. It has become a convenient shorthand formulation for all questions that have arisen since September 11 about the alleged conflict between civil liberty and national security.

But the Patriot Act is a real law, with real purposes and real provisions. Too much of the debate has focused on the Act not as it truly is, but as people perceive it to be. Most of the proposals for reform mistake the appearance of potential problems and abuse (the myth) with the reality of no abuse at all[87]—and, thus, the case for change has not been made.

The Security and Freedom Ensured Act of 2003 (the "SAFE Act")[88] is emblematic of this trend. It purports to be based upon an assessment of the necessity for change, yet its major substan-

86. See e.g. Audrey Hudson, "Cities in Revolt over Patriot Act," *Washington Times* (January 5, 2004). Jessica Garrison, "L.A. Takes Stand Against Patriot Act," *Los Angeles Times* (January 22, 2004), B4.

87. The Inspector General for the Department of Justice has reported that there have been no instances in which the Patriot Act has been invoked to infringe on civil rights or civil liberties. See "Report to Congress on Implementation of Section 1001 of the USA Patriot Act," 27 January 2004; see also "Report Finds No Abuses of Patriot Act," *Washington Post* (January 28, 2004), A2. This is consistent with the conclusions of others. For example, at a Senate Judiciary Committee Hearing on the Patriot Act, Senator Joseph Biden (D-DE) said that "some measure of the criticism [of the Patriot Act] is both misinformed and overblown." His colleague, Senator Dianne Feinstein (D-CA) said: "I have never had a single abuse of the Patriot Act reported to me. My staff ... asked [the ACLU] for instances of actual abuses. They ... said they had none." Even the lone Senator to vote against the Patriot Act, Russ Feingold (D-WI), said that he "supported 90 percent of the Patriot Act" and that there is "too much confusion and misinformation" about the Act. See *Senate Jud. Comm. Hrg.*, 108th Cong, 1st Sess. (October 21, 2003). These views—from Senators outside the Administration and an internal watchdog—are at odds with the fears often expressed by the public.

88. See S. 1709 (108th Cong.). The SAFE Act is co-sponsored by Senators Craig (R-ID), Durbin (D-IL), Crapo (R-ID), Feingold (D-WI), Sununu (R-NH), Wyden (D-OR), and Bingaman (D-NM).

tive provisions lack any factual basis for concluding that changes are necessary. Often the proposals rest on incomplete legal analysis and would make America's response to terrorism less effective. In the end, they appear to be little more than a political fig leaf, intended to allow politicians to assert that they have responded to the public will and "fixed" the Patriot Act.

But capitulating to hysteria is pandering, not leadership. The SAFE Act will not make America safer.

This paper addresses the three principal substantive provisions of the SAFE Act: Section 2, which would limit the use of roving wiretaps; Section 3, which would modify traditional authority to delay notification of a search; and Sections 4 and 5, which would limit the ability of law enforcement and intelligence authorities to secure business records relating to terrorist activity. Each of these proposed revisions is ill-conceived and ought, on the merits, to be rejected.

Roving Wiretaps: a Useful Tool

Section 206 of the Patriot Act authorized the use of "roving wiretaps"—that is, wiretaps that follow an individual and are not tied to a specific telephone or location—in terrorism investigations. America's original electronic surveillance laws (the Foreign Intelligence Surveillance Act ["FISA"] of 1978 and Title III of the Omnibus Crime Control Act of 1968)[89] stem from a time when phones were the only means of electronic communications and all phones were connected by hard wires to a single network.

Roving wiretaps have arisen over the past 20 years for use in the investigation of ordinary crimes (e.g., drug transactions or organized crime activities) because modern technologies (cell phones, BlackBerries, and Internet telephony) allow those seeking to evade detection the ability to change communications

---

89. The FISA governs applications for electronic surveillance in matters relating to foreign intelligence, espionage, counterintelligence, and terrorism. Title III governs applications for electronic surveillance involving the investigation of domestic crimes.

devices and locations at will. Section 2 of the SAFE Act would unwisely restrict the use of roving wiretaps in terrorism investigations.

Getting a FISA Warrant to Conduct Electronic Surveillance

To begin with, one must understand the general structure of laws governing when law enforcement or intelligence agents may secure authorization to conduct electronic surveillance relating to suspected foreign intelligence or terrorism activity. Title III (the statute governing electronic surveillance for domestic crime) allows a court to enter an order authorizing electronic surveillance if "there is probable cause for belief that an individual is committing, has committed or is about to commit" one of a list of several specified crimes.

FISA (the statute governing intelligence and terrorism surveillance) has a parallel requirement: A warrant may be issued if there is probable cause to believe that the target of the surveillance is a foreign power or the agent of a foreign power. FISA also requires that the government establish probable cause to believe that "each of the facilities or places at which the surveillance is directed is being used, or is about to be used" by the foreign power or the agent of the foreign power who is the target of surveillance. FISA court warrants thus are issued by federal judges, upon a showing of probable cause, and describe the things to be seized with particularity—the traditional three-prong test for compliance with the warrant clause requirements of the Fourth Amendment.[90]

Thus, no one can argue that these FISA warrants violate the Constitution. To the contrary, as the Foreign Intelligence Surveillance Court of Review recently made clear, the FISA warrant structure is "a reasonable response based on a balance of the legitimate need of the government for foreign intelligence

---

90.   For an articulation of this test, *see Dalia v United States,* 441 US 238, 255 (1979).

information to protect against national security threats with the protected rights of citizens."[91] This is so because, as the court recognized, there is a difference in the nature of "ordinary" criminal prosecution and that directed at foreign intelligence or terrorism crimes:

> The main purpose of ordinary criminal law is twofold: to punish the wrongdoer and to deter other persons in society from embarking on the same course. The government's concern with respect to foreign intelligence crimes, on the other hand, is overwhelmingly to stop or frustrate the immediate criminal activity.[92]

Roving Wiretaps and Section 206

Roving wiretaps (whether used in foreign intelligence or domestic criminal investigations) are, as noted, a response to changing technologies. Phones are no longer fixed in one place and can move across state borders at the speed of flight. Sophisticated terrorists and criminals can change phones and communications devices constantly in an attempt to thwart interception.

In response to these changes in technology, in 1986 Congress authorized a relaxation of the particularity requirement for the investigation of drug offenses. Under the modified law, the authority to intercept an individual's electronic communication was tied only to the individual who was the suspect of criminal activity (and who was attempting to "thwart" surveillance) rather than to a particular communications device.

Section 206 authorized the same techniques for foreign intelligence investigations. As the Department of Justice has noted:

> This provision has enhanced the government's ability to monitor sophisticated international terrorists and intelligence officers, who are trained to thwart surveillance by rapidly changing hotels, cell phones,

---

91.   *In re Sealed Case*, 310 F3d 717, 742 (Foreign Int. Surv. Ct. Rev. 2002).
92.   Id at 744.

and internet accounts, just before important meetings or communications.[93]

One important safeguard is that the FISA court may authorize such roving wiretaps only if it makes a finding as to the terrorist's actions — that "the actions of the target of the application may have the effect of thwarting the identification" of a terrorism suspect.[94]

The SAFE Act's Unnecessary Burden

The SAFE Act would modify the existing FISA requirements by, in effect, imposing an unreasonable and burdensome ascertainment requirement on law enforcement and intelligence agents. Under the Patriot Act, agents may seek authority for an interception even when the identity of the suspect is not known (so long as probable cause existed to believe the person involved was an agent of a foreign power). The SAFE Act would change that regime. If enacted, it would require agents seeking authority for a wiretap to specify the identity of the target and, if they were unable to do so, to describe with specificity the nature and location of the places where the interception would occur. In other words, in certain circumstances, intelligence agents would be unable to secure a warrant to conduct electronic surveillance because of the indefiniteness of their information.

The proposed modification of the Patriot Act misses the point completely — so much so that one doubts whether any of the authors is a serious student of either law enforcement or intelligence activity. To the extent the SAFE Act calls for specificity with respect to the precise location or facility where the communication is occurring, it is a non sequitur. Government agents use roving wiretaps only when the location or facility where the communication is occurring is not known with precision — for the

---

93. Department of Justice, *The USA Patriot Act: Myth vs. Reality* (2003), 3.
94. 50 USC § 1805 (c) (2) (b) (as amended by Sec. 206 of the Patriot Act).

simple reason that those under surveillance are attempting to thwart surveillance by constantly changing their location and means of communication. To call for specificity as to location imposes a higher burden on using roving wiretaps in terrorism investigations than in routine domestic criminal investigations.

The SAFE Act's proposal to require that the individual who is the subject of scrutiny be precisely identified is equally fool-hardy. In a domestic investigation, the identity of the suspect under scrutiny may often be well-known, though drug dealers do, of course, use aliases. The problem becomes substantially more acute in the shadowy world of espionage and terrorism, where the identity of the investigative subject is often obscured behind a gauze of deceit.

Terrorists change their identity with frequency and often pose as other, real-world individuals. Often, the only description that the intelligence agency will be able to provide to identify the suspect is an alias (or several aliases). Sometimes the description of the terrorism suspect may be nothing more than a physical description. And, on still other occasions, it may consist only of a pattern of behavior (i.e., the person who regularly uses this series of phones, in this order, every third day). To insist that intelligence and law enforcement agents precisely identify the individual under scrutiny or the facility he will be using is, in effect, to ban the use of roving wiretaps in terrorism investigations.

And that is the wrong answer—indeed, the SAFE Act reverses the proper analysis. It imposes a narrow law enforcement paradigm on the efforts to combat terrorism. That paradigm, however, no longer holds. Law enforcement efforts to combat terrorism are policing of a different form: preventative rather than reactive. There is little, if any, value in punishing terrorists after the fact, especially when, in some instances, they are willing to perish in the attack. Hewing to the traditional law enforcement paradigm of particularity in the context of terrorism investigations is a fundamental category mistake.

The traditional law enforcement model is highly protective of civil liberty in preference to physical security. All lawyers have heard one or another form of the maxim that "it is better that ten guilty go free than that one innocent be mistakenly punished." This embodies a fundamentally moral judgment that, when it comes to enforcing criminal law, American society, in effect, prefers to have many more Type II errors (false negatives) than it does Type I errors (false positives). That preference arises, at least implicitly, from a comparative valuation of the social costs attending the two types of error. We value liberty sufficiently highly that we see a great cost in any Type I error. And, though we realize that Type II errors free the guilty to return to the general population, thereby imposing additional social costs on society, we have a common-sense understanding that those costs, while significant, are not so substantial that they threaten large numbers of citizens or core structural aspects of the American polity.

The post-September 11 world changes this calculus, principally by changing the cost of the Type II errors. Whatever the costs of freeing organized crime boss John Gotti or serial murderer John Mohammad might be, they are considered less than the potentially horrific costs of failing to stop the next Al Qaeda assault. Thus, the theoretical rights-protective construct under which our law enforcement system operates must, of necessity, be modified to meet the new reality. We simply cannot afford a rule that "better ten terrorists be able to succeed in their attacks than that one innocent be mistakenly subject to surveillance." The SAFE Act's proposal to impose a traditional law enforcement construct misses this point altogether.

Nor is there any practical necessity for the SAFE Act's proposed revisions. Though Section 206 has been the law of the land for more than two years, there have been no reported instances of abuse of this authority.[95] Whatever else may be said about the

---

95.   See *supra* n. 1.

Patriot Act, even its most ardent critics must admit that they are basing their legislative proposals on fear rather than reality. But fear is not a basis for policymaking.

Searches and Seizures: Delayed Notification

One section of the Patriot Act that has engendered great criticism is Section 213, which authorizes the issuance of delayed notification search warrants—which critics call "sneak and peek" warrants. Section 3 of the SAFE Act would modify Section 213 by limiting the circumstances in which delayed notification warrants could be issued and by requiring burdensome, repetitive recertification requirements. Section 3 would also sunset (that is terminate) the provisions of Section 213 altogether on December 31, 2005.

Traditional Rules of Search and Seizure

Traditionally, when the courts have issued search warrants authorizing the government's forcible entry into a citizen's home or office, they have required that the searching officers provide contemporaneous notification of the search to the individual whose home or office has been entered.[96] Prior to September 11, some courts permitted limited delays in notification to the owner, when immediate notification would hinder the ongoing investigation. Section 213 codifies that common law tradition and extends it to terrorism investigations. Critics see this extension as an unwarranted expansion of authority—but here, too, the fears of abuse seem to outstrip reality.

Delayed notification warrants are a long-existing crime-fighting tool upheld by courts nationwide for decades in organ-

---

96.   This requirement has a long-standing provenance at common law. As the King's Bench court said in 1603: "In all cases where the King is a party, the sheriff ... may break the party's house, either to arrest him, or to do execution of the King's process, it otherwise he cannot enter. But before he breaks it, he ought to signify the cause of his coming, and to make request to open the doors." *Semanyne's Case*, 5 Co Rep 91a, 77 Eng Rep 194 (KB 1603).

ized crime, drug cases, and child pornography. For example, Mafia Don Nicky Scarfo maintained the records of his various criminal activities on a personal computer, protected by a highly sophisticated encryption technology. Law enforcement knew where the information was—and thus had ample probable cause to seize the computer. But the seizure would have been useless without a way of breaking the encryption. So, on a delayed notification warrant, the FBI surreptitiously placed a keystroke logger on Scarfo's computer. The logger recorded Scarfo's password, which the FBI then used to examine all of Scarfo's records of his various drug deals and murders.[97] It would, of course, have been fruitless for the FBI to have secured a warrant to enter Scarfo's home and place a logger on his computer if, at the same time, it had been obliged to notify Scarfo that it had done so.

The courts have approved this common law use of delayed notification. Over 20 years ago, the Supreme Court held that the Fourth Amendment does not require law enforcement to give immediate notice of the execution of a search warrant. The Court emphasized "that covert entries are constitutional in some circumstances, at least if they are made pursuant to a warrant." In fact, the Court stated that an argument to the contrary was "frivolous." [98] In an earlier case—the seminal case defining the scope of privacy in contemporary America—the Court said that "officers need not announce their purpose before conducting an otherwise [duly] authorized search if such an announcement would provoke the escape of the suspect or the destruction of critical evidence."[99]

---

97. *United States v Scarfo*, 180 FSupp2d 572 (D NJ 2001).
98. *Dalia v United States*, 441 US 238 (1979).
99. *Katz v United States*, 389 US 347 (1967).

Section 213 Adopts the Traditional Standard

Section 213 of the Patriot Act thus attempts to codify the common law authority given to law enforcement for decades. As summarized by the Department of Justice:

> Because of differences between jurisdictions, the law was a mix of inconsistent standards that varied across the country. This lack of uniformity hindered complex terrorism cases. Section 213 resolved the problem by establishing a uniform statutory standard. [100]

Now, under Section 213, courts can delay notice if there is "reasonable cause" to believe that immediate notification may have a specified adverse result. The "reasonable cause" standard is consistent with pre-Patriot Act case law for delayed notice of warrants. [101] And the law goes further, defining "reasonable cause" for the issuance of a court order narrowly. Courts are, under Section 213, authorized to delay notice only when immediate notification may result in death or physical harm to an individual, flight from prosecution, evidence tampering, witness intimidation, or otherwise seriously jeopardize an investigation.

In short, Section 213 is really no change at all; it merely clarifies that a single uniform standard applies and that terrorist offenses are included. Nor does Section 213 promise great abuse. Here, as in the past under common law, the officer seeking authority for delayed entry must get authorization for that action from a federal judge or magistrate—under the exact same standards and procedures that apply in getting a warrant to enter a building in the first place. And the law makes clear that in all cases law enforcement must ultimately give notice that property has been searched or seized. The only difference from a traditional search warrant is the temporary delay in providing notification. Here, the presence of oversight rules seems strong—

---

100. Department of Justice, *The USA Patriot Act: Myth vs. Reality* (2003), 11.

101. See e.g. *United States v Villegas*, 899 F2d 1324, 1337 (2d Cir 1990) (government must show "good reason" for delayed service of warrants).

certainly strong enough to prevent the abuse that some critics fear.

Section 213 Has Aided the Fight Against Terrorism

Nor can it be doubted that the delayed notification standards have performed a useful function and are a critical aspect of the strategy of prevention—detecting and incapacitating terrorists before they are able to strike.

One example of the use of delayed notification involves the indictment of Dr. Rafil Dhafir. A delayed notification warrant allowed the surreptitious search of an airmail envelope containing records of overseas bank accounts used to ship over $4 million to Iraq. Because Dhafir did not know of the search, he was unable to flee and he did not move the funds before they were seized. [102] In another instance, the Justice Department described a hypothetical situation (based upon an actual case) in which the FBI secured access to the hard drive of terrorists who had sent their computer for repair. In still another, they were able to plant a surveillance device in a building used by terrorists as a safe house. [103]

The SAFE Act Would Needlessly Limit the Use of Delayed Notification Authority

The SAFE Act would make two significant changes to Section 213. First, it would limit the circumstances under which delayed notification would be allowed. Second, it would impose upon the Department of Justice the burden of seeking reauthorization for the delay every seven days, regardless of whether circumstances had changed. Neither change is merited.

---

102. William E. Moscella, Asst. Atty. Gen. to Hon. Dennis Hastert, Speaker of the United States House of Representatives (July 25, 2003). See also "Four Indicted for Sending Funds to Iraq," *Associated Press* (February 26, 2003), http://www.chron.com/cs/CDA/printstory.hts/special/iraq/1796320.

103. Moscella, at 4.

The change in standards—limiting the use of delayed notification—is particularly pernicious. Under Section 213 (just as with wiretap or other electronic surveillance) delayed notice is appropriate only when immediate notification may result in:

- Death or physical harm to an individual,
- Flight from prosecution,
- Evidence tampering,
- Witness intimidation, or
- Otherwise seriously jeopardize an investigation.

The SAFE Act would delete this final catchall phrase because it is perceived as too broad and as providing too much leeway for Executive action. But this concern is overly cautious: One can imagine few circumstances in which an investigation would be "seriously jeopardized" that would not also satisfy one of the more specific listings of potential adverse consequences. And nobody disputes that those other consequences (flight, risk of harm, etc.) are appropriate grounds for delay.

Even worse, though, are logical implications of what the SAFE Act would do. Those who would adopt the SAFE Act and delete the catchall phrase are implicitly saying that they are willing to accept the frustration of legitimate investigations. If you advocate changing Section 213, you are advocating the view that, even if an Article III federal judge finds that an investigation would be seriously jeopardized without a delay, you will not allow a delay in notification to occur.

In other words, critics value the process of notification more highly than the substance of an impaired investigation. This reverses the more reasonable evaluation of the comparative values, especially when the result is validated by an independent federal judge.

Thus, proponents of the SAFE Act misunderstand the true nature of the issues at stake. The purpose of the notice requirement is twofold: (1) In typical searches, it allows a contemporaneous objection. The individual may say, in effect, "You've got the wrong house." (2) Following notification, it also allows for non-contemporaneous objections to be heard in court so that overzealous execution of the warrant, or a search beyond the scope authorized, may be challenged before a judge.

But in the context of a surreptitious entry and delayed notification, the first of those purposes can have no force. Except by accident, law enforcement or intelligence agents will not conduct a delayed-notice entry in a manner that affords contemporaneous notification—to do so would frustrate the precise purpose of the delayed notification. So the only way to effect the first of these two purposes is to prohibit delayed notification entry altogether—a rule that would have very significant costs. And it is equally clear that the second purpose—allowing subsequent challenge in court—is served so long as the law requires (as Section 213 does) eventual notification in all circumstances. The only real argument that critics can make is that Section 213 imposes costs by virtue of the time for which the notification is delayed—a true cost but a comparatively minor one when balanced against the substantial benefits that the process of delayed notification allows in appropriate cases.

The evident utility of the potential uses of Section 213, the provision for subsequent review in court, and the absolute absence of any evidence of abuse of this power suggest that several proposed repeals under congressional consideration are unwise. At worst, they would completely eliminate a long-standing investigative tool for all crimes—both terrorist crimes and traditional common law crimes. At best, the rejection of Section 213 would re-institute a dichotomy between traditional crimes and terrorist investigations—again, a mistaken one that oddly provides greater authority to investigate less threatening common law criminal acts.

Increased Investigative Authority and Business Records

Perhaps no provision of the Patriot Act has excited greater controversy than has Section 215, the so-called "angry librarians" provision. The section allows the Foreign Intelligence Surveillance Court in a foreign intelligence investigation to issue an order directing the recipient to produce tangible things.

The revised statutory authority in Section 215 is not wholly new. FISA has had authority for securing some forms of business records since its inception. The new statute modifies FISA's original business-records authority in a two important respects.

First, it "expands the types of entities that can be compelled to disclose information. Under the old provision, the FISA court could order the production of records only from 'a common carrier, public accommodation facility, physical storage facility or vehicle rental facility.' The new provision contains no such restrictions." [104]

Second, the new law "expanded the types of items that can be requested. Under the old authority, the FBI could only seek 'records.' Now, the FBI can seek 'any tangible things (including books, records, papers, documents, and other items).' "[105]

Thus, the modifications made by Section 215 do not explicitly authorize the production of library records; but by its terms, it authorizes orders to require the production of virtually any business record. That might include library records, though it would include as well airline manifests, international banking transaction records, and purchase records of all sorts.

Critics of the Patriot Act have decried this provision. As a consequence, Section 4 of the SAFE Act would limit the authority to seek records to those situations where the government can provide "specific and articulable facts" demonstrating that the person to whom the records pertain is the agent of a foreign

---

104. F. James Sensenbrenner, Jr., Chairman of the House Judiciary Committee (October 17, 2002), http://www.house.gov/judiciary/news101702.htm.

105. Department of Justice, *The USA Patriot Act: Myth vs. Reality* (2003), 16.

power. Section 5 would exempt library Internet services from surveillance that could be carried out on any other Internet system. The proposals are, again, an overreaction to the perception of a problem, mistaking the potential for abuse for the reality.

Section 215 Adopts Traditional Law Enforcement Practices

Section 215 mirrors, in the intelligence-gathering context, the scope of authority that already exists in traditional law enforcement investigations. Obtaining business records is a longstanding law enforcement tactic. Ordinary grand juries for years have issued subpoenas to all manner of businesses, including libraries and bookstores, for records relevant to criminal inquiries.

For example, in the 1997 Gianni Versace murder case, a Florida grand jury subpoenaed records from public libraries in Miami Beach. Likewise, in the 1990 Zodiac gunman investigation, a New York grand jury subpoenaed records from a public library in Manhattan. Investigators believed that the gunman was inspired by a Scottish occult poet, and wanted to learn who had checked out books by that poet. In the Unabomber investigation, law enforcement officials sought the records of various libraries, hoping to identify the Unabomber as a former student with particular reading interests.

Section 215 merely authorizes the FISA court to issue similar orders in national-security investigations. It contains a number of safeguards that protect civil liberties.

First, Section 215 requires FBI agents to get a court order. Agents cannot compel any entity to turn over its records unless judicial authority has been obtained. FISA orders are unlike grand jury subpoenas, which are requested without court supervision and are subject to challenge only after they have been issued.

Second, Section 215 has a narrow scope. It can be used only (1) "to obtain foreign intelligence information not concerning a United States person" or (2) "to protect against international terrorism or clandestine intelligence activities." It cannot be used to investigate ordinary crimes, or even domestic terrorism. Nor can it be used in any investigation premised solely on "activities protected by the First Amendment to the Constitution." [106]

This is narrower than the scope of traditional law enforcement investigations. Under general criminal law, the grand jury may seek the production of any relevant business records. The only limitation is that the subpoena may be quashed if the subpoena recipient can demonstrate that "there is no reasonable possibility that the category of materials the Government seeks will produce information relevant to the general subject of the grand jury's investigation." [107] There is no necessity of showing a connection to foreign intelligence activity nor any limitation against investigation of United States persons. Thus, unlike under Section 215, the grand jury may inquire into potential violations of any federal crime with effectively limitless authority.

Criticism of Section 215 Is Misguided

Critics make two particular criticisms of this provision: that the judicial review it provides for is a chimera, and that the provision of Section 215 imposing secrecy on the recipients of subpoenas issued pursuant to the section imposes a "gag rule" that prevents oversight of the use of the section's authority. Neither criticism, however, withstands close scrutiny.

Section 215 provides for judicial review of the application for a subpoena for business records. The language provides, however, that upon application, the court "shall" issue the requested

---

106. 50 USC §1861 (20) (B).
107. *United States v R. Enterprises*, 498 US 292, 301 (1991).

subpoena. From the use of the word "shall," critics infer that the obligation to issue the requested subpoena is mandatory and, thus, that the issuing court has no discretion to reject an application. Of course, if this were true (which, as discussed below, it is not), then the absence of any judicial ability to reject an application would reduce the extent of judicial oversight.

But critics who make this argument (even if it were the case) miss the second-order effects of judicial review. It imposes obligations of veracity on those seeking the subpoenas, and to premise an objection on the lack of judicial review is to presuppose the mendacity of the subpoena affiants. It is also to presuppose the absence of any internal, administrative mechanisms in order to check potential misuse of the subpoena authority. And, most notably, it presupposes that the obligation to swear an oath of truthfulness, with attendant perjury penalties for falsity, has no deterrent effect on the misuse of authorities granted.

But even more significantly, this criticism misreads the statute, which, while saying that the subpoena "shall" issue, also says that it shall issue as sought or "as modified." The reviewing judge thus explicitly has authority to alter the scope and nature of the documents being sought—a power that cannot be exercised in the absence of substantive review of the subpoena request. Thus, the suggestion that the provisions of Section 215 preclude judicial review is simply mistaken. To the contrary, Section 215 authorizes judicial review and modification of the subpoena request which occurs before the subpoena is issued. This is a substantial improvement over the situation in traditional grand jury investigations where the subpoena is issued without judicial intervention and the review comes, at the end, only if the subpoena is challenged.

Nor is judicial oversight the only mechanism by which the use of Section 215 authority is monitored. The section expressly commands that the Attorney General "fully inform" Congress of how the section is being implemented. On October 17, 2002, the House Judiciary Committee, after reviewing the Attorney

General's first report, indicated that it was satisfied with the Justice Department's use of Section 215: "The Committee's review of classified information related to FISA orders for tangible records, such as library records, has not given rise to any concern that the authority is being misused or abused." If it were—if, for example, the Department were conducting investigations based upon the reading habits of suspects, in violation of the First Amendment—we can be sure that Congress would have said so. That it has not demonstrates that, once again, critics' fears far outpace reality.

The second criticism—that Section 215 imposes an unwarranted gag rule—is equally unpersuasive. Section 215 does prohibit recipients of subpoenas from disclosing that fact—a precaution that is necessary to avoid prematurely disclosing to the subjects of a terrorism investigation that they are subject to government scrutiny. That prohibition might be independently justified, given the grave nature of the potential threats being averted.

But it need not be—for, again, the secrecy provisions of Section 215 merely extend existing rules in traditional law enforcement grand juries to the more sensitive intelligence arena. In the grand jury context, it is common for custodians of third-party records to be prohibited from disclosing the existence of the document request. Banks, for example, may be obliged to conceal requests made to them.[108] And it is clear, beyond peradventure, that these grand jury secrecy obligations are constitutional. For example, when the nanny of Jon Benet Ramsey was called to testify before a state grand jury, state law prohibited her from disclosing the substance of her testimony. When she challenged that law (on the ground that it infringed her freedom of speech), her challenge was rejected by the courts.[109]

---

108. 12 USC § 3604 (c)
109. *Hoffman-Pugh v Keenan*, 338 F3d 1136 (10th Cir 2003); see also *Hoffman-Pugh v Ramsey* 312 F3d 1222 (11th Circ 2002) (rejecting libel suit filed by nanny against the Ramsey family).

The SAFE Act Would Hobble Section 215

The SAFE Act proposes to require a showing of "specific and articulable facts" before a Section 215 order may be issued. That showing would impose a greater obligation on law enforcement in an intelligence investigation than under the simple "relevance" standard that applies to federal grand juries investigating ordinary criminal offenses. The purpose of the non-intrusive records request is precisely to develop the specific and articulable facts that warrant a greater intrusion, for if specific and articulable facts to seek the records exist, police will have sufficient probable cause to execute a search warrant—and under warrant there is less possibility that the required records will be destroyed.

In other words, the balance between the standard and the degree of intrusion is a tradeoff: The lesser the standard law enforcement must meet, the lesser the intrusion permitted. By altering that balance, the SAFE Act will have the perverse effect of providing law enforcement with the incentive to prefer more intrusive means.

In short, critics of Section 215 make a very difficult and, in the end, unpersuasive argument. They offer the view, in effect, that traditional law enforcement powers that have been used in grand juries for years to investigate common law crimes and federal criminal offenses ought not to be used with equal authority to investigate potential terrorist threats. To many, that argument seems precisely to reverse the evaluation—if anything, the powers used to investigate terrorism, espionage, and threats to national security ought to be greater than those used to investigate mere criminal behavior.

This is not, of course, to denigrate the significance and seriousness of many federal and state crimes; but it is to recognize that, however grave those crimes are, they do not pose the same risk to the foundations of American society or to the security of large numbers of citizens as the risks posed by potential terrorist acts.

Consideration of Section 215 should be grounded in a solid understanding of what the section actually authorizes. It should not be swayed by the public mythology that surrounds this provision. That myth has led to the rather absurd result that some librarians are destroying their borrowing records to prevent them from becoming available to the federal government. In other words, those charged in our society with protecting and maintaining knowledge and information are destroying it. The interest in protecting civil liberties must be high—but not so high that we lapse into hysteria.

Conclusion

The Patriot Act has become something of a political football in the past few months. One sees television commercials of anonymous hands ripping up the Constitution, with a voice-over blaming Attorney General John Ashcroft. Print ads show an elderly gentleman leaving a bookstore with text decrying the use of government powers to get his book purchase list. But the hysteria is based on false premises.

We cannot decide policy based upon an over-wrought sense of fear. Most of the steps proposed to combat terrorism were previously used to combat organized crime. And there is no evidence of any real abuse. No First Amendment liberties have been curtailed, no dissent or criticism suppressed. While we must be cautious, John Locke, the 17th century philosopher who greatly influenced the Founding Fathers, was right when he wrote:

> In all states of created beings, capable of laws, where there is no law there is no freedom. For liberty is to be free from the restraint and

violence from others; which cannot be where there is no law; and is not, as we are told, a liberty for every man to do what he lists. [110]

Thus, the obligation of the government is a dual one: to protect civil safety and security against violence and to preserve civil liberty.

In reviewing our policies and planning for the future, we must be guided by the realization that this is not a zero-sum game. We can achieve both goals—liberty and security—to an appreciable degree. The key is empowering government to do the right things while exercising oversight to prevent the abuse of authority. So long as we keep a vigilant eye on police authority, so long as the federal courts remain open, and so long as the debate about governmental conduct is a vibrant part of the American dialogue, the risk of excessive encroachment on our fundamental liberties can be avoided.

---

110. John Locke. *Two Treatises of Government*, ed. Peter Laslett (Cambridge: Cambridge University Press, 1988), 305.

CONCLUSION: BUSH, REAGAN, AND THE PIVOT OF HISTORY

ROD MARTIN

Rod D. Martin, editor with Aman Verjee of THANK YOU, PRESIDENT BUSH, *is Founder and Chairman of Vanguard PAC (www.VanguardPAC.org). A former policy director to Arkansas Governor Mike Huckabee and Special Counsel to PayPal, Inc. founder Peter Thiel, he is a member of the Board of Governors of the Council for National Policy and serves as Vice President of the National Federation of Republican Assemblies. He studied political and economic thought at Cambridge University, earned his J.D. at Baylor University, and is author of the forthcoming* VISIONS OF AMERICA.

Aman and I dedicated this book—a call for the re-election of George W. Bush—to Ronald Reagan. This choice meant more than you might think, both about us and about our current President.

For our parts, Ronald Reagan was not merely a great President: he was *the* great President, the formative political figure of our generation and the hero who defined our time. We do not bestow the comparison—even on a President we admire and support—lightly. For us, it is virtually the highest praise we are able to give.

But it is President Bush who earned that praise, and whom, dedication aside, this book lauds. While many dedications are almost throw-away lines, we see ours as integral to the book, precisely because the symmetry is becoming so very strong; and because we are convinced that, given a second term to complete his task, George W. Bush will give birth to a new and better era, one for which Reagan long hoped and of which he would be most proud. What's more, this younger leader comes to the stage not one moment too soon, because like Reagan—and for reasons which go far beyond 9/11—he (and we with him) stand at what might be termed the pivot of history.

The Reagan Legacy

Though you would never know it from the protestations of adoration poured upon him at his death, it was fashionable once—yea, mandatory—among media, political and cultural leaders of the Left to loudly proclaim Ronald Reagan a warmonger and a fool. Perhaps this is the best indicator of his Chuchillian stature; for like Reagan, Churchill was so maligned, and like Churchill, Reagan saved the world.

The Left, of course, credited Gorbachev for this, which resembled nothing so much as crediting Hitler's suicide for the end of World War II. Reagan's victory—and the fact that we are not now speaking Russian or buried ala Khrushchev under a smoldering ruin—was produced of a vision shared by no President before him, and a fortitude possessed by few.

He refused to accept the Left's received wisdom of "moral equivalence" between the Communist East and the democratic West: he called Russia the "evil empire" it was, and revived the moral courage essential for victory. His opponents, lesser men from Michael Dukakis to Michael Foot, hurled their epithets: "dangerous," "destabilizing," "cowboy." But Reagan understood the real danger was in a nuclear superpower bent on world conquest and in the throes of both economic and ethnic collapses its Western apologists refused to see.

He repaired a nuclear "deterrent" so badly eroded as to lack credibility and invite blackmail. Side by side with Margaret Thatcher, he stood down the Left's greatest-ever attempted appeasement—the nuclear freeze movement—and not only rearmed America but re-established its deterrent in Europe. The Soviets, playing off the terror of the times, threatened to walk out of stalled arms talks if he did so. In a move which stunned everyone, he wished them fond farewell. He would not be bullied; and when they realized it, they returned.

His certainty that people everywhere yearned for freedom and that free markets could always out-produce centrally-planned slavery drove his strategies where *realpolitik* could never go. He replaced both containment and détente with his "Reagan Doctrine," proclaiming America would actively roll back its foe by helping freedom fighters behind the Iron Curtain. From World War II until Reagan, not one square inch of ground had been recovered once lost to communism. Then all things changed, as Moscow was made to play defense, first in Grenada and Afghanistan, and ultimately from the Berlin Wall to the USSR itself.

Unwilling to play for less than total victory, he went for the Russian jugular. Realizing that over half of all Soviet hard currency came from the export of oil, he cut a deal with Saudi Arabia: weapons and other benefits previously unavailable, in exchange for an oil glut which would buoy the West and skewer the common foe. Combining this with an arms race, the keystone

351

of which was the high-tech Strategic Defense Initiative, he pushed Moscow over a cliff his opponents said did not—could not—exist. Gorbachev, coming in much too late after a string of dead General Secretaries, was left first to "restructure," then to dismantle his empire, and finally just to "wither away."

This is Reagan's greatest legacy, but it is hardly his only one. His supply-side faith in Arthur Laffer's lower marginal tax rates ignited a twenty-year boom in an America used to every-three-year recessions and facing real economic decline: the Club of Rome's famed "Limits to Growth" which, embraced by Carter and the commentariat, planned for the retreat of Western civilization to an almost pre-industrial level, were prompted not merely by sick ideology but by the fact that semi-socialist Keynesianism was burning out just like its more-evil Soviet cousin. His vision for tax-deferred retirement accounts transferred the "means of production" to the *proletariat* and destroyed the basis for class warfare: shareholders, a tiny fraction of the population in 1980, today are a large majority. The wealth his ideas created drove a technological boom unlike any the world had ever seen, and convinced billions previously susceptible to socialism that freedom really works.

It is there that Reagan's greatness really lies. To a bleak Orwellian world, he restored hope; and the chance not only that there would be a next century, but that it would be a good one. Today, standing on the shoulders of this giant, his successor has a chance not merely to continue that legacy, but to fulfill and extend it; and if he succeeds in that task, he like Reagan will define our nation for decades beyond.

Reagan's Heir

In the days surrounding Reagan's funeral, some questioned the validity of any comparison between these two men. Yet the facts speak for themselves, and speak powerfully. A brief survey is in order.

The End of the Rainbow: Missile Defense

This Fourth of July weekend, twenty-one years after Reagan's famous speech, America's first missile interceptor was finally loaded into its Alaska silo. What Reagan once dreamed—indeed, devoted much of his presidency to—George W. Bush has made real.

This will come as a surprise to the seventy percent of Americans who through the years have consistently believed Reagan deployed a working system in the 1980s. It comes as an equal shock to those millions of us who knew better, and who watched as Democrats pulled every trick in the book to prevent missile defenses ever being deployed. But there he was, on a cold December's day in 2001, George W. Bush, withdrawing us from the ABM Treaty by which Nixon had surrendered America's technological lead to Brezhnev, prohibiting America from defending herself; and there he was again this July, fulfilling Reagan's long ago promise.

He should be re-elected if only for this alone.

It's hard now to remember just how we all felt then, living under the daily threat not of what a bin Laden might do to one city or two, but of what history's most brutal dictatorship might do to us all. But it's even harder to imagine the insane logic of MAD, or Mutually Assured Destruction, which elevated that fear to the level of national strategy, the strategy in fact which most of America's liberal elite preferred as the bulwark of America's "defense" (the much smaller remainder of the Left, which demanded unilateral disarmament, can only be understood as terrified beyond reason or as a fifth column; and in fact, they were a good bit of both). MAD, simply put, said that if the Russians launched against us, we'd launch against them. It was a Strangelovian balance of terror, by which both sides held hundreds of millions of innocents hostage. Yet for wanting to end this surreal, sick nightmare through purely defensive means, the Left decried Reagan a madman, never quite seeing their own irony.

Their argument—which rested on the ideas that SDI would be "destabilizing" and that Russia's vast number of warheads would overwhelm any possible defense—would have held a great deal more credibility if they'd quit making it after the Soviet Union fell. But in fact, though the Evil Empire is gone, the new Russia is (mostly) our friend, serious bilateral nuclear disarmament has been in full swing for fifteen years, and the current and growing threats are entirely of accidental launches or unstable dictators with but a handful of missiles—neither of which can be meaningfully deterred—the Left has not, has never changed tunes. The Bill Clinton who once wrote that he "loathed the military," the John Kerry who returned from Vietnam accusing the majority of America's brave soldiers of war crimes, they and their allies did all they could to keep America undefended.

One can sympathize with the fearful, with those whose approach to the very real terror of nuclear attack was to hide their heads ostrich-like in the sand, raving about "the unthinkable." Never mind that Stalin's intentional terror famine in Ukraine was also unthinkable; Pol Pot's murder of half of Cambodia's population between 1975 and 1978 was also unthinkable; Hitler's "final solution" was also unthinkable. Some are constitutionally incapable of dealing with these issues, and likewise incapable of seeing that mass-murdering dictatorships are not an aberration but a constant of history. Though we disagree, we can understand how they feel, and be grateful for visionaries like Reagan, who could do their thinking for them and, in the process, remove the source of their fear.

But the willfully blind are another matter. It is not within the scope of this book to examine why Kerry or Clinton, Daschle or Kennedy wish passionately to leave America vulnerable to a North Korean missile; but it is within our scope to declare them unfit to lead. They are perfectly willing—and loudly demanding—that America gamble: that no one will launch a missile at her, that all attacks will be "like 9/11," unconventional and unpredictable.

And maybe they're right.

But in case they aren't—and since it's the job of our leaders to defend us to the best of their ability, not just bet on hunches and hopes—it seems quite self-evident that defending against the threat of the most dangerous weapons on Earth is indeed essential. And we finally have a President who has done it.

Letting Freedom Reign

Yet Reagan knew that merely defending America's homeland was not enough: "Fortress America" was inadequate at mid-century, ludicrous by the 1980s. The world would not be safe, America could never be safe, so long as the USSR remained, actively propagating its "dictatorship of the proletariat" by every means at its disposal. And likewise, merely replacing Soviet rule with "friendly" dictatorships, while occasionally unavoidable, was to Reagan no solution: the real goal was freedom. And free men everywhere, he believed, would lay down arms, take up tools, and given the chance, build a new, peaceful, prosperous world for themselves and their posterity.

In this measure too, Bush is Reagan's heir. Having defined his Axis of Evil, he quickly sought to diplomatically surround North Korea, and physically surround Iran (with bases encircling from Afghanistan and Central Asia to Iraq and the Persian Gulf). He lanced the endlessly festering boil of Iraq and established a democratic government which—at this writing—enjoys a roughly eighty percent approval rating. If it takes, it will surely inspire a cascade effect of freedom throughout a region without a single democracy, save Israel.

Again, the first domino to fall is likely Iran. Dissatisfaction with the mullahs is at an all-time high, a situation which has already had a positive influence in Iraq, where, despite a more than sixty percent Shi'ite majority, a mere eight percent want the sort of theocracy their neighbors have come to loathe. And most dangerous for the current regime, a majority of the Iranian population is younger than the revolution. Born after 1979, they know well the brutality of the extremely efficient ayatollahs, they know the Shah only as ancient history, and they know that many of their mothers had equal rights and studied in American universities. As the impossibly porous border with Iraq—and to a lesser degree Afghanistan—begins to spread fewer Iranian terrorists and more common Iraqis with a better, freer life, the lid will blow off Iran as though it were 1979 again.

Is Bush's Iraq/Iran policy American self-interest? Is it unabashed idealism? As with Reagan, it's both, reflected in Bush's twin beliefs in taking the battle to the enemy (the Reagan Doctrine perfectly parallels the Bush Doctrine) and in freedom as both subversive force and ultimate cure. The Left claims it is neither of these, but their claim rings increasingly hollow. As Victor Davis Hansen put it shortly after the handover of sovereignty:

> The oil pipeline in Afghanistan that we allegedly went to war over doesn't exist. Brave Americans died to rout al Qaeda, end the fascist Taliban, and free Afghanistan for a good and legitimate man like a Hamid Karzai to oversee elections. It was politically unwise and idealistic—not smart and cynical—for Mr. Bush to gamble his presidency on getting rid of fascists in Iraq. There really was a tie between al Qaeda and Saddam Hussein—just as Mr. Gore and Mr. Clinton once believed and Mr. Putin and [Iraqi Prime Minister] Allawi now remind us. The United States really did plan to put Iraqi oil under Iraqi democratic supervision for the first time in the country's history. And it did.

And when news of the handover of sovereignty to the Iraqis reached President Bush's ears, his smile told all, and his quickly dashed note to Condoleezza Rice—"Let freedom reign"—was heartfelt. It could not have been John Kerry. But it could have been Reagan.

Beyond Reagan's Vision

Trying to list the ways in which Bush is fulfilling Reagan's vision is the work of a book, not a chapter, and indeed that has been this anthology's very point. Yet the high points still impress. Surely no one has so firmly stood for America's sovereignty in ages: withdrawing us from the ABM Treaty, rejecting the International Criminal Court Treaty, and resisting Al Gore's Kyoto Protocol fantasy, Bush has stood like a giant, not merely refusing to be tied down by the Lilliputians, but stomping as many of them as possible under his feet. Likewise, he's been the most pro-gun President in memory, from his evisceration of UN efforts to impose a global gun ban to his reversal of the over-three-decades-old Justice Department position that the Second Amendment creates "no individual right" to gun ownership (and indeed, if it does not, it is utter nonsense).

He's been thoroughly pro-life, in his judicial appointments, in his reinstitution of the Mexico City Policy, in his signing of the Partial Birth Abortion Ban and the Laci Peterson Law, and most importantly in his constant, active encouragement of a culture of life. The fact that lifelong abortion activist Patty Ireland's own polls now show a pro-life majority *among women*—for the first time since *Roe v. Wade*—shows just how much impact he's had. And of course much of this book has been devoted to his revival of Reaganomics, a devotion to supply-side theory which—despite a recession and market crash inherited from his predecessor and the economic effects of 9/11 to boot—has created what the Associated Press this week called "the best economy in twenty years."

Will voters realize that fact before November? Maybe not; but one thing's certain: they did in 1984.

Yet perhaps the most enduring, transformative act remains a dream: real Social Security reform. This was surely the most unsung, yet dramatic achievement of Ronald Reagan's presidency aside from winning the Cold War: his championing of

Individual Retirement Accounts and 401(k)s, by which average Americans could save tax-free for their retirement, escape the slavery of the Social Security Ponzi scheme, and become real owners of the American Dream. Owners? Yes: when Reagan came to office, only 16% of American adults owned $5,000 or more of stock; by the turn of the century, that number had risen to an outright majority. On this flood of capital, markets soared, the economy boomed, small and large businesses alike exploded, homeownership soared, and Americans reached heights they'd never imagined. And perhaps most important of all, once again, the means of production had been transferred to the *proletariat*: America had become a *bourgeoisie* nation, and the fate of Marxian class warfare arguments had been sealed.

Building on this astonishing achievement—which the masses perceived but did not grasp—George W. Bush became the first major candidate to run on a platform calling for the individual ownership and direction of Social Security accounts. This went beyond touching the "third rail": it was grabbing the thing, ripping it from the crossties. And yet despite Al Gore's increasingly hysterical attacks, the public didn't punish Bush. Quite the contrary: even at the height of Enron and WorldCom and the bust, poll after poll showed majorities as high as seventy percent behind Bush's plan. Eventually, Democrats may realize that a sizeable portion of that majority is not Republican.

Like every major Western nation, America faces a crippling pension crisis. It has not saved a single penny of its people's Social Security "contributions", because the "Trust Fund" is a myth. Social Security is pay-as-you-go: everything that comes in is spent today, on everything from thousand dollar hammers to crucifixes dipped in urine. Nothing is saved, no one has a real account. Any company that tried this would be busted, its executives sent to jail. But America faces a day—soon and very soon—on which bazillions of baby boomers will regret the children they aborted, as their too-few living progeny cannot sustain their monthly checks. Those then-middle aged children, of course, will never receive anything at all.

It need not be this way. Private accounts work, because freedom works: a government pension system is designed as badly and works as well as a government steel mill. And if the poverty of a Social Security system in which the death benefit won't even buy a casket is not sufficiently clear, just look abroad. From Chile to Australia to Britain, our smarter neighbors have already pioneered this trail. We know exactly how to make private ownership work, and exactly what pitfalls must be avoided; and even more to the point, we know the power of the plan. After just a few years under the new system, Britain by itself had amassed a combined wealth in its private retirement accounts exceeding the total assets of all European government retirement systems *combined*.

Extending Reagan's legacy in dramatic fashion, George W. Bush looks to give every American the benefit of this experience. Politics, of course, requires starting smaller than the situation truly demands. However, a truly private retirement system could easily eradicate most poverty in America: more than that, it could transform America from a middle class nation to a nation of the rich. Even cautious estimates indicate that private accounts would enable the average American to live on a retirement income at least equal to his working-years salary, even after adjusting for inflation. More importantly, both spouses would get all the money they'd saved, and both could pass on everything they don't spend to their children, tax free. In this fashion—and through the similar Health Savings Account law just passed—nearly all Americans could accumulate true intergenerational wealth by the end of the century. It would be unlike anything in the history of the world.

The Pivot of History

It is in this manner—though not only this manner—that George W. Bush stands not merely as a good leader for his time, but truly at the pivot of history. Failure on the Social Security issue could doom America to a grim and dismal fate, as its internal economic crisis of escalating taxes and receding markets (as capital is withdrawn *en masse* from retirement accounts, much faster than can be replenished) comes to parallel Britain's decline after World War I, with an accompanying transfer of global dominance to the booming growth engine that is China. Yet success could easily inaugurate a golden age like nothing ever seen in all of time. George W. Bush stands at this pivot. The choice is not entirely his, but the credit or blame (properly) will be.

He also stands at the most polarized period in American life since 1864. The old consensus politics which grew out of the New Deal are gone: the Republicans have finally become a party of the Right, capable of balancing and meaningfully opposing a Democratic Party which moves further left by the day. This competition is at once frightening and exhilarating to liberals: they love the fight, they thrill at the opportunity to flex their considerable institutional muscles. And yet, they know they're losing power. That Americans think of Social Security in the way they now do, that welfare reform has worked so dramatically, that more numerous media outlets provide conservatives a national voice, all these things terrify the Left. It's not just about Congress, or about any particular institution: it's about the accumulated orthodoxy, built over a century, that says in a thousand ways every day to every American that liberalism is *right*. It is that which is slipping away. And that slippage is producing the polarization, on both sides.

Yet though the commentators speak of a 50-50 nation, it's not so simple as that. The gurus forever forget that, under the best of circumstances, only half of eligible Americans vote, that any party which can mobilize a decent number of non-voters can radically alter the landscape without swaying a single current voter.

They forget this because they believe that, in reality, pretty much every group is maxed out. And that's a pretty fair assessment. You'll likely never see a greatly increased percentage of African Americans voting than voted in 2000. The same holds for women, union members, gun owners, gays, or any other group you're likely to name. To the degree Hispanics are an exception, that is increasingly mitigated by the fact that Republicans are making significant gains within their ranks. This is the calculus, say the gurus: it's still all about winning the middle.

The problem is, their calculus is wrong. There is one truly enormous group which votes far less than its numbers suggest. Though many of its current voters still vote Democrat, that number is declining, while almost every additional voter they produce votes Republican. And no one sees it coming.

That group is Evangelical Christians.

There are 60 million Evangelicals in America, yet only 15 million of them vote. There are a number of reasons for this, most of which are theological in nature and not within the scope of this book. Yet every day that a baby is aborted, every time a Roy Moore gets attacked in the press, every place a homosexual "marriage" is performed, more Evangelicals find the resolve to enter the process and stand up for their values. And the polarization we see today is heaping mountains of fuel on the fire.

It is always positive when Americans participate in their government. Our system depends upon a vigorous debate in the marketplace of ideas: the effective self-exclusion of such a large group from its proper place in American life for much of the last century impoverished us all. In theory, at least, everyone should embrace the rise of Evangelical voting and applaud it as much overdue.

But it won't just be ideology that prevents the Left from enjoying this unfolding civics lesson.

Christians are coming into the process because they are out-raged. There's no question where their outrage is directed. Merely reaching the fifty percent voting strength one might expect of them would up-end the current political calculus: as they flood into Republican ranks, they will swamp the liberal and non-ideological hacks who run much of the party (this process has been accelerating over the past decade), and eventually they will dramatically add to Republican voting strength (not to mention activist strength) at general elections. And as everyone gains a powerful ownership stake in upward mobility through Health Savings Accounts and the proposed Personal Retirement Accounts, the number of Americans seeking distinctly free market solutions—and rejecting statism—is sure to increase as well. A 50-50 nation could easily turn 60-40 over the next generation.

For all these reasons, George W. Bush stands in a historically unique position: given another term, he can lay the foundation for a new American Century of such universal wealth and power as none have ever imagined; and at the same time, as a genuine Christian and a true supply-sider, he can dramatically propel those trends which would give his party an insuperable majority with which to see that project through. He has come to that point through faithfulness to Reagan's vision. Given just one more election victory, we will all learn whether he fulfills the promise he's shown, of reaching beyond that vision to one so much grander as to eclipse all which has gone before. But whether he does or whether he doesn't, we have seen that he can be trusted to try. His opponent, by contrast, will do everything possible to undo even that which we now have.

Conclusion

To borrow from de Tocqueville, George W. Bush has become a great man because he is first a good one. Even when he's erred, that goodness has shown through: he has consistently, obviously tried to do the right thing.

We believe in him. We appreciate him. We certainly support him. And perhaps most rare of all in politics, we thank him. He has earned our gratitude, as well as that of every friend of liberty throughout the world.

PUBLISHER'S NOTE

ERIC JACKSON

Eric M. Jackson is the president of World Ahead Publishing. A graduate of Stanford University with honors, he previously oversaw the marketing operations of Internet payment company PayPal, Inc., and currently serves on the boards of several organizations. Mr. Jackson is the author of an upcoming business memoir—THE PAYPAL WARS —which makes the case that regulators, lawyers, and criminals are threatening the future of American entrepreneurship.

When deciding whether or not to publish a book, a publisher must first meticulously consider a series of important questions: Is there a market for this idea? Is the book likely to turn a profit? Do I want to work with this author? Will it enhance my house's prestige? Does it complement the rest of my lineup?

My decision to go ahead with *Thank You, President Bush*—a project that I first conceived last December—was much easier. While I dutifully tinkered with profit and loss models, the question ultimately came down to a simple realization: this book is too important not to publish.

This book is important quite simply because the West is at war. And "war" is the only word to describe our predicament. Thousands of innocent lives ended when airplanes slammed into the World Trade Center, the Pentagon, and a Pennsylvania meadow. Islamic militants are committing increasingly brutal executions of foreign journalists and contractors and broadcasting them over Al Jazeera. Osama bin Laden has called it his "religious duty" to obtain nuclear weapons. Details have emerged that Saddam Hussein's regime not only had Al Qaeda ties but was also planning to carry out its own terror strikes against the United States.

While we have been forced into a war against savage foes, increasingly many of the West's political elites suggest otherwise. They're not always explicit about it, but their nuanced message is clear. Senator Hillary Clinton implied that Republicans are exaggerating the risk of terrorism: "If they get their way, you and I will be living in an America governed not by our hopes, but by our fears." Romano Prodi, president of the European Union, denounced the "American approach" to combating radical Islamists and proposed Europe find a more peaceful tactic: "It is clear that using force is not the answer to resolving the conflict with terrorists." Senator Ted Kennedy dubbed the war to remove Hussein—a despot who funded suicide bombings in Israel, sent envoys to bin Laden, gave sanctuary to Palestinian terrorist Abu Nidal, and previously used weapons of mass destruction against his own people—a scam: "This was made up in Texas ... This whole thing was a fraud."

These assertions by the West's liberal politicians may fly in the face of common sense, but they have also gone largely unscrutinized by the mainstream media. Whether it was extolling the "courage" of Richard Clarke when he conveniently released his book *Against All Enemies* prior to his televised testimony to the 9/11 Commission, or repeating Michael Moore's baseless accusation that family-oriented Disney wouldn't distribute his *Fahrenheit 9/11* diatribe because it feared Gov. Jeb Bush would rob their Florida operations of tax breaks, the media always seems to be talking about something political. Just not the Left's dangerous bout of self-denial.

Maybe that's because the media and the Left are one and the same. According to the Pew Research Center, national journalists are 70 percent more likely to call themselves "liberal" and 79 percent less likely to call themselves "conservative" than the public at large. And it turns out these persuasions do impact the way they report the news. A September 2003 quantitative study by Tim Groseclose of UCLA and Jeff Milyo of the University of Chicago concluded that mainstream media coverage has "a very significant liberal bias ... [that is] to the left of the average member of Congress." This systematic bias often shows itself in the form of omission. Consider that the media largely glossed over a foiled chemical bombing in Jordan last April. This attempted WMD attack had the potential to kill 20,000 people and was carried out by followers of an Al Qaeda agent stationed in Iraq, yet the near-atrocity received scant coverage despite the obvious WMD-Iraq-Al Qaeda links.

Evidently CBS, ABC, NBC, CNN, and *The New York Times* aren't going to make any effort to discuss the unpleasant truth of the war in which we find ourselves. Nor are the publishers cashing in on Leftist hatred of the President. If these giant conglomerates won't challenge the politicians and hucksters who trivialize the threat posed by Al Qaeda, Baathists, and their menagerie of fellow travelers, then I decided that my company would. Even if our book had to stand alone on bookstore shelves amidst dozens of Bush-bashing titles, I still wanted World Ahead to publish a book that explained why the stakes for this election are so high and why George W. Bush deserves more than just our votes: he has earned our gratitude.

The Democratic Party made my decision that much easier by nominating the nation's most liberal Senator for the nation's highest office. John Kerry said that the current struggle with terrorism "is not primarily a military operation. It's an intelligence-gathering, law-enforcement, public-diplomacy effort." Such an approach mirrors the philosophy that prevailed during the Clinton Administration, a belief that terrorism—like drugs and organized crime—was a law enforcement matter. Under this philosophy Team Clinton cranked out belated subpoenas while turning a blind eye to the foreign organizations actually orchestrating terrorism, thereby allowing civilization's foes to gather in strength and prepare to strike a sleeping nation.

Kerry's retro-security strategies are not the only shortcoming in his vision for America. On many other fronts, his gaze is transfixed on the failed policies of the past, causing him to miss the world of the present and the future.

Kerry and his party are advocating an "American Jobs Plan" that would rely heavily on publicly funded infrastructure jobs to get people back to work. Or, in other words, they want to do exactly what Japan futilely tried over and over to revive its moribund economy in the 1990s. But rolling back the clock to discredited Keynesian economics isn't enough for John Kerry; he wants to do the same with trade, too. Kerry proposed using the country's tax law to undermine the Reagan-Bush-Clinton free trade consensus by levying higher taxes on domestic firms that create overseas jobs. This implicit export tariff will not only hurt the competitiveness of American firms, but it will also stunt the economic progress of our trading partners, decreasing the demand for U.S. goods and services abroad while supplying grist to anti-American opportunists' mills.

Fortunately, in George W. Bush we have a man who is more than just someone other than John Kerry. Under his command U.S. soldiers have killed or captured most of the Al Qaeda and Iraqi leadership while ushering two nascent democracies into a part of the world that desperately needs a whiff of freedom. His tax cuts revived an economy that had been hit by multiple shocks, including a stock market crash, terrorism, and corporate scandals. With employment soaring and GDP posting its highest growth rate in two decades, Bush's low marginal taxes on income and investment will encourage accelerated growth for years to come. As of late, President Bush has also shown a renewed commitment to free trade, a welcome move coming several years after his rejection of the anti-growth Kyoto treaty. He's made incremental progress on medical savings accounts and school choice, signed a law to end the macabre practice of partial birth abortions, and proudly upheld America's respect for life by leading the effort to combat the international sex trade and the spread of AIDS in Africa.

The track record speaks well of Bush's vision, but his own words and actions speak just as highly of his leadership. Who can forget his rousing speech to the New York firefighters — "I hear you! The world hears you! And the people who tore down these buildings will hear from all of us soon!" — when he stood among the smoldering ruins at Ground Zero? Or the moral clarity of his address to the joint session of Congress the following week? "We're not deceived by their pretenses to piety... They're the heirs of all the murderous ideologies of the twentieth century. By sacrificing human life to serve their radical visions ... they follow in the path of fascism, Nazism and totalitarianism. And they will follow that path all the way to where it ends in history's unmarked grave of discarded lies." These are the words of a man speaking from his heart, his soul, and they uplifted and reassured the anxious nation that heard them.

But sometimes private actions, far away from the cameras, provide a more accurate measure of the man. And on this score Bush fairs just as well. I recently chatted with Bruce Vincent, the director of a non-profit group called Provider Pals that received the Preserve America Presidential Award in May, about his trip to the White House. He shared with me a heart-warming and insightful story:

> On our way out of the office I was the last person in the exit line. As I shook the President's hand, I did something that surprised even me. I said,

"Mr. President, I know you are a busy man and your time is precious. I also know you to be a man of strong faith and have a favor to ask you." As he shook my hand he looked me in the eye and said, "Just name it." I told him that at that moment my stepmother was having a tumor removed from her skull, and it would mean a great deal to me if he would consider adding her to his prayers. "So that's it," he responded. "I could tell that something is weighing heavy on your heart today. I could see it in your eyes." He pulled me out of the exit line and led me back toward his desk.

He asked about the surgery and the prognosis. I described her condition and he suggested that we pray right then and there. He motioned for his staff to leave and with his right hand reached for my head, which he gently placed upon his shoulder as he embraced my back with his left arm. He began to pray softly, at which point the emotion of the moment overcame me and I started to cry. He continued to pray as my body shook from the sobs, but he just held tighter. As he finished I stepped away from our prayerful embrace, slightly embarrassed and eager to wipe away the tears I left on his shoulder. But he paid them no mind. The President just looked into my eyes and smiled.

George W. Bush is a compassionate man who loves the people of his country and the world. But he also has a principled determination to pursue what he believes is right. He has led the willing nations in a fight against the evil men of our times, he has made our country and economy more free and prosperous, and he has liberated millions from totalitarian rule—a feat that will some day make him worthy of mention alongside FDR, Truman, and Reagan, the international emancipators of the prior century.

John Kerry is not a bad man and he certainly loves his country, but his vision harkens back to the failed policies of the past. Kerry does not understand the world ahead as George W. Bush does. And it is for this reason that World Ahead published the book you now hold.

World Ahead Publishing presents:

The PayPal Wars

Battles with eBay, the Media, the Mafia, and the Rest of Planet Earth

'Read this book and you'll be
amazed by PayPal's death-defying
origins and shocked by what they
tell us about the business
environment in America."
—*Dr. Michael New, Harvard-MIT
Data Center*

"*The PayPal Wars* offers an
inspiring story of how dedicated
entrepreneurs can both make a
profit and advance the cause of
liberty."
—*Doug Bandow, senior fellow,
Cato Institute*

When PayPal launched its online payment service and set out to
overhaul the world's currency markets, it survived the dot-com bust
and plunged into a fierce competitive struggle with the auction giant
eBay. But when hordes of government regulators, trial lawyers, and
organized crime rings targeted PayPal for destruction, its quest to
make Internet history turned into a desperate struggle for survival.

0-9746701-0-3 ▪ $27.95 ▪ 6 x 9 ▪ 360 pages ▪ In stores September 2004